PASSION AND VALUE
in Hume's Treatise

to Harpa

PASSION AND VALUE
in Hume's Treatise

PÁLL S. ÁRDAL

EDINBURGH
UNIVERSITY
PRESS

© P. S. Árdal 1966, 1989

Edinburgh University Press
22 George Square, Edinburgh

Printed in Great Britain by
Redwood Burn Limited
Trowbridge, Wilts.

British Library Cataloguing
  in Publication Data
Árdal, Pall S.
Passion and value in Hume's Treatise. – 2nd ed.
  1. Scottish philosophy. Hume, David, 1711–1776: Treatise
of human nature
I. Title

ISBN 0 85224 641 2

CONTENTS

PREFACE

This book is an altered version of a Ph.D. thesis accepted by the University of Edinburgh in 1961. I have expanded the discussion of the main theme – the relation of the passions to the evaluation of character – and omitted parts of the thesis that seemed to me to have little or no bearing upon this topic.

I owe a great debt to all the works I mention – no less to those that have provoked me to criticism than to those with which I have found myself in agreement.

I am extremely grateful for the encouragement given to me by Professor Emeritus A. D. Ritchie who supervised my thesis. My debt to colleagues and students is enormous, but special thanks are due to the following: Mr G. P. Morice who read the whole of the book in typescript and made a great number of helpful criticisms, and Mr Errol Bedford, Dr G. E. Davie, and Mr H. S. Eveling, all of whom made many valuable comments upon large parts of the book in typescript. I also wish to thank Professor W. H. Walsh for critical comments on the second chapter of the book and Mr I. R. Wilson for helping me to make many improvements in the last chapter. Mrs Judith Stoothoff and Miss Jean Allan provided invaluable assistance with typing.

I have given page references to both the Everyman's Library edition and the Selby-Bigge edition of Hume's *Treatise* in that order. I have followed the more modern spelling of the Everyman's edition, although I have, on a few occasions, adopted the punctuation of the Selby-Bigge edition when it seemed to me preferable.

P. S. Á.

Edinburgh, March 1966

ABBREVIATIONS

PDH   N. Kemp Smith, *The Philosophy of David Hume*, Macmillan, London 1941.

EHU   David Hume, *Enquiries Concerning the Human Understanding and Concerning The Principles of Morals*, ed. L. A. Selby-Bigge, Oxford, at the Clarendon Press, 2nd ed. 1902.

HI   J. A. Passmore, *Hume's Intentions*, Cambridge, at the University Press, 1952.

DH   A. H. Basson, *David Hume*, Penguin Books, Middlesex 1958.

THN   David Hume, *A Treatise of Human Nature*, in two vols., Bk. I in Vol. I and Bks. II and III in Vol. II, Everyman's Library, Dent, London 1911; and ed. L. A. Selby-Bigge, Oxford, at the Clarendon Press, 1888.

PE   G. E. Moore, *Principia Ethica*, Cambridge, at the University Press, 1903.

FTET   C. D. Broad, *Five Types of Ethical Theory*, Kegan Paul, Trench & Trubner, London 1930.

ET   Richard B. Brandt, *Ethical Theory*, Prentice Hall, N.J. 1959.

N of S   Max Scheler, *The Nature of Sympathy*, translated from the German by P. L. Heath, Routledge & Kegan Paul, London 1954.

TMS   Adam Smith, *The Theory of Moral Sentiments*, in *The Essays of Adam Smith*, Alex Murray, London 1872.

EPHM   Dugald Stewart, *Elements of The Philosophy of the Human Mind*, in *The Collected Works of Dugald Stewart*, Vol. III, Edinburgh 1854–60.

HTPM   A. B. Glathe, *Hume's Theory of the Passions and of Morals*, University of California, Berkeley 1950.

PWTR   Thomas Reid, *The Philosophical Works of Thomas Reid*, James Thin, Edinburgh 1895.

DHTK and M   D. G. C. MacNabb, *David Hume, His Theory of Knowledge and Morality*, Hutchinson, London 1951.

LDH   David Hume, *The Letters of David Hume*, ed. H. Greig, Oxford 1932.

PAS(SV)   *Proceedings of the Aristotelian Society*, Supplementary Volume.

BM   *British Moralists*, ed. L. A. Selby-Bigge, Oxford, at the Clarendon Press, 1897.

R and C   Rachael Kydd, *Reason and Conduct in Hume's Treatise*, Oxford, at the Clarendon Press, 1946.

LE   John Locke, *An Essay Concerning Human Understanding*, Routledge, London 1900.

SHE   Ingemar Hedenius, *Studies in Hume's Ethics*, repr. from *Adolf Phalén in Memoriam*, Uppsala 1937.

Ethics   P. H. Nowell-Smith, *Ethics*, Penguin Books, Middlesex 1954.

PML   Jeremy Bentham, *An Introduction to the Principles of Morals and Legislation*, Hafner, N.Y. 1948.

A   David Hume, *An Abstract of a Treatise of Human Nature* (1740) reprinted with an introduction by Keynes and Straffa, Cambridge, at the University Press, 1938.

Enquiry   is always used to refer to *The Enquiry Concerning the Principles of Morals*.

PR   *The Philosophical Review*.

ACKNOWLEDGEMENTS

I wish to thank the following publishers for permission to use quotations from works listed above: Macmillan, The Clarendon Press, Cambridge University Press, Penguin Books, Routledge and Kegan Paul, Prentice Hall, Hutchinson, Hafner, Dent.

I also wish to thank Mrs D. Moore for permitting me to quote from G. E. Moore's *Principia Ethica*, Professor J. A. Passmore for permission to quote from his *Hume's Intentions*, Mr A. A. Kassman, the Honorary Secretary of the Aristotelian Society, for permission to quote from the Society's published proceedings and Professor H. B. Acton, the editor of *Philosophy*, for allowing me to include in the final chapter of this book material that appeared in the October 1964 issue, and for allowing me to quote from articles in other issues of that journal. My thanks are also due to Professor Ingemar Hedenius from whose *Studies in Hume's Ethics* I have quoted.

INTRODUCTION TO THE SECOND EDITION

I

Importance of the indirect passions

Since the first publication of *Passion and Value*, few commentators on the *Treatise* have challenged the main theses of the book: that there is philosophically interesting material in the book 'Of The Passions' and that reading it is vital for proper understanding of the book 'Of Morals'.[1] There is, however, considerable disagreement about the central importance I claim for four of the indirect passions: love, hatred, pride and humility. But, my error was the opposite of the one with which I have been charged, for I now believe that my claim for the importance of these passions was too modest. They certainly are at the heart of Hume's account of judgments of virtue. But, since, as I shall argue, the concept of virtue is fundamental to Hume's epistemology, love, hatred, pride and humility, when they are judgments of virtue, have their place at the deepest ontological level of the science of man. These passions are the basic favourable and unfavourable evaluations of persons: virtues and vices are qualities of mind or character loved or hated, when they belong to another person and causes of pride and humility, when they belong to oneself. Not only is Hume's moral theory based on this theory of the passions in Book II, but the discussion of virtues and vices in Book III also throws a great deal of light upon some aspects of Book I. Thus, Hume's account of natural beliefs, such as the belief in a world of objects and causal regularities, can be understood, only if one pays attention to what he says about virtues and vices in the later books. The idea of virtue is also essential for understanding that Hume abandons the Cartesian view that fundamental beliefs about reality must be proved to be true to be acceptable. The truth of natural beliefs can neither be established by perception nor by reasoning, and an appeal to the traditionally conceived reason as an infallible faculty of truth begs the question in favour of the Rationalists. Yet Hume holds these natural beliefs to be reasonable, in that the person who allows himself to be guided by them helps to secure his success as an agent, and is generally 'loved' for that reason, whereas we 'hate' a person who shows no concern for his own or other peoples' interests. Such is the mental condition of one who prefers 'the destruction of the whole world' to 'the scratching of his finger.'[2] His is a form of madness, an unhealthy mental condition. Natural beliefs are in general the signs of a healthy mind. The mad person, suffering from delusions, mistakes his ideas for reality. This is a condition we can understand, for it happens to all of us, although in most cases the condition is fortunately temporary and thus different from the condition of some insane people. Hume writes: 'Thus, in sleep, in fever in madness, or in any very violent emotions of soul, our ideas may approach our impressions.'[3] It is of course debatable whether one can have beliefs in a dream. But, since believed reality is revealed to us in the form of strong and violent perceptions, our beliefs are a poor guide for actions in these special conditions.

It is clear that we are not using the term 'love' in any of its most customary senses when we say that a person is loved for possessing mental sanity. The oddity of the use of 'hatred', in this context, is even more striking. To say that one hates the insane for their condition seems not only odd but cruel. We do not, or at least ought not, to blame and hate an insane person. He is rather to be pitied. Hume would agree with this. Our evaluation of the insane person's life is of a different kind. We are pained by the thought of the insane person's condition. The 'hatred of him' for being in this condition *consists in* rating his life as of poor quality. Hatred of him as of blameworthy character would not be fitting. If the 'judgment' that a person has a vice or a defect or some other undesirable characteristic is an emotion, Hume needs a word for an emotion that captures the undesirability of the insane person's condition, covering blameworthy behaviour while not necessarily carrying the implication of blameworthiness. The outline of Hume's view, so far given, looks strained due to the fact that 'passion', 'virtue', 'love', hatred', 'pride' and 'humility' are all given a special, unusual meaning in Hume's account. It is a main

x

theme of this introduction to reveal some of the implications of the tensions in Hume's terminology.

Seeing 'judgments' of virtue as indirect passions is in harmony with Hume's claim that actions are never valued, or approved of morally, except as signs of qualities of mind or character, i.e. as signs of virtues in the agent. Here one must remind oneself that a virtue is, on Hume's account, a quality of mind or character that is immediately pleasing to the person himself or to others, or useful to the person himself or to others. The opposite characteristics are the source of vices or defects.[4] Insanity would be a defect (vice) in that it is neither useful to the person himself nor to others, but is likely to be harmful as well as immediately painful to the person himself and to others. The indirect passions are aroused only when the cause is relatively closely connected with the object of the passion for a reasonable period of time. Thus, I can be proud of the beauty of my homeland, but not of a country to which I am making a casual visit. It may be seen as a confirmation of the view that Hume thought evaluations of people were indirect passions if he overemphasises the unreasonableness of holding people responsible for actions out of character. One might want to claim that an action shown to be out of character may still be morally assessable. Hume sometimes seems to be denying this view. It would weaken Hume's account, but strengthen my account of what 'judgment of character' involves for Hume, if Hume can be seen to have been misled by treating judgments of character as indirect passions. It is of course not debatable that our interest in some morally undesirable behaviour may not focus upon judging the character of the perpetrators. One may think the damage has been done and be primarily concerned that the undesirable behaviour will not repeat itself. But there is an important minimum requirement that all actions must meet if they are to be considered morally assessable. Thus one's moral indignation does not cease when the physical action is hindered, so long as everything else (including intentions) remains. If we are making a moral assessment of an action one must consider the action relevant as an indication of a quality of mind or character, although it may not be immediately clear what character trait of which person is being displayed. To illustrate this one can take post-hypnotic suggestion. When the subject sees an apparently kind action as indicative of a quality in the hypnotist the action ceases to make him proud. If anyone deserves praise, it is the hypnotist, assuming the action is praiseworthy. No one may deserve praise, for an apparently kind action performed by the subject may consist in the hypnotist giving a small sum of money out of the subject's pocket. As soon as you see the action as evidence of a quality of the character of the hypnotist, it ceases to look generous. The hypnotist would not be loved for generosity and you would have nothing to be proud of.

It should not be too difficult to persuade a contemporary speaker of English that emotions can amount to judgments of character. Both 'love' and 'hate' are frequently used in precisely this way. We may love one person for his endearing qualities and hate another for his insensitivity. Pride and humility are also clearly forms of self-evaluation, although humility may, to some people, suggest undue modesty, and to others a virtue. We shall come back to further consideration of the nature of the four indirect passions I am claiming to be basic to Hume's account.

II

Technical terms and ordinary language

In reading the *Treatise*, one must constantly bear in mind the difference between asking what Hume had to say about what he means by a certain term and what Hume had to say about what we mean by the same term. I am encouraging you to bear these two questions in mind, in all your attempts at understanding the *Treatise*. In developing the science of human nature, Hume gives new technical meanings to certain terms or restricts or expands their usual meaning. Even the word 'passion' is given a new meaning, as was noted by Thomas Reid, who writes about desires and affections: 'When they are so calm as neither to produce any sensible effects upon the body nor to darken the understanding and weaken the power of self-command, they are not called passions.'[5] Reid claims that this meaning is more in accordance with common usage than the use given to the word 'passion' by David Hume, who, he thinks, erroneously allows for the possibility of calm, enlightened passions, whereas passions are, in their very nature violent. Reid writes: 'Passion, or violent appetite, first blinds the understanding, and then perverts the will.'[6]

Most modern readers will find themselves in sympathy with Reid's observations. But, Hume was producing a new science of human nature and he needed terms that he could not find ready-made in

xii

English. Hume may have thought that his novel theory, that reason cannot be in conflict with passions, is best expressed by unmistakably claiming that what people had taken for reason was nothing but a certain calm passion or in other words, 'reason improperly so called'. The usage draws attention to the fact that there are not two kinds of mental causes, reason with authority, and blind, subservient emotion. When an emotional determination has become a settled principle of action we may mistake this for a God-given faculty of calm judgments, whereas what we have is only calm passions that may involve so little conscious emotional disturbance as to be more known by their effects than their immediate conscious feeling. Hume wants to display that there is so much conscious difference between passions, at one end of the scale, and reason, improperly so called, at the other, that the impropriety is easily missed. The expression 'calm passion' brings out the radical nature of Hume's doctrine. It also reveals a certain difficulty in the concept of passion. The passions, Hume says, are simple impressions, but they may become settled principles of action that move to action independently of conscious awareness. To produce an alternative to the theories of the Rationalists Hume had to distinguish *motivating power* from conscious strength, excitement or vivacity.

Since any quality of mind or character is a virtue, if it makes you proud when it belongs to yourself and makes you love another person when it belongs to him/her, there are bound to be a great number of virtues. Since any valuable quality of mind or character is a virtue, one cannot avoid concluding that to be a responsible language user is a virtue and the tendency to believe in a continuously and independently existing world is another virtue. To be the kind of person that is guided in his actions by observed regularities is to possess another valuable quality of mind, or, in other words, a virtue. Hume is not only saying that nature has not left it to chance whether we believe in a world of objects, or look for causes. The tendency to have these beliefs is both a general quality of human nature and a valuable characteristic that greatly helps to secure our survival and effective agency. The justification for treating these tendencies as virtues is to be found in Hume's wide conception of virtue. Qualities of mind or character that cause the indirect passions are virtues and vices and there seems to be no ground at all for excluding from the class of virtues, the fundamentally valuable dispositions, or natural beliefs mentioned above. The following quotation from the *Treatise* justifies this claim. Hume writes about the sources of pride and humility: '. . . we may observe that their most obvious and remarkable property is the vast variety of subjects, on which they may be placed. Every valuable quality of the mind, whether of the imagination, judgment, memory or disposition; wit, good sense, learning, courage, justice, integrity; all of these are the causes of pride; and the opposites of humility.'[7] To be a quality of mind that causes love is to be a virtue.

Hume is trying to show us that 'judgments' of virtue can be explained without the need to postulate special orders of value or special intuitive powers. If Hume can identify the basic passions from which we develop the special passions that make us praise or condemn people for their character, his account would seem much more persuasive. Thus, if thinking a man is a good man is to love him in a certain way, then it may be claimed that judgments of virtue have turned out to be no more puzzling than loving, and no one has thought it necessary to postulate special powers or orders of value independent of man to show how loving is possible. Hume thus has a strong motive to claim that the indirect passions of love, hatred, pride and humility are easily identifiable in our experience. Incidentally, a distinction can be drawn between the pride *of something* that characteristically finds its expression in boastfulness and the pride that is shown by a person's stubborn resistance to being helped, the insistence upon standing on your own feet. Hume may have thought this stubbornness a character trait that does not have any necessary relation to pride as an evaluation of oneself. Suffice it to say that the existence of a rational, ethical intuitive faculty is to be rejected because it is unnecessary. To postulate such a special power will cease to seem tempting when judgments of virtue have been explained as a development from uncontroversial phenomena, something we are all perfectly familiar with. Incidentally, the explanation of moral evaluation as a development from already familiar emotions, also makes it unnecessary to postulate a moral sense.

Pride and humility have oneself as their object, whereas the object of love and hatred is *another person*, another *sensitive being* or another *thinking being*. Inanimate objects are explicitly ruled out and Hume would seem to be committed to ruling out plants as well for, although animate, they are neither thinkers nor persons. It is not so clear that plants have no sensitivity, but Hume wrongly uses the different characterisations of the objects of these passions as if there were no problem in treating them as interchangeable. However, some animals,

xiv

Hume thinks, can experience these passions, and animals are not commonly thought to be persons, and although sentient, they are usually only considered capable of relatively elementary thinking.

Hume is quick to point out that the existence of self-love does not furnish a counter-example to his claim. He insists that, in using language in this way one is not using 'love' in its proper sense.[8] To strengthen this claim Hume points out that there is little in common with 'that tender emotion, which is excited by a friend or mistress'. But, it is questionable whether the love that Hume describes as an indirect passion has much in common with our tender feelings towards our friends or mistresses. Hume's prime example is our love or admiration for virtue, but he also talks about love of beauty, and our love or esteem for the rich and powerful. To be consistent with his general account of the objects of the indirect passions he should really talk about the love of someone for being virtuous or beautiful. It is doubtful whether any of these kinds of love is the kind of love we have for a friend or a mistress. The love which constitutes an indirect passion is love for the possession of a special quality that is found independently pleasing. But the love of a mistress is generally taken to have some sexual component and Hume treats love between the sexes as a separate complex passion. The love which characterizes true friendship is again different in that it typically involves loyalty which survives the discovery that your friend is perhaps not altogether an admirable person. A true friend wants to improve your moral condition and the fact that other people tend to avoid contact with you because of your bad character becomes an added reason for trying to lead you to mend your ways rather than abandon you. It is characteristic of a true friend to be loyal beyond what is demanded by the friend's virtues. There is nevertheless a good reason why Hume should decide to exclude self-love. In his system, self-love, as high self-esteem, *is pride*, whereas self-love as selfishness is a motive or a motivational attitude, but none of Hume's indirect passions love, hatred, pride and humility are motives. Motives, however, mark an important difference between pride and humility on the one hand, and love and hatred, on the other. Love and hatred are associated with benevolence and anger, benevolence and anger being conceived of as the desire for someone's happiness and unhappiness respectively, but pride and humility are 'pure emotions in the soul' in no way attached to the desire to make happy the proud person or unhappy the humble one. When you love a person for his virtues you naturally want to make him happy for that reason alone, whereas it seems inappropriate to desire to be rewarded for moral virtues in oneself.

The more refined the distinctions are that characterize evaluations the less plausible it is to appeal to special evaluative faculties. There is a flexibility in human responses that is not captured by typical objects of so-called rational intuition such as goodness and badness, rightness and wrongness. One may not always agree with Hume's explanation of the phenomena, but he certainly had a keen eye for evaluative social responses. Thus a relation's love for you makes you proud only when the love is seen by you to be merited. But your love of him, in so far as it is seeing him to have value, makes you proud. You are permitted to claim the increased self-worth that pride involves, without having done anything to merit it. The exploits of friends, family ancestors, fellow citizens and other relations are legitimate causes of pride. Although this may seem to make the criteria for legitimate pride too permissive, and thus irrational, there may be human situations in which this permissive emotion has a proper place. Effective social action by members of an underprivileged nation may need pride as based upon a kind of fiction, in order to gain the objectives that really justify pride, such as your own virtue and accomplishments. Thus pride is a form of self-evaluation that tolerates a certain degree of bias. If one claims to be proud because one possesses a virtue, such as courage, one must actually be courageous to be justly proud. But the courage may be entirely native to you, due to your inherited nature rather than any admirable exercise of your will. On Hume's account, it is not a precondition for the moral value of a virtue that it be acquired by voluntary effort.

Hume considers the view that love of another person must always be caused by his intentional actions. In this connection he draws a distinction between qualities inherent in a person's character, on the one hand, and actions on the other. If you find someone a boring person you treat this as a defect without considering whether this defect was intentionally acquired. Indeed, if you conclude that the person was intentionally boring you, you have not settled whether he is a bore or not. Being a bore is boring people whether one intends to do so or not. However, in general unintended action taken in isolation is frequently not closely enough related to the agent to cause an emotion towards him. A person may be acting out of character due to ignorance or inattention. A polite, tactful person may say something impolite and tactless due to blameless ignorance or complete inattention to certain features of a situation. When the same behaviour is intentional it is an *indication* of the character trait of tactlessness or rudeness in the agent that remains when the action is completed, and may lead to the expectation of similar future behaviour from the person in question. It is a strong consideration in favour of the claim that judgments of virtue are to Hume indirect passions, that actions are morally evaluated only in so far as they issue from a relatively constant quality of mind or charscter. This feature of the cause of the indirect passions was stressed in Hume's account of these passions.

III

Truth and reasonable belief

The account I am giving of Hume's theory downgrades the philosophical importance of truth as correspondence and upgrades that of reasonable belief.[9] The Cartesian error was to think that our beliefs had to be proved to be true before it was reasonable to adopt them. Our right to take our clear and distinct ideas to be true of, or correspond to reality ultimately rested upon proof of the existence of a God who is not a deceiver. Although Hume thought we can form a relative idea of God, he rejected the possibility of any proof of God's existence. To him, therefore, going down the road of Cartesian doubt was a one-way street. The existence of a world of objects could neither be proved by reasoning nor revealed by our senses. Only in fevered delirium or madness can this belief be shaken, with the exception of the momentary illusion of philosophers, when they are alone with their thoughts in their study. But the illusion of suspending this belief is dispelled as soon as the philosopher returns to society from his relatively short excursion into the world of pure thought. To be sane in the world is a quality of mind that is useful to the person himself or to others as well as immediately pleasing to the person himself and to others. Thus sanity is a virtue that derives its value from all these four considerations.

It is at this point that the four indirect passions come into the picture, for thinking well of a person because he possesses a virtue is to love him for that reason. The love which is an indirect passion is an evaluation of a person for a reason. In so far as the opposite of virtue is vice, to be mad in the world would be a vice. 'Fault' or 'defect' would seem much more appropriate as the opposites of 'virtue' in Hume's extended use of that term. To Hume, the important question is 'which qualities of mind or character cause love, esteem and approbation?' Hume is clearly not using the terms 'virtue' and 'vice' with the meaning we now give to these terms. We certainly would not call wit a virtue and being a bore a vice. The wide sense given by Hume to 'virtue' makes the claim that the concept of virtue is central to his epistemology much less startling and implausible. I am drawing attention to what Hume's account of virtue and the indirect passions commits him to. One can therefore not conclusively refute my thesis by pointing out that Hume does not explicitly state the view I am attributing to him. One cannot expect original thinkers to be fully aware of all the implications of their novel doctrines.

Hume's view that moral evaluations only consider actions in so far as they indicate some quality of mind or character of an agent has considerable implications. Intentional actions and omissions are clearly indicative of qualities of mind or character. Deliberate harm is blame-worthy, but so is the deliberate failure to prevent harm. But total failure to be interested in the welfare of your fellow human beings is also blameworthy. Insensitivity and apathy are moral flaws, and on Hume's view, there is nothing surprising about this. One may find the hard-hearted abhorrent. Their behaviour is out of tune with the situations that call for a certain response. That is enough; behaviour need not be intentional and voluntary to be seen as an indication of a character defect. To be forgetful about important matters is to have a defect although the forgetfulness is neither deliberate nor can be traced to a deliberate choice of the forgetful person. Hume's concept of virtue is wider than our own. Being intelligent and witty are virtues and the opposite of virtue is vice. These terms, with their wider significance, must be understood in the context of Hume's theory.

It may help to drive home the importance of Hume's doctrine to draw attention to the fact that Kant's 'Categorical Imperative' pre-supposes a different view about that for which people are responsible. The injunction that one should act only on that maxim one can will to become through one's will a universal law presupposes that the action can be legitimately seen as done on principle. This could be made to include deliberate inactivity, but it could not cover omissions due to forgetfulness, apathy, insensitivity or being a bore. To Hume it is important to accept responsibility for these defects in that the self-hatred generated may lead the agent to try to become a different, more adequate person. Kant's notion that one can be responsible for one's character only if it is chosen leads to difficulties. If the real self is the rational self, as he sometimes suggests, the difficulty is to understand how a rational self can choose to become defective. The reality of evil would seem to presuppose something like original sin. Each person's temporal existence would represent such an underlying choice made by a real self that is non-temporal. But the price you pay is that anything like a moral conflict has been pushed out of the agent's temporal life.

I have been arguing that Hume's four terms for basic passions evaluating people are best considered to be technical terms, although Hume suggests otherwise. This makes the theories that I and Donald Davidson have attributed to Hume, not so much an aspect of Hume's theory of pride as theories suggested by Hume's text.[10] It is perhaps not accidental that no one has discovered in Hume a cognitive theory of love, humility and hatred. These passions and pride are the four basic ways of evaluating people for a reason. In his choice of words to stand for the four indirect passions of his scheme Hume has decided upon terms that are related in meaning to the technical sense his account requires. It is unfortunate that Hume himself is partly responsible for the mistaken view that he is analysing the very emotions that, independently of his theory, are called love, hatred, pride and humility.

IV

Varieties of 'justice'

In dealing with Hume's theory of justice one cannot but notice that Part II of the *Treatise* is called 'Of Justice and Injustice', but this is also a chapter heading. It is thus suggested by Hume both that justice includes all the artificial virtues and that justice refers exclusively to the distribution of property rights. Hume usually refers to justice in this narrower sense and is criticized for this. He would not entirely escape censure if we take him to have used 'justice' to refer to all the artificial virtues. It is most implausible to suggest that the rules governing modesty and chastity are rules of justice, and Hume himself suggests that these rules are unfair to women, depriving them unfairly of sexual pleasures. In doing this he seems to be using ordinary rather than theory-laden language. He can thus be said both to have had a too narrow and too wide a concept of justice. Once the distinction is drawn between what Hume calls justice and what we call justice it can be readily seen that issues of justice have a much greater part to play in the *Treatise* than those that criticize Hume for too narrow a conception of this virtue seem to realise. Thus, the indirect passions, pride, humility, love and hatred are all naturally biased in favour of friends and family. This bias is in one sense an injustice and in another not. Hume thinks we should be more concerned about the welfare of those close to us than total strangers. This is the natural bent of the passions of which we approve on reflection. But, when the bias *affects judgments of virtue*, and interferes with our judgments of peoples' qualities of mind or character, it is an injustice. Hume talks about the difficulty of giving our enemies due credit for the virtues they possess. If, as I have argued, the indirect passions are judgments of virtue when they are caused by qualities of mind or character, a basic problem of the book 'Of Morals' is to show how we can *do justice to* the real qualities of mind or character of people, how the natural bias of the passions can be overcome.

V

The attack on reason

In assessing the place Hume allots to reason, one must guard against the error of thinking that Hume is allowing that we have reason, but that we have tended to overestimate what reason can do. It is the very existence of an infallible faculty of reason that Hume is calling in question. Reason he claims is nothing but the discovery of truth or falsehood. Reason's infallibility explains why Hume calls it a discovery. You can only *discover* what really is the case. But, notice that Hume does not say that reason is the *power* to discover truths and falsehoods. He is anxious, whenever possible to avoid appealing to faculties, or hidden powers. There is, he says, no distinction to be drawn between power and the exercise of it, and he defines the will as the impression we feel when we knowingly give rise to some thought in our mind or movement of our body. Hume clearly thinks we have an immediate experience of doing things as opposed to things happening to us. But this is not to be equated with awareness of causal power. Not that

Hume thinks our actions are not the result of causes. He, on the contrary, thinks that it would be entirely irrational to love or hate people for their actions, unless the causes of actions are some qualities in us. What is more, one praises and condemns people after the action is completed. The cause of the action for which the person is praised or condemned, must thus be presumed to remain after the performance of the action. We are responsible for our actions only if they are caused, a cause is required for accountability, not just compatible with it. This is all fully understood when one remembers how the cause was distinguished from the object of the indirect passions. You love the person for possessing the quality that causes the action.

The traditional concept of reason that Hume was attacking was not only infallible, but also versatile. It enabled us to do mathematics and science and revealed to us moral standards. Hume tried to show that the unreasonableness of the immoral person is quite different from the condition of the person who accepts falsehoods. To understand the importance of Hume's claim, one must keep in mind that it was not uncommon in the eighteenth century to maintain that it does not really matter whether one thinks of actions as right or wrong or as true or false.[11] Since reality was the creation of God it had to be perfect. Thus, right actions had to be in conformity with reality, just as true statements and beliefs corresponded to reality. Kant saw the importance of Hume's attack upon the versatility of reason and tried to give reasons for thinking that the same principle of reason set the standard in logic, science and morals. Reason, he thought, was the faculty of laws.

VI

Persons and natural beliefs

Animals are sensitive to each other's pains and pleasures as is shown by the way they avoid hurting each other in often violent play. Sympathy is shown by the manner in which animals prefer the company of members of their own species. The reason why we do not think animals capable of judgements of virtue is that they cannot form the concept of a quality of mind or character. That concept makes it possible to compare the virtue of people living in different ages and to abstract from the special relation you may have to the object of the emotion. Hume uses our own experience to interpret the behaviour of animals. This results in upgrading the life of animals. Hume makes them seem quite closely similar to humans, capable of a variety of passions, and he may well have thought it reasonable to presume in people a natural instinctive awareness of members of their own species. It is entirely possible that the statement that the minds of men are mirrors to each other is meant to suggest that our belief in persons, is a natural belief, the tendency to which is a virtue. If we take the Cartesian doubt seriously, we certainly cannot prove the existence of persons, for persons are physical objects and we cannot prove the existence of physical objects, if the assistance of God is unavailable, and it certainly was unavailable to Hume. But, Hume believes that there is an inner and outer side to those physical objects we call persons, although we only perceive the outer side of other people. But it is characteristic of natural beliefs that they cannot be proved to be true. The claim that our minds are mirrors to each other strongly suggests that we see other people *as having minds*. It is not something that needs to be proved, for which we have some evidence. No evidence could adequately support the enormous strength of this belief. In addition to describing the minds of men as mirrors to each other Hume says our emotions are transmitted like sounds, reverberating, sounding sympathetic notes and dying away gradually as they fade away, moving from their original centre. The concept of reverberation captures better than that of a mirror image that it is taken for granted with absolute certainty that in our social life we are in constant inter-action with other persons. Not only are the 'minds of men mirrors to each other', but the following quotations show how deeply essential to human beings shared experience is. Hume writes: 'Every pleasure languishes when enjoyed apart from company and every pain becomes more cruel and intolerable.'[12] He adds a little later:

> Let all the powers and elements of nature conspire to serve and obey one man: let the sun rise and set at his command: The sea and rivers roll as he pleases, and the earth furnish spontaneously whatever may be useful and agreeable to him: he will still be miserable till you give him some one person at least, with whom he may share his happiness, and whose esteem and friendship he may enjoy.[13]

When a person is deliberately harmed by another person part of the harm is done by the ill-will that the action expresses. Since the minds of men are mirrors to each other it is not easy to escape the hostile

xxii

feelings of our fellow men. And since we need others to share our experience, our fortunes are inextricably dependent upon the good will of others.

Hume dramatically characterizes Nature as a teacher in the opening paragraph of the important section of the *Treatise* 'Of Scepticism with Regard to the Senses.' It captures perfectly the naturalist, anti-sceptical interpretation of Hume that I favour. Hume writes:

Thus the sceptic still continues to reason and believe, even though he asserts, that he cannot defend his reason by reason; and by the same rule he must assent to the principle concerning the existence of body, though he cannot pretend by any arguments of philosophy to maintain its veracity. Nature has not left this to his choice, and has doubtless esteemed it of too great importance to be trusted to our uncertain reasonings and speculations. We may well ask, what causes induce us to believe in the existence of body? but it is in vain to ask, whether there be body or not? That is a point which we must take for granted in all our reasonings.[14]

Here we have a clear statement of the claim that natural beliefs are of fundamental importance for us. It is fortunate that we should have these beliefs for having to base these fundamental beliefs upon fallible reasoning would leave us much worse off. Hume thinks human life is social at the deepest emotional level. All natural beliefs are stronger than reasoning can support. If nature thought it was too important to leave establishing the reality of physical objects to reasoning, would it not be even more important for us to be furnished with a natural belief in persons with whom we must share our experience? The notion of nature as an intentional guide is of course not to be taken literally, for there is no reason to presume a consciously devised plan behind nature. But, in following our natural bent we come to develop such socially invaluable features as language, property and civic society. Thus following nature guides us towards wise living and preservation of life although nature was not designed to serve these ends.

VII

Truth, calm passions and general rules

People need to be educated to take up the point of view that licences expressions like 'John is a good man'. The behaviour that can be seen as our duty may be difficult and the propaganda of parents and politicians may have to be sought to achieve the necessary social stability through general adherence to the artificial virtues. But, ideally, when challenged, the person has to be guided by what he finds himself approving and disapproving of on reflection. Since there is not always time for the necessary reflection people can frequently do no better than to follow the general rules of behaviour that society has adopted. Hume seemed to think that in the case of all the artificial virtues one should follow the rules in preference to each individual attempting to calculate the consequences of his behaviour in particular cases. Thus, in spite of the ultimate individualism that I have been attributing to Hume he tends to be rather conservative, insisting upon the need to follow the rules that have come to be adopted by society.

If value judgments are emotions and emotions are neither true nor false, then assessing their propriety and impropriety must be different from assessing their truth. This is precisely what Hume seems to emphasize: the passions, unlike beliefs, have no representative quality but a person's love or hatred, pride or humility may still be challenged. People may be asked to reconsider their attitude and as a result of this reconsideration they may come to feel quite differently about the person and his attitudes and actions. The attempt to overcome personal biases may be described as the demand of reason, but Hume attempts to go behind this apparent appeal to a faculty and trace the tendency to objectivity to the need for co-operation in society and the need for communication. Taking up an impartial point of view, abstracting from the special relations to yourself and your personal peculiarities, is the work of that calm passion Hume calls reason improperly so-called. I believe this is the crucial concept, not only underlying Hume's theory of virtue and obligation but also when it comes to the *justification* of the so-called natural beliefs. Reasonable beliefs are not necessarily known to be true beliefs in the sense of accurately reflecting an independently existing reality. Hume held a correspondence theory of empirical *truth* and at the fundamental level neither reason nor perception can establish this correspondence. It is experience alone that teaches us which beliefs we should take seriously in our lives. If we do not allow ourselves to be guided by regularities in nature our desires are less likely to be satisfied, including that desire which characterises philosophers, curiosity, or the love of truth. For although the hunt for truth may ultimately not succeed, philosophical pursuits give pleasures similar to the pleasures of the hunt, a philosophically inclined individual would be disadvantaged if he did not join the hunt and Hume tells us that he philosophized so as not to become a loser in point of pleasure. This is not to deny that philosophy is a noble pursuit. Hume's point is that one cannot in advance know the value of one's philosophical speculations. What we know is that some people have a craving for knowledge and understanding and the process of hunting for these, though perhaps ultimately doomed to failure, may nevertheless be well worth while because of the pleasures of the activity. The hunter's time has not necessarily been wasted though the quarry escapes.

VIII

Meaning and property

There is no discussion in *Passion and Value* of the kind of account Hume would have to give of the nature and function of language.[15] I only make the negative point that Hume's theory of 'morals' in the *Treatise*, is a theory about the nature of evaluations of agents, not a theory about the nature of language. I still believe this to be essentially right. But I had not seen then, what I have seen now, that the analogy Hume draws between meaning and property, treating meaning as a conventionally acquired causal property of sounds and visible marks, strengthens my case against the subjectivist account of moral judgments often attributed to him. Although it is in Book III that Hume reveals his views about the place of language in our lives, he rejects in Book I the view, wrongly attributed to him, that the meanings of words are ideas conceived of as images. Antony Flew states this view clearly. He traces Hume's overestimation of the importance of mental imagery to 'an approach to language, and hence to philosophy, which is wholly inverted.'[16] 'The first' [incorrect] approach 'begins with the logically private realm of one man's experience; the second [correct] view starts from the common public world of physical things and events, the world of 'the reality of things' and of transactions between people.'[17] Since, on this view, the meanings of words are private mental images, communication is made impossible and any knowledge of the world is equally impossible since it is confined to the knower's private world of images. But, a close look at the chapter 'Of Abstract Ideas' reveals a different view. Hume stresses that the meanings of words cannot be images since we can distinguish between the thought of a figure with 999 sides and one with 1 000 sides and yet we could not distinguish between images of these two figures. And, instead of finding Hume arguing from the private world of ideas to a public world of material objects we find him arguing from the known determinacy of physical objects both with regard to quality and quantity, to a similar determinacy of ideas or images. Hume is not just stating the obvious, that the forming of an image is a datable occurrence and thus particular. He is making the much more interesting claim, that all ideas are of particulars. He rejects the view that abstract ideas are possible on the ground that they would be of something that could not have separate existence. People with strong visual imagination may be able to imagine such a thing as a line by projecting it on to a wall of determinate length. But it seems clearly false that all images must be of determinate character. It seems possible to form an image of an object such as a table, without the image being of a particular table. Of course, if I form an image of a particular table, the image is of something determinate because physical objects are necessarily determinate with respect to quantity and quality. Hume is arguing from known characteristics of physical objects to a conclusion as to what must be the characteristic of images. He most assuredly does not argue from the characteristics of a private world of images to a conclusion about physical objects. He appeals to a principle generally received in philosophy, that everything in nature is individual . . . and he adds: 'If this . . . [that something exists that is not determinate with regard to quality and quantity] be absurd in *fact and reality* it must also be absurd *in idea*'.[18] Hume is clearly presupposing knowledge of a world of physical objects and he goes wrong in attributing to the subjective world of images characteristics of this known objective world. So much for Hume's alleged inverted conception of philosophy. It is impossible to make sense of Hume's description of the way in which we give people a simple idea except by presupposing a physical world. You give someone the idea of the taste of a pineapple by providing him with a pineapple to eat. Hume rightly considers it absurd to try to give someone the impression by providing him with the idea. The very notion is absurd. But even if we assume that a person who has never tasted a pineapple could try to form an image of the taste, it is hard to see how he could in this way learn to identify pineapples by their taste.

In 'Of Abstract Ideas' in Book I, Hume is attempting to show how general thoughts are possible, although all ideas are of particulars. What happens is that the same sound is used to cover a range of particulars that are similar in certain respects although different in some other respects. Gradually a customary association is formed between the sound and these objects in such a way that the hearing of the sound calls to mind an image of one or other of these particulars. Most of them are there in power only. The range of particulars may be indeterminate, but it is the power to call to mind particulars that control the application of a term that constitutes knowing the meaning of the term. People that speak the same language have learned to apply the terms in roughly the same way. It may be argued that Hume overstates the case for the use of images in the controls that are operative in the communicative use of language. But Hume himself points out that images may become unnecessary and he never suggests that the meanings of words are ideas or images. Thus Hume writes

. . . that in talking of GOVERNMENT, CHURCH, NEGOTIATION, CONQUEST, we seldom spread out in our minds all the simple ideas, of which these complex ones are composed. It is however observable, that notwithstanding this imperfection we may avoid talking nonsense on these subjects as well as if we had a full comprehension of them. Thus, if instead of saying, *that in war the weaker always have recourse to negotiation*, we should say *that they have always recourse to conquest*, the custom, which we have acquired of attributing certain relations to ideas, still follows the words, and makes us immediately perceive the absurdity of the proposition, in the same manner as one particular idea may serve us in reasoning concerning other ideas, however different from it in several circumstances.[19]

Thus, when a language has been mastered images play a lesser part in our thinking. The thought that the weaker have recourse to conquest is incoherent and cannot possibly be true. It is not of course sufficient for effective communication that we avoid this kind of nonsense. Responsibility in the use of language is a necessary condition for effective communication. If language were primarily used to deceive, communication would break down. Since communication is essential to build and maintain the co-operation that gives the human race sufficient strength to make up for human physical weaknesses, being a responsible language user is an important virtue. A possessor of this virtue does not only refrain from making deliberately misleading utterances, but also makes sure not to get sloppy in his use of language. Each language user has a duty to use language responsibly and others have a right to expect this of him/her.

In drawing an analogy between the origin of the virtue of respect for property rights and being a responsible language user Hume shows these to be artificial virtues. In each case he thinks there is a necessary training called for, or what he calls propaganda of parents and politicians. Individuals are likely not to perceive the enormous importance of abiding by the standards of responsible use of language and respect for property. Hence the need for special training or propanda. Hume takes it as an advantage in his account that the obligation to use language in such a way as not to deceive is not without exception. Lies are not only permitted on certain occasions, but may even be morally required. If only a lie can save innocent life, a lie ought to be told.

Meaningful use of words becomes possible by convention and convention also gives rise to property rights. A convention is a practice that arises gradually and develops through awareness of a common interest in preserving the practice. To quote Hume:

> Nor is the rule concerning the stability of possession the less derived from human conventions, that it arises gradually, and acquires force by slow progression, and by our repeated experience of the inconvenience of transgressing it. On the contrary, this experience assures us still more that the sense of interest has become common to all our fellows, and gives us a confidence of the future regularity of their conduct: and it is only on the expectation of this, that our moderation and abstinence are founded. In like manner are languages gradually established by human conventions without any promise.[20]

A promise is a speech act and thus presupposes language. Hume's procedure would be circular if convention were not sharply distinguished from promise and contract.

IX

The ontology of obligations

It must be remembered that Hume does not believe judgments of virtue exhaust the class of moral judgments. It is true that he seems to agree with Kant that an action that is in conformity with duty, but does not seem to be an indication of a valuable quality of mind or character does not have moral value. Both Hume and Kant made the concept of virtue central to their theories, although of course they had very different ideas about the nature of virtue. But, Hume also has a doctrine of moral obligation or duty and the crucial passage encapsulating his view is to be found in the chapter 'Of Promises' in the *Treatise*. He writes:

All morality depends upon our sentiments; and when any action, or quality of the mind, pleases us *after a certain manner*, we say it is virtuous; and when the neglect, or nonperformance of it, displeases us *after a like manner*, we say that we lie under an obligation to perform it.[21]

The crucial words here are 'after a certain manner' and 'after a like manner'. Hume is again careful to remind his readers that not all pleasures and displeasures are of the kind that make us praise and condemn. But Hume here further strengthens the connection between his account of virtue and vice on the one hand, and his account of obligation and duty, on the other, by calling judgments of duty a form of self-hatred. Humility is having a low opinion of yourself, but self-hatred, because of a lack of certain qualities, involves active condemnation and not just failure to admire. Hume's concept of humility seems to cover both. His account would have been more accurate if he had drawn finer distinctions between vice and mere failure to come up to a sufficiently high standard to merit being called virtuous. One can contrast positive virtue on the one hand, and vice on the other. The fact that 'faults are but minor vices' does not entail that no distinction is necessary between lack of virtue and a positive vice. We tend to think of virtue as the possession of more than the minimum standard of some excellence. Behaviour that merely comes up to an acceptable standard is neither vicious nor virtuous. On Hume's account this is reflected in his claim that conduct which is neither pleasing nor displeasing neither causes pride nor humility in the person himself nor love or hatred in others. Qualities that are shared by most people, and are in no way special, are not proper causes of the indirect passions. There is thus a middle ground when neither virtue nor vice is properly attributable to a person. Following the quotation from the chapter 'Of Promises' Hume goes on to say that for there to be a change in our obligation due to a voluntary act, such as promising is supposed to be, a change must be effected in our sentiments and we cannot change our sentiments at will. If Hume were a realist this would be a strange claim for the obligation would then arise from the act of promising, independently of any feeling in the promiser, or anyone else. Even if sentiments or feelings are caused by a promise and thus furnish a clue to there being an obligation, the feeling or sentiment would merely have an epistemological function. To make the sentiment a necessary element in the obligation is to give up the realist position. The sentiments that constitute thinking that one has an obligation are clearly those of the judge, although the judge and the judged may be the same person, the promiser.

Notice that Hume is describing the conditions that entitle us to say that a person is virtuous or vicious, or that an action is a duty or not a duty. Hume's view is that there is no such situation discoverable as *being under an obligation*. There are simply conditions that entitle us to say this is so or not so. But clearly we do not have feelings of the kind Hume mentions every time we say that persons have a virtue or that certain obligation is incurred by them. Hume is well aware of this. It may be difficult for us to achieve the degree of objectivity that is needed to overcome the natural bias of our passions 'we must fix on some *steady* and *general* point of view'. To learn how to make judgments of virtue and vice is to learn to adopt a shared point of view with others. This will, we hope, correct our sentiments, or at least our language as the following well-known passage suggests. Hume writes:

> Experience soon teaches us this method of correcting our sentiments, or at least, of correcting our language, where the sentiments are more stubborn and inalterable. Our servant, if diligent and faithful, may excite stronger sentiments of love and kindness than *Marcus Brutus*, as represented in history; but we say not upon that account, that the former character is more laudable than the latter. We know that were we to approach equally near to that renowned patriot, he would command a much higher degree of affection and admiration. Such corrections are common with regard to all the senses; and indeed it were impossible we could ever make use of language or communicate our sentiments to one another, did we not correct the momentary appearances of things and overlook our present situation.[22]

In this passage we have a clear indication that judgments of

character involve contrary to fact conditional judgments. What determines our evaluation is whether or not we would have feelings of
approbation or disapprobation, love or hatred, under specifiable conditions. But once the customary relation has been established between
a certain kind of quality and a certain evaluation the appearance of the
quality may determine your language and your behaviour, although
your emotions may be more stubborn. People have a tendency to be
determined by general rules and this may lead a person to call valuable
some character about whom he finds he does not have feelings of
approval. The general rule comes to dominate. The habit of falling in
with the attitudes of one's fellows is too strong. But, if this evaluation
should be seriously challenged the only correct procedure is to try as
far as one can to overcome the bias of personal relations and personal
peculiarities of one's own character. There is of course no guarantee
that unanimity will result, but Hume thinks that human nature is
much the same in all times and places and although on the surface
there may be vast differences between people's behaviour in different
centuries, and in different parts of the world, the principles from which
these behavioural differences developed are found to be basically the
same.

X

Explicit and tacit promises

Insisting that promises are not natural acts, Hume poses the problem
about the nature of promises by asking what function the expression
'I promise' performs. Promises come into existence when a certain
form of words has conventionally acquired the function of laying the
speaker's reputation for dependability on the line. 'Let me never be
trusted again, if I fail to do what I am promising to do' catches the
essence of promising. When the usefulness of the practice of giving
and keeping promises has come to be appreciated a moral motive is
added. Since most people are not sufficiently reflective and perceptive
to be motivated by the general utility of the practice of promises and
the prudential motive, a special training in faithfulness to promises is
needed. '*Public interest, education and the artifices of politicians . . .*'[23]
have the same effect in creating a moral motive to respect property
rights and keep promises: Hume identifies the question 'What is a
promise?' with the question 'What is the function of the expression

"I promise"?' He seems to limit the class of promises to explicit promises. This is very much in the spirit of his doubts about tacit consent or tacit promise as a source of political obligation. An actual promise to obey the government may be a good, perhaps the best, source of political obligation, but tacit consent or tacit promise is not, unless what constitutes the promise somehow does duty for, or is an extension of, language. Hume does, it is true, think tacit promises possible in the sense that actual words are not used. 'The will' he says, 'is signified by other more diffuse signs than those of speech.'[24] Thus, even in a tacit promise there is of necessity, communication by the use of signs or symbols. Although Hume was arguably wrong to think a special formula is needed to make a promise, he was right to claim that promises are linguistic acts or acts using signs or symbols doing duty for language. The following stories are meant to illustrate this point. Only in the fourth, fifth and sixth stories does Kant, the main character of the stories, promise, for only in these stories does he perform the kind of symbolic act that constitutes a promise.

First story. There is a vacancy in the Department of Philosophy at the University of Königsberg. Jobs in Philosophy are very hard to come by, and Hume, in spite of his shaky German, decides to apply for the post. Kant, who has been waiting for this vacancy, gets very upset about this, for Hume is the only thinker he knows of who would be a serious competitor. Kant with his customary cunning and conveniently forgetting the evil nature of the dear self, thinks up a plot that would secure his success. He, with fiendish ingenuity, makes full use of his knowledge of certain facts. Hume, he has found out, has no watch and is planning to decide with a number of Königsbergians to use the fact that Kant can be depended upon to be jogging round a certain corner at precisely 8 a.m., but Hume's interview for the job was at 8.30. Kant's habit is so firmly established, and well known, that Hume relies on it with complete confidence. Kant knows that punctuality is considered an essential quality by the selection committee and, although finding it painful to break his jogging habit, deliberately rounds the crucial corner at 8.30 a.m. on the day of the interview, thus making sure that Hume would be late for this important appointment and therefore have no chance to get the post.

Second story. On arrival in Königsberg to be interviewed for the job mentioned in the first story, Hume anachronistically phones Kant from his hotel room to tell him the news. Hume is furious because the customs officers had confiscated his new watch, claiming that, super-ficial appearances notwithstanding, it could be a vegetable and as such a carrier of certain diseases.

But, Hume adds: 'my dear Immanuel, thanks to you, I have found the perfect solution to my predicament. The hotel receptionist has told me that you will be jogging round the corner of Königstrasse and Wilhelmstrasse at precisely 7 a.m. I shall be looking out for you and congratulate you on your having added yet another wonderful regular-ity to nature, a regularity moreover that furnishes me with invaluable guidance for action.' Kant is pleased, not only because of the compli-ment, but because he knows that the corner Hume mentioned cannot be seen from Hume's hotel window, and that Hume will be watching a corner Kant will come to half an hour later. Suppressing a malicious chuckle the wily Prussian says nothing. He is particularly delighted to discover that his interests can be served without the need for a lie or a false promise, for that would not have been permitted by his beloved 'Categorical Imperative'.

Third story. Kant hears that Hume is coming to town. Having always been grateful to Hume for Hume's success in waking him from his dogmatic slumbers and, also wanting to practice his English, he offers to put Hume up, believing that Hume was on a diplomatic mission. To his consternation he discovers on Hume's arrival, not only that Hume's Scottish accent makes him useless as an English instructor, but also that Hume is coming to Königsberg to be interviewed for the job that Kant had been fully expecting to get. Since he thinks he has a right to the job, he believes a rational agent would here be looking for a hypothetical imperative to guide his action. To make sure that Hume is late for his interview, which would ruin his chances, Kant not only brings in ample supplies of claret, but ostentatiously sets his alarm clock for 7 a.m., when the claret has begun to elicit deep yawns from his guest, and an expressed wish to retire. Not a word is spoken by Kant, but he makes sure Hume sees him set the alarm. As soon as Hume's snoring indicates that the claret has had its desired effect, Kant sets the alarm for 9 a.m. Again Hume's chances of the job have been ruined.

Fourth story. Everything is exactly the same as in the third story, except that Hume asks Kant 'Will you make sure to wake me up at 7 a.m.?' and Kant, not remembering his own views about the alleged right to tell lies, the nasty things he said about his dear self, and the respect he had advocated for the 'Categorical Imperative', perfidiously says 'Certainly, my good man'. But, although knowing that Hume would be a better man for the job, Kant sets off jogging at 7 a.m. without waking Hume up, the dear self having once more triumphed over the 'Categorical Imperative'.

Fifth story. In the fifth story, Kant is not only shocked by Hume's inability to understand Kant's German, but finds that his (Kant's) attempt at imitating an Oxford accent totally baffles Hume. As a result, Hume has great difficulty in communicating to Kant the request for being woken up in time for the interview and Kant is not sure how he can promise to do so. But, being a couple of pretty bright, though linguistically poorly equipped fellows, they manage to communicate by the use of sign language. Hume looks at Kant, replacing his customary vacant stare with a questioning one, while he points at 7.30 on the alarm clock, puts both hands under one cheek and pretends to snore. Kant raises his hand with a loud 'Aha' and nods vigorously. Since neither here issues a word it might be thought that no promise was made. However, this would be an error. There has here been an overt symbolic communication between our two friends, though language has strictly speaking, not been used. This is my main reason for preferring to say that promises are symbolic acts, though not necessarily linguistic, in a strict sense of the term 'linguistic'.

Sixth story. We may assume the facts to be the same as in the fifth story apart from the fact that each of the two gentlemen has no difficulty in expressing himself in a language intelligible to the other. Just before retiring Hume confides to Kant that his obesity has now reached a stage such that he has great difficulty waking up in the morning. He adds 'I know you get up early to jog and I am assuming that you will tell me now if there is any reason why you cannot wake me up. I am depending on you.' Hume knows that Kant hears him perfectly well and naturally assumes that Kant's silence indicates that there is no problem, that Kant will for sure wake him up, his good will shining like a jewel in spite of Kant's jealousy, and that once again an unconditional good will be brought into the world, Kant's dear self notwithstanding. Kant's silence has the force of a promise. The significance of the silence is due to conventions and the silence is thus also a linguistic act. If this is taken to be a tacit because silent promise then tacit promises are overt symbolic acts.

In the final story Hume is quite overwhelmed by Kant's simple goodness. He would have expected some jealousy. For, although the job was given to neither of them, Hume certainly was a dangerous rival. But, there was no trace of jealousy. Quite the contrary. Kant seemed to take great delight in showing Hume the various sights of Königsberg, and teaching him to play cards and snooker, claiming all along that he was doing no more than his duty. Hume was quite unable to get Kant to accept gifts for his kindness, for Kant insisted that it was not good for one's character to accept gifts for doing one's duty. But, Hume felt overwhelmingly indebted to Kant and could not be stopped from saying as they parted: 'My dear friend, not only shall I never forget all you have done for me, but I promise you that, if you ever come to Auld Reekie, I shall show you the sights of that beautiful city.'

In each of the first six stories Kant is guilty of an immorality that consists in deliberately misleading a person or allowing a person to be deceived about the future to that person's probable detriment. The 'vice' or character defect is dishonesty although in each case malice is evident as well. In the second and third stories there is reason for Hume to believe that Kant knows that he (Hume) is depending upon him and that Kant's behaviour justifies this belief. This makes Kant's actions in this respect similar to a typical case of promising and yet it is only in the last four stories that a promise is given. The reason for this is that it is only in these cases that overt symbolic acts are performed. Hume's promise seems perfectly honest, although it may not be. Kant's behaviour in the first six stories is deceitful. However, making false promises is not the only way in which we can culpably mislead people about the future. One can talk of promises only when language, or some other conventionally adopted means of communication, is used. Arranging the world in such a way as to mislead but not using any words or symbols to do this, can of course be just as immoral a case of deception as making a lying promise.

If Hume fails to do what he says he is going to do in the last story, he has clearly broken a promise. This story may indeed be taken to illustrate a typical case of a promise. Hume owes a debt of gratitude to Kant and a promise was not needed to create that obligation. But, the promise nevertheless strengthens the obligation, in that Kant has a right to depend upon Hume's word, as well as upon his gratitude. There may frequently be a prior obligation to do what people promise to do. The obligation to keep promises cannot in these cases be wholly decided by the previously existing obligation, for the promise tends to add weight to the commitment.

The Hume and Kant stories display what kind of act promising is. Promises essentially involve conventionally determined, or agreed upon communication. To call them speech acts is only acceptable with qualifications that the stories should help us to remember and understand. And, Hume's consistency is clearly vindicated. Tacit promises are made by signs or symbols doing duty for language. The man who simply does not leave a country is not thereby performing any symbolic act, and is thus not promising in any sense. As a source of obligation to obey the government his behaviour is not promisory in nature.

One can I believe look upon the Hume and Kant stories as a way of displaying the impressions from which an idea is derived. But I hope they may also remind us of the fact that the pursuit of pleasure was the motive for Hume's philosophizing.

Hume's treatment of emotions as evaluations displays the richness of our value-laden existence. The most efficient way of displaying and exploring important concepts may be the telling of stories exhibiting the core of the concepts and drawing their boundaries. But is philosophy not concerned with truth? Are these stories not fiction? Perhaps this is not a defect. One is baffled by the question 'Is Hume's *Treatise* true?' It seems more appropriate to ask whether it is enlightening or stimulating. Truth suggests that there is only one perspective that really displays the nature of the universe and our place in it. Members of different 'schools' of philosophising are liable to maintain their method to be the only one that can penetrate to the core of reality. Philosophers of the analytic school, of whom I am one, should be mindful of the fact that art is in some important sense also concerned with throwing light upon reality. I don't think philosophers should see art as an alternative to analytic philosophy, something for others, but not for them. Why should they not take artistry in their service? In doing so, I believe they would be acting in the spirit of David Hume, who saw the pursuit of pleasure as the origin of his philosophy. We tend to forget that written philosophy is literature and international philosophical conferences are rather like gigantic theatrical workshops. It would, I believe, be wrong to see no value in analytic philosophy. There is, however, room for concrete illustrations as well as 'abstract' analysis. Abstract analysis can lose contact with the richness of reality, but without analysis one may drown in meaningless detail.

I believe we should follow Hume and pursue philosophy for pleasure. We could contribute to the enjoyment of the philosophical enterprise by attempting to adopt a more light-hearted, humorous style in place of the boring ponderous pomposity that so frequently characterizes our philosophical performances.

When we escape from our methodological prejudices it may seem less strange to attribute metaphysical importance to love, hatred, pride and humility. It gives metaphysical pride of place to ourselves as persons. Hume's world is not a world of objects in which there happen to be people. It is a world of persons in constant emotional interaction. This makes sense of Hume's claim that of the three books of the *Treatise*, it is the book 'Of Morals' that deals with the most fundamentally important material. I should like to conclude by suggesting that Hume's stress upon the emotions involves a perspective from which we can profitably explore the nature of our conscious being in the world.

Perhaps seeing human nature as essentially governed by instincts, desires and emotions will deepen our understanding of the human predicament. Hume has at least taught us that it is more than doubtful whether human beings have the right to claim the possession of a versatile and infallible faculty of reason.

Notes

1. A noteworthy exception is Lois E. Loeb's 'Hume's Moral Sentiments and the structure of the *Treatise*', *Journal of the History of Philosophy*, Volume 15, Number 4, October 1977. I have nothing to add to my response to Loeb in 'Another Look at Hume's Account of Moral Evaluation' in the same issue. My article also contains comments upon Thomas K. Hearn's 'Ardal on the Moral Sentiments in Hume's Treatise', *Philosophy* 48 (1973): 290. 'Another Look . . .' also contains some comments upon Jonathan Harrison's failure to consider my view as a possible interpretation of Hume's account of moral judgments. Harrison and I were colleagues when I was developing my views on this topic. He was familiar with my ideas, which makes it surprising that he should entirely mislead his readers about the content of *Passion and Value*. He observes in a footnote that *Passion and Value* contains a discussion of sympathy of no relevance for Hume's moral epistemology, whereas the book is clearly concerned with Hume's account of judgments of virtue and the evaluation of persons. See also Jonathan Harrison *Hume's Moral Epistemology*, Oxford University Press, 1976.

2. *A Treatise of Human Nature* by David Hume, Book I edited by D. G. C. MacNabb, Books II and III in one volume, ed. Páll S. Ardal, Fontana/Collins 1972 and ed. Selby-Bigge, second edition with revised text by P. H. Nidditch. Page references to both editions in the order listed (*Treatise* II, 157, 416).

3. *Treatise* I, 45, 2.

4. For a fuller discussion of this issue see Páll S. Ardal, 'Some Implications of the Virtue of Reasonableness in Hume's *Treatise*' in *Hume: A Re-Evaluation*, edited by Donald B. Livingstone and James King, Fordham University Press, 1976.

5. 'Essays on the Active Powers of Man' in *The Works of Thomas Reid*, edited by Sir William Hamilton, Edinburgh: James Thin, p. 573.

6. Ibid.

7. *Treatise* II, 40, 279.

8. *Treatise* II, 83, 329.

9. See Ardal, 'Some Implications . . .' cited above.

10. See Donald Davidson 'Hume's Cognitive Theory of Pride'. First published in *The Journal of Philosophy*, 75, 1978. Reprinted in *Actions and Events*, Oxford University Press, 1980, pp. 277-90. Davidson independently arrived at an account of Hume's analysis of pride that is remarkably similar to mine. However, there is one difference worth mentioning in this context. Davidson states that for Hume 'self-esteem, self-applause constitute pride' (D.284). And a little later we read: 'Hume equates approbation with judgment of merit' (D.284). This is followed by the claim that 'the self-approbation that is pride may . . . be expressed by a judgment that one is praise-worthy'. On my view the criteria for justified pride may be frequently satisfied when the cause for pride does not entitle the person to claim to be praiseworthy. However, it should be remembered that Davidson does not endorse Hume's use of the word 'pride', which he does not think reflects any usage in English. Thus Davidson's own view about the analysis of pride as we know it, may possibly be closer to mine than the analysis extracted from Hume's text.

11. See Páll S. Ardal's Introduction to the Fontana edition of the *Treatise*, cited above.

12. *Treatise* II, 112, 363. For an interesting comparison of Hume and Wittgenstein see Peter Jones, 'Strains in Hume and Wittgenstein' in *Hume: A Re-Evaluation*. Notice the similarity between Hume's account of natural beliefs and Wittgenstein's statement that 'our ordinary certainty is something that lies beyond being justified; rather it is something animal'. *On Certainty*, ed. G. E. M. Anscombe and G. H. von Wright, Oxford, 1969.

13. Ibid.

14. *Treatise* I, 238, 187.

15. See 'Convention and Value' by Páll S. Ardal in *Hume: Bi-Centenary Papers*, Edinburgh University Press, 1977 for a more thorough discussion of this topic.

16. *Hume's Philosophy of Belief* by Antony Flew, Routledge and Kegan Paul, London, p. 37.

17. Flew, op. cit., p. 39.

18. *Treatise* I, 63, 19.
19. *Treatise* I, 67, 23.
20. *Treatise* III, 221, 490.
21. *Treatise* III, 245-6, 517. For a sound treatment of Hume on Obligation see Knud Haakonssen, 'Hume's Obligations' in Hume Studies, Volume IV, Number 1, April 1978.
22. *Treatise* III, 302, 582.
23. *Treatise* III, 251, 523.
24. *Treatise* III, 272, 547.

INTRODUCTION

The main purpose of this book is to show that some aspects of Hume's discussion of the passions in Book II of the *Treatise* are both philosophically interesting and of vital importance for the correct interpretation of Hume's views about the evaluation of human character. The reader will be disappointed if he expects either a detailed analysis of the whole of Book II or a complete account of Hume's moral theory.

The study of a limited aspect of Hume's *Treatise*, such as a strand of his theory of moral value, must involve a grave risk of misrepresenting his thought. The three books of the *Treatise* possess a singular unity, in spite of the fact that commentators have found it easy to draw attention to certain apparent inconsistencies among doctrines in the different books. Thus in Book II, the impression of the *self* plays an indispensable part although, in his discussion of personal identity in Book I, Hume emphasizes the impossibility of finding such an impression (PDH, 171). This is a notable example of Hume's alleged inconsistency, but many others could be cited. They have, indeed, been found to be of such gigantic proportions that it has been considered hard to say whether Hume ' . . . taught, or did not teach, this or that particular doctrine' (EHU, vii).

Some later commentators have agreed with L. A. Selby-Bigge's estimate of the difficulty of interpreting Hume's works, and have concluded that he taught different and incompatible doctrines in different parts of his philosophical writings (HI, 2). It is neither my purpose directly to challenge the view that Hume had many intentions in writing his philosophical works, nor to deny that these may have led to inconsistencies in his published work. J. A. Passmore warns that too much emphasis on the lack of unity in Hume's thought has its dangers. He stresses that, although Hume may have had many intentions in writing his *Treatise*, 'there is a unity in his work; it is dominated by a single overriding intention' (HI, 2). With this I agree: Hume's main aim in the *Treatise* is to establish the science of human nature on a firm foundation.

A modern reader, brought up to believe that a philosopher must emulate the scientist by developing a strictly defined technical terminology, is likely to consider Hume's use of language loose and unscientific. It must be remembered that although he sought to introduce the 'experimental method into Moral Sciences', he was essentially a man of letters, writing for the educated reader of his day, and not a specialist addressing himself exclusively to other specialists. The style is varied according to the context; the same doctrine is expressed in many different ways. It is essential to try to follow the drift of the argument, rather than to take a forceful statement of doctrine out of context, on the assumption that it contains the essence of Hume's thought at the time of writing.

In what follows I shall concern myself exclusively with doctrines as expressed in the *Treatise*. One obvious reason why it is undesirable to quote the *Treatise* and the *Enquiries* indiscriminately, when dealing with any aspect of Hume's theory of value, is the change in style. One cannot assume that terms that bear a special technical sense in the second two books of the *Treatise* have the same meaning in the *Enquiry Concerning the Principles of Morals*, for Hume retains little of his subtle psychological analysis in the later and more popular work.

This would be of relatively small importance if all aspects of his theory of value could be understood without reference to the psychological analysis. I hope, in the course of this book, to show that this is not the case. Hume's moral theory is an aspect of the more general account of man's emotional nature. Hume, in the second two books of the *Treatise*, is concerned with an attempt to discover those psychological laws that explain human emotions (including moral emotions) and the behaviour of people in society. There is no neat division between Hume's psychology and his moral theory. Although he is undoubtedly seeking psychological explanations, it is quite misleading to conclude, with A. H. Basson, that most of Hume's writings on morals

are psychologically interesting but of no philosophical importance:
> It is assumed, then, that the only parts of Hume's moral philo-
> sophy that are of real importance are (i) his theory that moral
> judgments are a matter of feeling and not of rational conviction,
> and (ii) his belief that the doctrine of free will is irrelevant to
> morals. Hume's discussion of the particular virtues and vices is
> psychologically interesting, but not philosophically important.
> (DH, 17)

If this view were accepted, all that the *Treatise* contains relevant to
moral theory is to be found in the three first sections of Book II Part III
and Part I of Book III. It is often thought that Hume's moral theory
can be mastered by reading these parts of the *Treatise* as a supplement
to the *Enquiry Concerning the Principles of Morals*. To approach the
interpretation of his moral theory in this way may easily lead one to
attribute to him views that he never held. Surely it is possible that
Hume may have altered his views in the period between writing the
two works? I shall not try to prove that he did so, but the mere possibility in itself makes suspect the attempt to derive a composite theory
from the two works. At any rate, the first step must be to find out what
he thought when he wrote each of them. I shall try to convince the
reader that certain features of Hume's constructive moral theory in the
Treatise can be understood only if the second and third books of the
Treatise are studied together, for the sub-title of the *Treatise* must be
taken seriously. Hume is attempting to introduce 'the experimental
method of reasoning into moral subjects'. In the *Abstract*, where his
purpose is to give a simplified account of the main argument of the
Treatise, he begins by making the point that

> it is at least worth while to try if the science of *man* will not admit
> of the same accuracy which several parts of natural philosophy are
> found susceptible of. There seems to be all the reason in the
> world to imagine that it may be carried to the greatest degree of
> exactness. (A, 6)

Passmore emphasizes the unity of the first two books of the *Treatise*,
quoting Hume's words in the Advertisement that 'the subject of the
understanding and the passions make a complete chain of reasoning by
themselves'. But it is misleading to claim that these two books had to
be published together because these two topics are to be distinguished
as a unity by 'the fact that in both cases association is the source of
order and complexity' (HI, 106). This is not an adequate reason for

suggesting that the relation between Books II and III is not as close as the relation between the first two books. It is unlikely that Passmore wanted to give this impression, for he correctly emphasizes that Hume's main interest was in the 'science of man', and describes this as 'the science which concerns itself with the human mind and with human relationships in society' (HI, 4). This, indeed, describes admirably the subject matter of the last two books, whereas Passmore himself considers the first book to be largely concerned with methodological topics: 'Without anachronism, we can think of it [the first book] as Hume's methodology of the social sciences' (HI, 6). Although partly true, this is an oversimplification, for Hume discusses in Book I many topics that are not strictly speaking methodological, such as knowledge of the external world, and personal identity. In Books II and III, the main doctrines of Book I are indeed presupposed, but the two later books have a peculiar unity, in that both deal with the active or 'passionate' side of human nature rather than the understanding.

It seems clear to me that, although there is less explicit mention of the principles of association in Book III of the *Treatise*, one is not justified in concluding that it plays no fundamentally important role in the argument. Book III is to be understood in the light of the arguments in the earlier books. I consider it a mistake to place too much importance upon Hume's statement in the Advertisement to Book III:

> I think it proper to inform the public that tho' this be a third
> volume of the Treatise of Human Nature, yet 'tis in some measure
> independent of the other two, and requires not that the reader
> should enter into all the abstract reasoning contain'd in them.

Notice first of all that Hume claims for Book III only 'some measure' of independence and that it is not necessary to understand 'all the abstract reasoning' in the earlier books. But the most important point to bear in mind is this: Hume considered that the first two books of the *Treatise* had been badly received. All one may assume from his words is that he is anxious that prejudice against the earlier books will not deter people from reading the book on morals. It is not unreasonable to see in the following words, quoted from the opening chapter of the book on morals, Hume's fear that people may prejudge it. A certain bitterness against the reading public can also be detected:

> What affects us, we conclude, can never be a chimera; and, as our
> passion is engaged on the one side or the other, we naturally think
> that the question lies within human comprehension; which, in

other cases of this nature, we are apt to entertain some doubt of. Without this advantage, I never should have ventured upon a third volume of such abstruse philosophy, in an age wherein the greatest part of men seem agreed to convert reading into an amusement, and to reject everything that requires any considerable degree of attention to be comprehended.

(THN III, 165-6/455-6)

I have so far tried to point out only that it is prima facie not unplausible to suggest that Hume's discussion of the passions and emotions may be relevant to the understanding of his moral theory as expressed in the *Treatise*. The following brief description of the main topics covered in different chapters of this book may prove helpful. It will show clearly how selective I have been. The fact that I say next to nothing about the function of reason in Hume's moral theory, and do not even mention most of the artificial virtues, must not be taken to indicate that I consider these, and other topics that I do not discuss, unimportant.

CHAPTER 1 Hume maintains that the passions are simple impressions. The concept of simplicity is explained and defended against the charge that it is radically incoherent. Hume's method is determined by what can be said about simple impressions.

CHAPTER 2 The account of the four indirect passions, pride and humility, love and hatred, is discussed with special emphasis on the concept of pride. It is suggested that these passions are four basic, though biased, ways of valuing people and are thus of importance for Hume's account of evaluation of character. Hume's discussion of pride is shown to be rich in interest for those who concern themselves with conceptual analysis.

CHAPTER 3 The principle of sympathy has to be distinguished from benevolence, pity, and compassion. It is discussed with reference to various phenomena that could be said to involve sympathy in some form. Mixed passions, such as malice and pity, are briefly discussed and it is pointed out that the principle of comparison has effects opposite to those of sympathy. The allegation that Hume is a psychological egoist is considered, special attention being paid to the charge that Hume's account of the principle of sympathy implies such egoism.

CHAPTER 4 Hume's 'determinism' has some peculiar features and is here discussed primarily to illustrate Hume's attempt at explaining actions without reference to faculties. The will is described as an impression. Some features of the discussion tend to support the emphasis placed upon the indirect passions in chapters 2 and 6 of this book. CHAPTER 5 It is claimed that the concept of a calm passion has been misunderstood. An alternative interpretation is suggested. Hume is again shown to be much concerned to avoid reference to hidden powers. His main purpose is to distinguish the motivating power of a passion from conscious emotional intensity. An interpretation of the famous 'slave' passage is briefly suggested.

CHAPTER 6 Approval and disapproval of character are treated as objective variants of the indirect passions. The problem of objectivity is discussed and the influence of sympathy and the imagination. Special attention is given to Adam Smith's account of the nature of sympathy and its relation to evaluation. Certain points of comparison with Hume's views are mentioned.

CHAPTER 7 The view that approval is a species of sympathetic consciousness is discussed. The charge that sympathy need be referred to in accounting for only some virtues is critically examined. The limits of the concept of virtue are briefly considered.

CHAPTER 8 Hume's view that actions derive their virtue from virtuous motives seems to be inconsistent with the admission of an artificial virtue. Prominence is given to Hume's attempt to show that there is a separate virtue of justice which is not reducible to benevolence and prudence.

CHAPTER 9 In the *Treatise* Hume is mainly concerned with the nature of evaluation. He does not pay a great deal of attention to the function of evaluative language. Emotivism and Subjectivism are here treated as theories about the function of evaluative language. 'Emotionism' and 'Reflectivism' are introduced to refer to two theories about the nature of evaluations themselves with which Emotivism and Subjectivism might be confused. It is argued that Hume is advocating Emotionism, and reasons are given for the difficulty of ascertaining Hume's view about these issues.

1

THE PASSIONS AS SIMPLE IMPRESSIONS

It is important to clear up, at the outset, certain points regarding Hume's method in the two later books of the *Treatise*. A careful look at his initial classifications and characterization of the passions should convince us that a reductivist analysis of the passions is not to be expected. The point is important, for Hume is undoubtedly a naturalist, and yet there is a sense in which it is implausible to foster on him a naturalistic theory of morals. If naturalism in morals is understood as the doctrine that a *definition* can be given of all moral concepts in terms of non-moral concepts, Hume is not a naturalist, for no passions can be defined – at least not in G. E. Moore's sense of 'define'; and moral approval and disapproval are in this respect no exceptions. The concepts of moral approval and disapproval are, for Hume, basic and indefinable.

It may be recalled that, for Moore, to define is to analyse. After discarding several senses of 'define' as irrelevant to the sense in which he wants to emphasize that 'good' is indefinable, he says:

We may mean that a certain object, which we all of us know, is composed in a certain manner: that it has four legs, a head, a heart, a liver, etc. etc., all of them arranged in definite relations to one another. It is in this sense that I deny good to be definable. I say that it is not *composed of any parts*, which we can substitute for it in our minds when we are thinking of it. (PE, 8)

Yellow and good are alike indefinable in that they are not *composed of any parts*. Hume would have agreed with this. It will appear later that he argues that moral approval and disapproval are different from all other emotions though very similar to some other passions. It would be peculiarly irrelevant to quote Bishop Butler against him to the effect that 'everything is what it is, and not another thing'; for Hume is much inclined to maintain that for each meaningful term standing for a passion there must be a different impression. He certainly believed that 'morally good' and 'morally bad' derive their meanings from specific impressions, although they are not the impressions of qualities in the object evaluated (except in the case of self-valuing). In a similar way Hume maintains in Book I that the notion of causal necessity is derived from an impression in the person making the causal inference and not from an impression discoverable in the objects between which the causal relation holds. All simple impressions have this also in common: that one can not understand the terms referring to them unless one has experienced the relevant impressions.

In an introductory chapter Hume indicates certain principles of classification. Referring back to the distinction between impressions and ideas in Book I, the passions are obviously impressions, he tells us. But impressions were there distinguished into two kinds, impressions of sensation and impressions of reflection: 'Of the first kind are all the impressions of the senses, and all bodily pains and pleasures: of the second are the passions, and other emotions resembling them' (THN II, 3/275).

The impressions of sensation are original in that they do not arise from other impressions or ideas. They make their appearance 'without any introduction' (THN II, 3/275). This does not mean that they have no causes, although they must be regarded as ultimate data from the point of view of the science of the mind. A causal explanation of these impressions would belong to 'anatomy and natural philosophy' (THN II, 3/276). We are not to be treated to an account of bodily fluids which gives such an archaic flavour to the account of the passions in Descartes and Malebranche. Hume begs to be excused from tackling these subjects. He is concerned only with explaining the origin of those impressions which arise from other impressions or from ideas. His explanation is to be psychological and not physical or physiological.

Bodily pains and pleasures are not themselves passions although passions arise from them. It is possible to distinguish the passions into two kinds according to the way in which they arise. If they arise immediately from pleasure or pain they are called direct, whereas additional qualities are needed in order to give rise to the so-called indirect passions. It goes without saying that the explanation of the indirect passions is more complicated, and the first two parts of the book are concerned with this topic, whereas the direct passions are discussed much more briefly. Hume, hardly consistently, elsewhere includes among the direct passions some that do not arise from pleasure and pain. Among these he lists 'the desire of punishment to our enemies, and of happiness to our friends; hunger, lust, and a few other bodily appetites' (THN II, 149/439). He also mentions, as not arising from previous pleasures and pains, certain original instincts such as 'benevolence and resentment, the love of life, and kindness to children' (THN II, 129/417). Thus the classification of passions into those that arise directly from pleasure and pain, and those that need other qualities as well, cannot be considered exhaustive. Let us, following Kemp Smith's terminology, call *primary* those passions that do not arise from pleasure or pain.

One further distinction is introduced by Hume. He points out that passions are either calm or violent: 'the sense of beauty and deformity in action' are instanced as calm passions (THN II, 4/276). The distinction between calm and violent passions is, in important respects, different from the distinction between direct and indirect passions. The latter distinction refers to the way in which the passions arise; no passion can, on some occasions be direct, and on others indirect. On the other hand, the *fundamentum divisionis* between the calm and the violent is the intensity of the feeling considered as an impression. Thus a calm passion is distinguished by the fact that it is experienced, on most occasions, at a low emotional intensity. Hume's statement is quite explicit on this point. I shall have occasion to say more about calm and violent passions later on, but attention must be drawn to the fact that 'the sense of beauty and deformity in action, composition and external objects' consist in passions according to Hume. From this it follows that these, like all other passions except the primary ones, arise either directly or indirectly from pleasure or pain.

The following brief classification of the passions is too compressed to be fully intelligible except in the light of the arguments of later chapters. Close attention to it at this point is not essential for the understanding of what follows; but some readers may find it interesting to compare the classification of the passions here suggested with that advocated by Kemp Smith (PDH, 168). The most important difference between the two accounts results from a difference in the interpretation of the concept of calm passions and the importance I attach to the indirect passions in relation to Hume's account of the evaluation of character.

PRIMARY PASSIONS

These, like the impressions of the senses and bodily pains and pleasures, do not arise from pleasure or pain. These passions arise from 'a natural impulse or instinct' which is 'perfectly unaccountable' (THN II, 149/439). From the point of view of the science of man they must be treated as ultimate inexplicable constituents of our emotional life. These can be either calm or violent. One can, following Hume, divide them as follows:

(1) Violent[1]: the desire of punishment to our enemies and of happiness to our friends; hunger, lust, and a few other bodily appetites.

(2) Calm: benevolence, resentment, the love of life, and kindness to children. In the place where this list is given Hume also lists as calm passions 'the general appetite to good and aversion to evil'. By 'good' and 'evil' he here means pleasure and pain. He does, however, seem to distinguish them from the original instincts. We can only develop these general appetites and aversions after having experienced pain and pleasure. These passions, though calm, are thus not to be considered primary.

SECONDARY PASSIONS

These are aroused by a preceding impression of pleasure or pain or the ideas of these. They are distinguishable into the direct and the indirect.

I. *Direct*

(1) Direct and violent: listed are desire and aversion, joy and grief, hope and fear, despair and security. Hume also includes volition among the list of violent passions, although his views on the nature of volition hardly make it useful to include volition among them. To the extent, however, to which he treats volition as an impression, the question obviously arises as to what sort of impression it is. If it is an impression that ever causes action it seems it must be a passion of some sort. It is doubtful whether Hume thinks the will ever does determine action by itself; he seems to think the will is

---

[1] By the term 'violent' I only want to indicate that these are not listed among the calm passions. Thus all the passions can be exhaustively divided into calm passions and violent passions.

always determined by motives, impressions other than the impression we are referring to when we talk about the will.

(2) Direct and calm: here we must list the general appetite for good and aversion to evil. Hume himself calls the calm primary passions direct. This seems confusing, for the notions of direct and indirect both involve necessary reference to a preceding pleasure or pain as a cause of these passions. Kemp Smith includes in this category the moral and aesthetic sentiments as proceeding from the contemplation of actions and external objects. There is, perhaps, some justification for doing this, but as I understand Hume these calm direct passions are certainly not to be equated with the basic moral sentiments.

II. *Indirect*

These arise from preceding pleasures and pains, in conjunction with other qualities.

(1) Indirect and Violent: 1_1 Basic: pride, humility, love and hatred. 1_2 Others mentioned are ambition, vanity, envy, pity, malice, generosity, 'with their dependents' (THN II, 4/276-7).

(2) Indirect and calm: approval and disapproval of persons. These passions can be considered special cases of the basic indirect passions.

Hume emphasizes the uniqueness of each different passion as a simple impression. Speaking of pride and humility he says ' . . . it is impossible we can ever, by a multitude of words, give a just definition of them, or indeed of any of the passions' (THN II, 5/277). Thus a passion is a simple impression, and can obviously not be constructed out of simpler elements. Passmore is, therefore, more than a little misleading when he says 'the central psychological problem is to construct the more complicated "indirect passions" out of the direct passions, with the aid of the associative principles' (HI, 124.). Direct and indirect passions are equally simple, as Hume's words indicate. There is no analogy at all between the relation of these two classes of passions to each other and the relation of simple to complex ideas. One can justify saying that complex ideas are constructed out of simple ideas.

But if we consider Passmore to be using the term 'construct' in a somewhat extended sense, he can perhaps be acquitted of confusion. In the usual sense of 'construct', the material out of which we construct is part of the completed structure. Thus the timber out of which a building is constructed is part of the building itself. It may be said that this account of the relation between 'construct' and the resultant structure is misleading: if we have been shown all the rooms of a house we have been shown all the parts of that house, although a great deal of the material used in its construction has remained hidden. Therefore, what the house is constructed out of is no part of the building. Perhaps what Passmore has in mind is that, in accounting for the origin of the indirect passions, reference must be made to the direct passions, just as, in explaining how the rooms of a house come to be there, reference must be made to building materials. If this is the case, he has not made himself very clear. But Passmore's failure to appreciate that the passions are simple impressions can perhaps be more clearly seen from the following quotation:

He does not think that *all* the passions consist in the association of certain perceptions with pleasure or with pain. (HI, 123)

The answer is that, according to Hume, no passion consists in such an association, though it may be necessary to appeal to the principles of association in order to give a causal explanation of a passion.

It is fairly obvious that Hume's contention that the passions are simple impressions determines the kind of 'analysis' we can expect in the two later books of the *Treatise*, where he is engaged in constructing his 'science of man'. The simple cannot be reductively analysed, for such an analysis would be tantamount to the denial that the simple really is simple. The analysis given is indeed meant to be causal in nature, and free appeal is made to the principles of association. Since, however, association cannot work unless simple impressions can be described as similar, something must be said about the charge that similarity is inconsistent with simplicity, that the similarity of two perceptions is inconsistent with the simplicity of each of them. If this charge can be upheld, it must be concluded that the whole of Hume's account of the passions is based upon a simple logical mistake.

A simple perception cannot be analysed into distinct parts. Yet Hume thinks it can be characterized by pointing out its similarity to other simple perceptions or its difference from them. One can also state the conditions under which it is found to arise, or, in other words, its causal conditions. Thus, for Hume, a simple perception is not just something that can only be pointed to and given a name. Many things may be predicated of it. I shall, indeed, emphasize that the bulk of the second book of the *Treatise* is concerned with stating the causal conditions for the emergence of simple impressions, and indicating various similarities between them.

Hume first introduces this doctrine in a long footnote when discussing abstract ideas. The correct understanding of Hume's view of this point is important for our purpose and consequently it seems justifiable to quote this footnote in full:

> It is evident, that even different simple ideas may have a similarity or resemblance to each other; nor is it necessary, that the point or circumstance of resemblance should be distinct or separable from that in which they differ. *Blue* and *green* are different simple ideas, but are more resembling than *blue* and *scarlet*; though their perfect simplicity excludes all possibility of separation or distinction. It is the same case with particular sounds, and tastes, and smells. These admit of infinite resemblances upon the general appearance and comparison, without having any common circumstance the same. And of this we may be certain, even from the very abstract terms *simple idea*. They comprehend all simple ideas under them. These resemble each other in their simplicity. And yet from their very nature, which excludes all composition, this circumstance, in which they resemble, is not distinguishable or separable from the rest. It is the same case with all the degrees in any quality. They are all resembling, and yet the quality, in any individual, is not distinct from the degree. (THN I, 28/637)

It will be argued later that much of Hume's trouble arises from treating each passion as a simple impression of which he can only give a causal explanation and point out its similarity or similarities to other passions. At present, however, I am not concerned with a special application of this doctrine, but with the theoretical plausibility of the doctrine regarded as a general thesis about simple perceptions.

Hume's view has met with severe criticisms by a recent commentator, Professor J. A. Passmore. Passmore thinks Hume should have concluded from the observation that all simple ideas resemble each other at least in being simple 'that there are no simple ideas' (HI, 109). His ground is that 'the least which can possibly confront us would be something simple, vivid (or faint) and, for example, blue, i.e. a complex idea' (ibid.). This does not seem to me a just criticism, for it must be remembered that Hume's reason for treating particular tastes, sounds, smells, and colours as simple is that they 'exclude all composition'. Would Professor Passmore then want to argue that the idea of a particular shade of blue is composed of vividness, blueness, and simplicity? If we use the word 'compose' here it would be manifestly different from the sense in which certain philosophers (for example G. E. Moore) have thought that the complex idea of a horse would be composed of the ideas of its various parts in certain relations.[1]

It seems to me that Professor Passmore is wrong when he maintains in criticism of Hume 'that it is quite unintelligible to assert that an idea can have various distinguishable characteristics without any sacrifice of its simplicity . . .' (HI, 110). The whole point rests on the assumption that to say that x resembles y is to say that x and y have a certain characteristic in common. Since x and y are *ex hypothesi* different and also have a characteristic in common, neither can be simple. Each would be split up into that quality which is the same in each and the quality which makes them different.

But is this assumption a just one? Hume obviously did not subscribe to it, and I think his position perfectly defensible. Let us take the example of the colours: Hume is surely right in claiming that it makes perfect sense to say that blue and green are more similar than blue and scarlet. Would this statement be considered justified only if it could be pointed out that blue and green had something in common? Would one not rather say: 'They have nothing in common. They are just similar.'? The same situation would often be met with in dealing with smells. Some smells are more alike than others, but to be asked what similar smells have in common is puzzling.

It is not out of place to emphasize here that when we are not satisfied that we have conveyed to a person the idea of a certain smell, or colour for that matter, we point out the causal conditions, the circumstances within which it arises. A large part of Hume's account of the passions is not unnaturally concerned with this topic.

In the case of force or vividness, it is not easy to see what it is that

---

[1] It is irrelevant that Moore may have been quite wrong in thinking that defining a horse is analysing it into parts. One might, for example, say that horselike behaviour was just as much a part of the concept as having the various anatomical parts of a horse. Some, indeed, are fairly inessential: a threelegged horse is still a horse. But Hume uses the notion of composition and when, in Book I, he first mentions complex ideas he takes the ideas of particulars, the cities of Paris and the New Jerusalem. 'I can imagine to myself such a city as the New Jerusalem, whose pavement is gold and walls are rubies, though I never saw any such. I have seen Paris; but shall I affirm I can form such an idea of that city, as will perfectly represent all its streets and houses in their real and just proportions?' (THN I, 13/3). Simple ideas are exact copies of simple impressions, but complex ideas are not. The imagination is free to combine simple ideas in various ways. Here it is plausible to say that the complex ideas contain within them ideas of all the parts of a city ultimately analysable into elements not composed of distinguishable parts.

vivid olfactory, auditory, and visual images have in common. If we use the same word here we presumably see a resemblance, though not a characteristic which is identically present in each. What of 'a cold colour', 'a warm colour'? There is a reason for using these expressions; but try to find an identical characteristic in a cold colour and a cold drink. I am not suggesting that it is never plausible to analyse similarity in terms of partial identity, only that this is not always plausible. Thus, one might have two squares, each divided into four equal squares. The top right hand square in each is coloured red. This is a repeated characteristic of the two squares, which might not be shared by a third divided square, where the corresponding quarter was not coloured. If, in this case, I say the two squares are similar this is plausibly interpreted as an assertion of partial identity. An intermediate position would be that of father and son who are said to have 'exactly the same nose'. This is normally not to be taken strictly to refer to partial identity; the two noses do not have all qualities in common. They are generally, one would think, not precisely qualitatively identical; but the similarity between the two persons is more plausibly analysed as partial identity than is the similarity between two smells. All one can say is that similarity looks more like partial identity in certain cases than in others.

It seems to me clear that it is not absurd to suggest that simplicity may be consistent with similarity, unless you want to define a simple idea as that which can only be named and not described in any sense of 'describe'. Hume does not use the term 'simple' in this way, and I see no very obvious reason for claiming that he ought to have done this. In fact he always holds that you can 'describe' a simple idea in at least three ways: (1) by using a scale of intensity, (2) by pointing out its similarity or difference from other simple ideas, and (3) by describing the conditions under which it arises. It must be admitted that the notion of intensity, vividness or force is an obscure one. Hume recognizes this, but can do no better than appeal to the reader's experience. Perhaps we can make something of the appeal. Sometimes emotions seem to involve a violent disturbance of our conscious state. We all know what it feels like to become violently angry. If we contrast this with the peaceful contemplation of a beautiful landscape, we can see what Hume is driving at. The second emotion involves hardly any 'disturbance in the soul'.

In this chapter I have stressed the importance of seeing what consequences follow from Hume's contention that the passions are simple impressions and consequently indefinable. Since the basic moral concepts of approval and disapproval are passions, it follows that Hume is not a naturalist, if by naturalism one understands the view that all moral concepts are definable in terms of non-moral concepts. The view that the passions are simple impressions also restricts the kinds of things than can be said about them. They cannot be analysed into their constituents for they have no constituents. Hume is indeed trying to explain their occurrence; he is giving their causal conditions.

2

THE INDIRECT PASSIONS

Exponents of Hume's ethical doctrines have, generally speaking, paid relatively little attention to the passions dealt with in this chapter. This neglect of Hume's account of the indirect passions is no doubt largely due to a combination of the two mistaken beliefs, that the bulk of Book II of the *Treatise* is of no philosophical interest, and that Book III is fully intelligible without reference to the doctrines of Book II. But commentators have not just ignored this aspect of Hume's work, for it has been explicitly maintained that Hume's discussion of the indirect passions in Book II of the *Treatise* is of little importance for his treatment of ethical problems. Thus Professor Kemp Smith says:

> More than a third of Book II is employed in the treatment of four passions which have no very direct bearing upon Hume's ethical problems, and play indeed no really distinctive part in his system – pride and humility, love and hatred, viewed as operating in and through a complex double process of association.
> (PDH, 160)

Kemp Smith seems to consider the discussion of the indirect passions as important only because it illustrates Hume's attempt at proving that 'the laws of association play a rôle in the mental world no less important than that of gravity in the physical world' (PDH, 160). He therefore emphasizes that there is here a connection with the account of causal inference in Book I, although he does not seem to think that the discussion of the indirect passions is important for Hume's ethical doctrines. This view can be challenged, and it will be argued hereafter that a great deal can be learned about Hume's views on the nature of evaluation from his discussion of the indirect passions.

It is perhaps not wholly clear that the passage quoted above represents Kemp Smith's considered opinion, for he writes a little later that there is a close 'connection between Hume's theory of the passions and his ethical teaching' (PDH, 161). This connection can hardly be too strongly emphasized. I hope, furthermore, to show that this part of the *Treatise* is not entirely devoid of intrinsic philosophical interest.

Hume begins by drawing a distinction between the object of a passion and its cause. The object of both pride and humility is the self. There is really nothing very surprising in this terminology, for Hume is thinking of the direction of our thought or attention when we feel proud or humble. Hume, it is true, misrepresents the relation between the indirect passions and their object, but Kemp Smith's criticism of Hume's terminology is nevertheless not entirely well founded:

> Hume speaks of the self as being the 'object' of pride and humility: we should have expected him rather to say their 'subject'.
> (PDH, 180)

But do we not talk quite naturally of 'the object of our attention' or 'an object of thought'? The object of love and hatred is, according to Hume, some other person, and these passions are, in this respect, contrasted with pride and humility, where the object is self. It is much more natural to talk of a person we love as 'the object of our love' rather than 'the subject of our love'. Hume is using 'object' as a technical term. His terminology seems quite well suited to bring out the contrast he has in mind. Pride and humility are directed to oneself as their object, in the way in which love and hatred are, according to him, directed towards others.

A syntactical point may perhaps further vindicate Hume's terminology. We can on some occasions use interchangeably the two verbal expressions 'I am proud of x because of y' and 'x's (possession of) y makes me proud'. Thus a man can either say 'I am proud of my son because of his learning' or 'My son's learning makes me proud'. The two sentences would convey the same thought. This reduces the strength of the objection to Hume's terminology, since the oddity of calling self the object of the passion of pride appears to be derived from the fact that 'I' is the grammatical subject of the sentence 'I am proud of x'. The point may not seem of any great importance, but it is clear that Kemp Smith's complaint might incline people to the view that Hume is thinking of self as qualified by pride, whereas he is thinking of self as the object of pride in a quite different sense. For love qualifies the person loving whereas the *object* of love is the person loved. This distinction is more easily overlooked in the case of pride and humility, for they are directed towards the very person that has the passion.

It is necessary to distinguish Hume's use of 'object' in this context from the use of 'object' when we talk of objects of our desires. Desires are aimed at bringing something about, a change in, or the continuation of, a certain state of affairs. They can be satisfied (it is proper to talk in these terms although one may believe desires to be insatiable), and what satisfies them is their object. But the object of an indirect passion, whether oneself or another, is something real, not something to be realized, and it makes no sense to talk of it as satisfied by the realization of its object. It would seem, then, that the indirect passions are not desires, and their object is not something to be brought about. Hume suggests they have objects only in the sense that our attention is drawn to a particular object when they are aroused.

Hume's account of the nature of the indirect passions, and their relation to their objects, may be criticized in more than one way. Let us concentrate our attention on pride. His treatment of the passions as particular experiences or impressions leads him to overlook the fact that 'pride' and 'proud' are used in different though allied ways.

Consider the difference between the following statements:

(*a*) 'John is a proud man'
(*b*) 'He refused the offer with a proud gesture'
(*c*) 'He strutted about proudly'
(*d*) 'John is proud of his skill at chess'
(*e*) 'John suddenly felt his breast swell with pride' (when this is, for example, a description of John's feelings on being presented to the Queen).

In sense (*a*) the proud man is one who has certain character traits. He has a great tendency not to want to be helped by other people, even though he may need their help. There may be a hint involved that accepting help would, in his estimation, indicate a certain inferiority, so there may be a reference to self-evaluation. But 'He was too proud to accept our help' focuses our attention on a man's character and behaviour and it is not necessarily implied that he is proud *of* anything. There is no special reference to the cause of pride.

It appears that to be proud, in this sense, is not equivalent to having a certain experience or impression. I do not want to deny that a proud person may be prone to special 'feelings of pride'; but generally speaking we regard behaviour as being decisive and we seem relatively uninterested in the way the proud man feels or how he would describe his feelings. We certainly do not think the proud person is in a specially favourable position to know whether he is proud or not. It does not even seem unreasonable to suggest that a proud man's pride is in general more conspicuous to others than it is to the person himself.

Pride as a character trait may involve a somewhat stubborn refusal to accept that one is in any way in need or deficient. But this is a negative thing and there need be nothing such a man is proud of. Although a man may be proud in this sense without being proud of anything, it may be true that those who are proud *of* many things may tend to be proud men in this sense, because they are considering themselves to have a positive value, and will therefore be more reluctant to admit deficiency or need. This would often be the case when a person considers himself superior to his fellows irrespective of special circumstances. Thus the proud man might be a member of the aristocracy, although otherwise undistinguished, or he might be a business man who has seen better days. But it must not be forgotten that people who in no way feel superior to others may be described as too proud to accept assistance; they do not want to feel indebted to others. This makes them feel inferior and is seen as a threat to their self-respect. A person who persistently refuses assistance may be properly described as a proud person. It is more than doubtful whether pride in this sense necessarily involves ever having any special feeling identifiable as the feeling of pride.

(*b*) and (*c*) 'Proud' or 'proudly' are sometimes used to describe an individual action or a gesture. 'It was a proud action' may simply mean 'the action typical of a proud man', and 'proudly' often refers to the external demeanour or the physical changes characteristic of either a proud man (sense *a*) or a man proud of something – the look of disdain on a face when assistance is offered, or the strutting about of a man who thinks he has achieved something. These are usually not consciously decided upon.

Hume on the whole gives little attention to the physical aspects of the passions such as the proud man's expanding his chest and throwing back his head. He does, however, mention this in discussing pride and humility in animals. But there, typically, he considers these as signs of an inner experience, as the effect of a felt pride. He talks of the 'marks' of pride and humility, and says:

> It is plain, that in almost every species of creatures, but especially of the nobler kind, there are many evident marks of pride and humility. The very port and gait of a swan, or turkey, or peacock, show the high idea he has entertained of himself, and his contempt of all others. (THN II, 48/326)

The causes of these passions are supposed the same as in human beings 'making a just allowance for our superior knowledge and understanding' (THN II, 49/326). Thus in a turkey and a peacock, pride is to be thought of as derived from the beauty of the birds – 'the pride always attends the beauty, and is discovered in the male only' (THN II, 49/326).

The proud strutting of a peacock is a *mark* of pride, a mark of an inner impression which constitutes the pride. It is because we find similar behaviour in man accompanying the impression of pride that we are justified in making the inference from one to the other.

(*d*) A proud man is not necessarily proud of anything, although he may be; and an 'of' clause cannot follow the use of 'proudly' and 'with pride' when these are used to describe an action, although the cause of the behaviour in question may, of course, be given in other ways. But 'John is proud of his skill at chess' describes the way in which a person values himself because of a certain skill. One would not, however, say that John is proud of his skill at chess *only* when he is talking or thinking about chess, that he ceases to be proud of this when you direct his attention to other things, or when he falls asleep. The case is similar to loving or knowing. A man continues to love his wife even when absorbed in his work and he knows the multiplication tables even when he is not called upon to display this knowledge.

Of course when 'proud' is used to describe character it likewise does not refer to special behaviour on a special occasion. A man is a proud man even when he is not displaying or showing this. But more is needed than simply to establish that a man is proud if we want to verify the statement we are now considering. What he is proud of must also be established. Similarly, the behaviour that would tend to verify it is rather different. A man may be very proud of certain things, such as the beauty of his wife, without being at all a proud man in sense (*a*). Of course there is a sense of 'proud man' that attributes pride to a person at a particular time or period, though not necessarily implying that his character is that of a proud man. 'He is a proud man these days: his wife has just had twins' would be an example. But the behaviour expected from such a proud man would involve much less insistence on his self-sufficiency and dignity, and much more boasting and what people often describe as 'showing off'.

(e) 'John suddenly felt his breast swell with pride.' Here 'pride' could be thought of as an impression. John could recall how on this occasion he was glowing with pride. This is something he may keep to himself, though there will no doubt be a tendency to strut, to boast, and perhaps to be disdainful of any suggestion that one may in any way be deficient or in need of assistance. But I do not accept that pride is simply the name for this inner feeling and that all these other things are only indications that one is experiencing it. A man is not only proud when he is, and so long as he is, experiencing the glow of the feeling of pride, and he may in fact be proud though he sincerely claims that he does not have this glow. We cannot know how a person's special glow of pride feels and yet we can attribute pride or proud behaviour to people in any of the senses mentioned and know what kind of consideration would settle the matter. These considerations by no means always involve asking the man to describe his conscious state. In most cases we should not really attribute much relevance to such a description, and in many cases we should consider it quite irrelevant. A man is not at all the best judge himself as to whether he is a proud man. People are often poor judges of their own character, and even in the case of a man being *proud of* some particular thing, he may often fail to face up to his pride and think, for example, that his constant comments upon the merits of his children are simple, unbiased, objective observations, rather than inspired by pride. And yet, it must be admitted, we do expect people in such situations to have a certain conscious emotion. We should certainly be very surprised if someone told us that he felt *angry* when he was proudly dwelling on the glowing virtues of his children. We expect that a man who is proud of something will both behave in a way characteristic of pride and have certain feelings of pride. In the case of demeanour such as the strutting of a peacock, I do not see how we can attribute pride to such creatures unless our criteria are certain observable characteristics. We know what we mean when we describe an animal as a proud one, and I suggest that we do not mean that they experience special glowing feelings.

There is no doubt that Hume radically misrepresents the relation between pride and its object, even in the only case when it seems at all remotely plausible to think of pride as naming or essentially referring to a unique inner experience. A man glows with pride when he is presented to the Queen: the passion is supposed to have an object, in the sense that the attention of the proud person is always turned to himself.[1] But is this so? Is it not more likely that his attention at that time is focused on all the magnificent things he is in the presence of on this unique occasion in his life? It makes him think more highly of himself, and a proud man will no doubt tend to dwell on the characteristics that make him proud, because he likes to think of his self-importance. He can be described as a man who thinks a great deal of himself; but this is not properly characterized by saying simply that pride draws your attention to yourself. It is a form of self-valuing, and in this sense it has an object. But the object is not something separate from the pride, something one thinks of after one is already proud. This mistakenly suggests that the relation between pride (for Hume an impression) and its object is a contingent one. Talking of pride and humility Hume says:

> It is evident, in the first place, that these passions are determined to have self for their *object*, not only by a natural, but also by an original property. No one can doubt but this property is *natural*, from the constancy and steadiness of its operations. It is always self, which is the object of pride and humility; and whenever the passions look beyond, it is still with a view to ourselves; nor can any person or object otherwise have any influence upon us.
>
> (THN II, 7-8/280)

It is obvious from this passage that Hume thinks of the relation of pride and its object as a contingent relation. One might be proud and yet not think of oneself. It is his insistence on the simple nature of the passions as impressions that obscures for him the fact that the relation is a logical one. But, contrary to Hume's view, one must insist that it would be logically absurd to suggest that a man might have the passion of pride, and, at the same time, that the object of this pride (in Hume's sense of 'object') is another and not the person himself. Hume, who in most places appears to think of pride as a form of self-valuing, ought to have seen that 'to think highly of *oneself* because of *y*' and 'to be proud of *y*' are two ways of saying almost the same thing, and that the relation to oneself is a logical aspect of pride without which it could not be pride

---

[1] This feature of Hume's doctrine has been noticed by P. L. Gardiner in a broadcast talk published in *David Hume, a symposium*, London, 1963. See also Anthony Kenny: *Action, Emotion and Will*, p. 24.

at all. The closest he comes to realizing this is when, in the paragraph following the quotation above, he describes the relation to self as 'a distinguishing characteristic of these passions'.

Hume argues unambiguously that, because the self is the object of both pride and humility, it cannot be their cause, for these two passions are opposites and two opposite passions cannot have the same cause. If we have our value enhanced and diminished in our own eyes at the same time by a cause equally suited to produce both pride and humility, the effects would cancel each other. The two opposed emotions would leave the mind in equilibrium.

The influence of Newtonian mechanics upon Hume's thought about the passions is evident here. The passions are opposed to each other in the same way as opposing gravitational forces. The more complex model of the emotional life common at the present time allows the possibility of, for example, loving and hating a person at one and the same time, and the result is tension and inner turbulence and not equilibrium at all. But this is by the way, and the important point to note is that qualities of a great variety of subjects can cause these passions. We may be proud because of some quality we possess ourselves, but we may also be made proud by qualities of other persons or objects, if they are closely enough related to us. Thus, I might be proud of my skill in golf or dancing, but my garden or the exploits of my family might also arouse my pride. Nothing arouses pride in a person unless it is closely related to him. If the subject which arouses my pride is my beautiful garden, one can distinguish between the object itself, the garden, and the quality it possesses which arouses my pride; for unless the garden has a quality which is an independent source of pleasure it would not arouse my pride. This last condition is most plausible if to be an independent source of pleasure is to be independently valued. Thus the object must have a close relation to a person, and also be thought to possess some valuable quality if it is to arouse his pride.

The fact that Hume talks of beauty as a quality in an object must not mislead us into thinking that he is contradicting his later refutation of objectivism or intuitionism. All he needs to prove his point is the admission that an object does not make a man proud unless it is an independent source of pleasure, and that this is part-cause of the pride.

Hume thinks he is giving the causal conditions for the creation in our consciousness of a unique simple impression. The ultimate criterion for deciding whether a man is proud or not would be the presence or absence of this impression. We have already seen that this is a questionable criterion, for it is often true that a person is proud, in spite of his sincere claim that he is not. This is the case if it is accepted that a person is not always himself the best judge as to whether he is proud or not. It seems that Hume could not allow this, for he felt that an impression is in its very nature such that one cannot be deceived as to its presence or absence. Only verbal mistakes would be possible: a man might not know what a particular impression is called. If this is the case, it would have to be admitted that Hume has not given us the causal conditions for *being* proud, and one is forced to make the distinction between feeling proud and being proud. Hume, one might say, has stated the causal conditions for *feeling* proud, although admittedly some people *are* proud though they do not *feel* proud. The answer to this is that Hume most certainly did not draw this distinction. To be proud is, for him, to feel proud. His account is vitiated because he thinks of being proud as equivalent to *feeling an impression of pride*.

Hume turns to an account of the principles that must be assumed to be at work in the creation of the impression of pride. It would be absurd, he argues, to think that each object arousing pride was, by nature, suited to arouse this passion, and we must, therefore, attempt to find a common principle which will explain why pride arises in any of its occurrences. The principles of association are now appealed to. We are familiar with the association of ideas from the first book of the *Treatise*, but the association of impressions is here first introduced. The only relation by which this operates is resemblance, although *noticing* a resemblance is no part of the operation of the association. The relation here is a natural and not a philosophical relation. We notice only reflectively that passions that resemble one another in a certain way follow one another in our experience.

If Hume had thought the 'association' depended upon a reflective comparison it might have been odd for him to talk of the 'association of impressions'. But, that the association does not depend upon a prior conscious comparison is clearly shown by the fact that an impression is on its first occurrence supposed capable of giving rise to an associated impression which has not been previously experienced. Hume states this principle thus:

All resembling impressions are connected together, and no sooner

one arises than the rest immediately follow. Grief and disappointment give rise to anger, anger to envy, envy to malice, and malice
to grief again, until the whole circle be completed.
(THN II, 10/283)

Taken literally this statement is obviously absurd, though it may be
true that disappointment *tends* to make a person angry with anyone
responsible for it, and an envious person might easily become malicious.
Any one passion may resemble a number of other passions. Hume is,
therefore, in real difficulty, for if the association of impressions operates
by resemblance only, it becomes hard to explain why any one of a
number of resembling impressions should be aroused in a given case.
Let us consider the way in which pride or humility arises. Hume says:

When an idea produces an impression, related to an impression,
which is connected with an idea, related to the first idea, these
two impressions must be in a manner inseparable, nor will the
one in any case be unattended with the other. It is after this
manner that the particular causes of pride and humility are
determined. (THN II, 16/289)

If thinking of x pleases me, and x is related to me, then the pleasure
gives rise to pride, which is related to pleasure by similarity. Pride in
turn is *naturally* such as to make one think of oneself. We thus have a
double association, between oneself and the object related to oneself and
pleasure and pride, which is itself a pleasant passion. This double association is conceived as a mechanism by which the passion is produced.

It may be helpful to represent some of the relations between the
basic indirect passions by drawing up a square according to Hume's
description (THN II, 54/333).

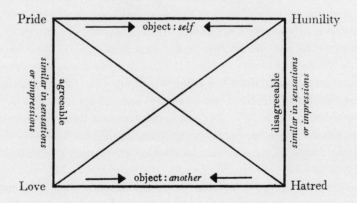

Each diagonal indicates both difference in sensation or impression and difference in the object. The device works well enough within its limitations. It fails to represent the fact that the causes of agreeable passions are agreeable and those of the disagreeable passions disagreeable. The square also fails to show that in each case the subject must be specially related to the object of the passion. By 'subject' Hume means whatever has the quality or characteristic that is the cause of the passion. If a man is proud of his son, then his son is the subject of his pride.

Hume talks as if the relation between pride and its object were purely contingent. We might have had the impression of pride and this might have been directed at others if we had been differently constituted. The thought of self and the passion of pride are only *naturally* connected; one always follows the other. One can only note this but not explain it; association does not help here at all. I have already suggested that what is here called a natural relation is, in fact, logical.

Although one may feel sceptical about Hume's argument considered as an account of the causal conditions for the emergence in consciousness of a special impression contingently related to the thought of self, some of the things he says are, with minor modifications, quite admirable as pieces of conceptual analysis. Let us take his contention that pleasure must be independently aroused by the cause of pride in order to give rise to that passion. Here Hume writes again as if he were simply stating the *de facto* relation of two events with no special logical relation at all. It is as if he were doing mechanics. The experience of pleasure, in certain specifiable situations, gives rise to the experience of pride, because these two are similar. It is simply that similar experiences follow each other. But the insight here so confusedly expressed is this: a man who is proud of something cannot be proud of it unless he values it. To be proud of something involves thinking of it as having a certain value or as indicating some value in you. As to the condition that the subject of pride must be related to the object of pride, it is certainly true that I could not claim to be proud of the late Sir Winston Churchill unless I implied that I stood in some special relation to him. If *per impossibile* I were his father, this relation would certainly be close enough. Members of the same nation might be taken to be closely enough related to enable them to say that they are proud of any one member of that nation. It becomes a bit more doubtful whether an Icelander could claim to be proud of Churchill even though he were a member of the Icelandic Conservative Party. It is certainly the case that one cannot claim to be proud of a person simply because one thinks that person has valuable qualities. One must also think that one stands in some special relation to that person. What sort of relation would be necessary? For Hume, it seems, the three relations of causality, contiguity in space or time and resemblance could all, if close enough, give rise to pride. Since we are considering how far Hume's causal story can lead us to certain conceptual insights, we must distinguish between the following two questions: (1) Under what conditions is it proper to give the name 'pride' to an emotion? and (2) Under what conditions is pride justifiable?

As regards the first, it is important to see that it is not the actual relation between subject and object which is relevant, but rather what the object *thinks* is his relation to the subject.[1] A man cannot (logically) be proud who thinks neither that he stands in any special relation to the subject of pride nor that this subject has any special value nor shows any special value in him (the object). But he might be proud even if he were mistaken about all these. Thus he may be proud of the exploits of a person he believes to be his son and to have achieved some important feat, although it may turn out later that he was mistaken in both beliefs. In such a case, one might say with pity 'And he was so proud of the fellow'. One would not say he thought he was proud of the person he believed to be his son, but could not in fact have been proud of that person because he did not in fact stand to that person in the requisite relations nor, indeed, did the person have the necessary value.

One could further examine the relations Hume thinks necessary for arousing pride, by drawing attention to the difference between pride and joy, which he emphasizes. An object must be related to us to give us joy; in this it resembles pride. But a much closer relation is required for the production of pride. A dinner party may give us joy, but in most cases it would make only the host proud. An occasion where merely being a guest at a dinner party causes pride could be due to the fact that it was a mark of honour to have been invited. But here, we should be closely related to the party, in contrast with all the people who are left out. It is where the cause of joy is no more closely related to me than it is to a great number of other people that it may furnish no reason for pride. Return to health gives rise to joy, but it is not very

1 I here use Hume's terminology.

often that it is an occasion for pride, because it is shared with such vast numbers. Hume explains this as follows:

> The reason why pride is so much more delicate in this particular than joy, I take to be as follows. In order to excite pride, there are always two objects we must contemplate, viz. the *cause*, or that object which produces pleasure; and self, which is the real object of the passion. But joy has only one object necessary to its production, viz. that which gives pleasure; and though it be requisite that this bear some relation to self, yet that is only requisite to render it agreeable; nor is self, properly speaking, the object of this passion. Since, therefore, pride has, in a manner, two objects to which it directs our view, it follows, that where neither of them have any singularity, the passion must be more weakened upon that account than a passion which has only one object. Upon comparing ourselves with others, as we are every moment apt to do, we find we are not in the least distinguished; and, upon comparing the object we possess, we discover still the same unlucky circumstance. By two comparisons so disadvantageous, the passion must be entirely destroyed. (THN II, 18-19/292)

It is fairly obvious that Hume thinks of his account as an explanation of the origin of the passions of joy and pride respectively. Two unfavourable comparisons will weaken a passion more than will one, and may in fact destroy it. The passion is thought of as separable from its *object* and its *cause*. He is making a perfectly valid point, but expressing it misleadingly because of his predisposition to state a logical point in causal terms. The difference between joy and pride to which Hume is drawing our attention, has surely to do with the justification of pride, the attempt to meet the challenge 'How can you be proud of *x*?' It is certainly the case that a man can be joyful though the source of his joy has no very close relation to him; but the challenge 'You have nothing to be proud of' cannot be met unless there is something special in the relation between the cause of pride and its object. Thus, my return to health might justify pride if it were due to a certain exceptional courage or effort of my own. If this effort were no greater than could normally be expected of the average person, I could not be said to have justified my pride in it. But, and this is an important point, unless the person *thinks* that there is a special relation between the cause and the object of pride, he simply cannot be proud of it. It is not just that his pride would not be justified, for to be proud of *x* is, partly, to think there is a special relation between oneself and x. It is essential for pride that a special relation should be thought to exist. On the other hand I can quite legitimately claim to experience joy at the thought of objects I do not consider to have any special relation to me. Joy, but not pride, can logically arise from the contemplation of any purely imaginary objects.

Hume does not explore sufficiently the possible relation between the closeness of the relation and the value of the cause of pride. He insists that the agreeable object that gives rise to pride must not only be 'closely related, but also peculiar to ourselves, or at least common to us with a few persons' (THN II, 18/291). This is hardly the whole truth, for the kind of value that gives rise to the pride does affect the logical issue. Let us assume that a man has a little garden to which he devotes great care. It need not necessarily be a very splendid garden for us to recognize that it is logically proper for the man to claim to be proud of it. On the other hand, a member of the same village could not be said to be closely enough related to the garden to claim to be proud of it unless it were a specially beautiful garden, something that would seem to add distinction to his village, so that some credit could rub off on him. Similarly, the president of the USA could hardly say without absurdity that he was proud of a garden owned by the Soviet premier, however splendid the garden might be. On the other hand he could say, on the occasion of a Soviet space flight, 'This achievement should make the breast of every human being swell with pride.' The point is this: the kind of achievement in question here is of *international* importance. It is something that could be taken to be a mark of increased importance of the human race, and could therefore be the source of pride for any member of that race.

It is obvious from this that people can be proud when they do not consider themselves to be causally responsible for the value of the related object. Thus people are often proud of the exploits of a local football team although they may have contributed nothing to its success. A father is closely enough related to his son for pride to be possible. He may, of course, be thought causally responsible for the son's qualities, even although, as regards the purely hereditary aspect, it may be unreasonable for him to claim any special credit. More surprisingly, a son is entitled to claim to be proud of his father, whose virtues he may not at all consider to be due to any praiseworthy efforts of his own. Mere contiguity in space, such as 'coming from the same part of the world', we recognize as the sort of relation that would make pride possible. We should not even challenge the propriety of such a pride given the right sort of value in the related subject. This, however, does not entail that our procedure is *reasonable*.

We may now turn our attention briefly to the question 'Under what conditions can a man justify his pride?' One might be inclined to think that pride is justifiable only when the person can claim to have been in some sense responsible for the realization of what is taken by him to be the *cause for* pride. We do not, however, demand this condition. But if to be proud of x is, or involves, thinking highly of oneself because of x, it seems reasonable to demand that we bear some responsibility for the realization of whatever it is that we claim as the justification for our pride. That we do not demand this condition for the justification of pride does, I think, show that there is a difference between the two concepts of 'being proud' and 'thinking highly of oneself'. Let us imagine a conversation about Mr Jones, a Welshman. A: 'Jones thinks very highly of himself.' B: 'Why?' A: 'A Welshman won a gold medal at the Olympic Games recently.' B: 'But this is no reason for *Jones* to think highly of himself. He had nothing to do with his compatriot's success.' B's remark seems here quite reasonable. Jones is not justified in thinking highly of himself, here, because he had nothing to do with his compatriot's feat. But the case is different with pride. A: 'Jones is a very proud man these days.'[1] B: 'Why?' A: 'A Welshman won a gold medal at the Olympic Games.' B: 'Why should that make *Jones* proud?' Here this question is unreasonable if we know that Jones is a Welshman. Every Welshman has a right to be proud of this great achievement of a fellow Welshman. He does not have to show further that *he* actually helped to bring it about. I do not think all this entails that to be proud in cases such as the above is not a form of self-valuing. But it is a special kind of self-valuing that we allow to be justified even when strictly speaking the proud person can take no credit for the cause of his pride.

I have already mentioned two of the limitations to the rule that whatever is an independent source of pleasure and related to oneself causes pride. I have critically examined Hume's reasons for maintaining that a 'closer relation' is needed for pride than joy, and his contention that the subject of pride is always peculiar to the proud person or only shared with a few other persons. All the limiting conditions are

---

[1] A is indicating that Jones is proud of something, not that his character is that of a proud man.

also supposed to apply to humility, although the cause is different, unpleasant rather than pleasant. The third limitation mentioned by Hume makes it clear that pride and humility are forms of self-valuing, and is really making an appeal to the influence of sympathy, although this principle is not explicitly mentioned. The happiness of others tends to make us happy, and this is why the fact that the object is pleasing to others increases the happiness we derive from it:

> This circumstance, like the two foregoing, has an effect upon joy as well as pride. We fancy ourselves more happy, as well as more virtuous or beautiful, when we appear so to others; but are still more ostentatious of our virtues than of our pleasures. (THN II, 19/292)

Happiness derived from sympathy with the happiness of others becomes a form of valuation only when it arouses a separate passion, in this case pride. This already suggests an analogy between evaluation in the form of moral and aesthetic judgments, and the indirect passions. I shall later try to show the importance of this analogy, and how it can help to clear up some puzzles in the interpretation of Hume's views on the function of sympathy in moral and aesthetic valuation.

The fourth point made by Hume refers to the fact that in order to arouse pride or humility the cause must have a certain degree of constancy: 'What is casual and inconstant gives but little joy, and less pride' (THN II, 19/293). The following emphasizes still more how pride and humility are forms of valuation: 'It seems ridiculous to infer an excellency in ourselves from an object which is of so much shorter duration, and attends us during so small a part of our existence' (ibid.). The implication seems to be that unless we can infer some excellency in ourselves we cannot be proud. But I do not think Hume really thinks the evaluation of ourselves is an *inference* from the qualities observed in ourselves, or in objects closely related to us. The expression 'it seems ridiculous to infer . . .' could be taken to indicate merely that Hume is insisting that one could not justify pride unless one could point out valuable qualities of a relatively constant kind. One must, after all, rule out flukes. But I take this to be another instance where Hume is vaguely aware of what makes his observations plausible, although he is still concerned to state the conditions under which pride arises, that is causal conditions. Indeed, pride and humility are, for him, equivalent to feeling satisfied or dissatisfied with oneself: ' . . . I observe that by *pride* I understand that agreeable impression, which arises in the mind, when the view either of our virtue, beauty, riches, or power, makes us satisfied with ourselves; and that by *humility* I mean the opposite impression' (THN II, 23/297). What gives rise to the evaluations of oneself gives rise to these passions, for they are the evaluations. I shall later examine the connection between these and the other directed indirect passions on the one hand, and approval and disapproval on the other.

Hume's final observation regards the important concept of 'general rules' which have considerable influence on the passions. He seems to have in mind that people are occasionally proud of things which do not give them any sensible enjoyment. Hume's example is, however, curious, for it regards the esteem of the rich and powerful. We esteem a rich man because of his riches, even though he does not derive any enjoyment from them. This is because our esteem is governed by the general rule that riches are a source of enjoyment to the possessor, even though the particular case in question may be an exception to the rule. But the same rule may be seen to apply in the case of the rich man himself. He may be proud of his riches even though they no longer give him any enjoyment, for 'custom and practise . . . have settled the just value of everything; this must certainly contribute to the easy production of the passions, and guide us, by means of general established maxims, in the proportion we ought to observe in preferring one object to another' (THN II, 20/294). We esteem the rich because riches are pleasing to the possessor. But although this is the ultimate source of the valuing of riches, a rich man may still value his riches, even when they no longer furnish him with any enjoyment. His evaluation is governed by the general rule which determines the value of riches as such. We can only understand this as a reference to 'objective evaluation' which disregards the special point of view of the person evaluating. The rich man disregards the circumstances that, in his own case, riches are no source of pleasure to him personally.

I have, so far, focused my attention almost exclusively on pride. This is because Hume's account seems to throw rather more light on the analysis of pride than on the analysis of humility. It becomes clear that Hume thinks of these as the two opposite ways of self-valuing: thinking highly of oneself and having a low opinion of oneself. But the ordinary concept of humility as self-valuing seems in general to involve having an *unduly* low opinion of yourself and, further, it does not obviously have a subject in quite the same way as pride. A man is proud *of* something, but cannot be humble *of* anything. This syntactical point may, however, not be very significant, for humility certainly can have special causes. Thus a man may be humbled by his relative inability to perform a special task; and one could say 'It was a humbling experience to discover that I could not solve a simple mathematical problem'. In these cases there is no obvious indication that one has an unduly low opinion of oneself. Thus there may be, although there need not be, some special characteristics that make the man humble. This is also true of pride as a character trait: a proud man need not be proud *of* anything. But this is not the kind of pride which seems to have been most prominent in Hume's mind. It is clear from his account of humility that he is not really interested in the ordinary concept of humility; his concern is with self-valuing. Humility to him is essentially the opposite of thinking highly of oneself (pride), and these passions are in each case induced by pleasure-creating or pain-arousing characteristics in something belonging to, or closely related to, the proud or the humble person. It may be suggested that Hume should have used the word 'shame' rather than 'humility' to stand for the opposite of pride. People are often ashamed of their appearance, their lack of intelligence, or of their families. It seems much less plausible to suggest that these characteristics and relations make people humble.

In giving an account of the passions of love and hatred Hume again emphasizes that these, like other passions, are simple impressions and hence indefinable. They are rightly classed with pride and humility as indirect passions, because a double association of impressions and ideas is necessary for their production. Some important differences are to be noticed, however, for the object of love and hatred is always 'some sensible being external to us' (THN II, 51/329). The object of pride and humility is always the proud or humble person. If it be objected that, in self-love, the object is surely the person himself, Hume's answer is that this is not, properly speaking, love at all. Substantiating this claim he simply appeals to introspection. The sensation self-love produces has not 'anything in common with that tender emotion which is excited by a friend or mistress' (ibid.). It is striking that here Hume uses 'love' to mean 'tender emotion', whereas for the most part he means by 'love' 'thinking highly of', just as by pride he usually means high self-esteem. The final distinguishing characteristic of a passion is the intrinsic quality of the feeling or emotion itself. This intrinsic quality cannot be the pleasantness, for this is common to the two passions under consideration love and self-love.

The object of love and hatred is the same,[1] and consequently it cannot be identified with the cause, since these passions are opposites in the same way as pride and humility are opposite passions. The cause is, in both cases, a quality of the subject[2] which arouses a separate pleasure and pain. The causes of the two pairs of passions are alike, but the difference lies in the object. It is to be noticed that Hume is not concerned with any other love than the love of human beings. The love he concerns himself with is always directed at another person as its object. The relation of the cause to oneself excites pride or humility, whereas if related to some other person it causes love or hatred. Hume points out that the connection between pride and vanity confirms this, for the vain person desires the love and esteem of others, and tries to gain this by exhibiting to them those qualities which are the cause of his pride. This procedure is deemed sensible, but would be completely irrational if the cause of pride and the cause of love and esteem were not the same. Any quality which, when we possess it, makes us proud, arouses love when it belongs to another.

But this is hardly the whole story, for people may win our love by pleasing us, though we might not be proud of the quality from which the pleasure arises if it were ours. 'Whoever can find the means, either by his services, his beauty, or his flattery, to render himself useful or agreeable to us, is sure of our affections; as, on the other hand, whoever harms or displeases us never fails to excite our anger or hatred' (THN II, 67/348). This emphasizes that a person who pays us compliments arouses our love or good will even though we might not be at all proud of our own characteristic as flatterers if we possessed it. Here it is the fact that the person pleases me, rather than the fact that he possesses a pleasing or a valuable characteristic, that arouses my love. This is important, for it draws attention to the essentially biased nature of many of our passions. We find it difficult, not only to love our enemies, but to form an unbiased view of their qualities. One of the central problems of the moral evaluation of people is to explain how objective evaluation arises from the biased forms of valuing involved in being proud or humble, in loving or hating. 'Biased' has often a derogatory connotation: a biased judge is a bad judge. But there is nothing wrong with a biased emotion in the sense in which I here use 'biased'.

---

[1] Not the person who loves or hates but another person. I am not, of course, suggesting that a person loved is always also hated.

[2] The word 'subject' is used here in the technical sense given to it by Hume.

'Biased emotion' is in this way similar to 'biased binding'. But the biased emotions may lead to unfair evaluation. Thus a man may mistake his love for approval based on objective assessment.

Perhaps pride, unlike love, is not so often or so obviously biased, for the proud man is making a claim to be enhanced in value, and the cause of the pride must thus be obvious to others as a source of pleasure, or perhaps more correctly, as something valuable. In this connection Hume himself considers it necessary 'that the pleasant or painful object be very discernible and obvious, and that not only to ourselves but to others also' (THN II, 19/292). It seems this is more a condition that would help one to justify one's pride, or to make it reasonable to *show* pride in something. Under special conditions a man might be proud of a thing which was not highly valued by other people, but in this case people would no doubt wonder how he could be proud of it. The biased nature of love and hatred is, indeed, very obvious. We do not love people in proportion to merit, for those more closely related to us arouse our love to a higher degree than strangers, even although we may be aware of the superior merit of the latter. Thus love can lead to a wrong evaluation, or, when this is not the case, it may be aroused even when the object possesses no very obvious pleasing qualities. This is brought out clearly by the love of relatives for 'whoever is united to us by any connection is always sure of a share of our love, proportioned to the connection, without inquiring into his other qualities' (THN II, 71/352).

The fact that a kinship existing between two persons seems to be sufficient to produce love appears to contradict the doctrine that a double association of ideas and impressions is necessary for the production of an indirect passion; it does not seem to be necessary for the cause of love to be an independent source of pleasure. Hume tries to explain this in terms of the enjoyment derived from company or the enjoyment of being in close association with others. This is hardly sufficient, for a man who only hears of the exploits of a son he has never seen and does not know would often be likely to overestimate these. One might, indeed, say that the lack of social relation might tend to increase the pride. It would be a mistake to think the closeness of relation always makes the passion biased in one direction. It seems, all the same, that the quality of being closely related to a person may sometimes be sufficient to arouse a separate pleasure which could account for the emergence of love. No wonder, therefore, that the passion of love is not aroused in direct relation to merit, for contiguity in space or time, or the causal relation of kinship, are deemed irrelevant in deciding upon the merit of any object.

However difficult it may be to distinguish between the pleasant feeling of love and the independently produced pleasure that leads to it, Hume still has to maintain this distinction to support his theory that a double association of impressions and ideas is necessary for the production of the indirect passions. A certain uneasiness is betrayed on this point, as the following quotation shows:

> It is not so evident at first sight, that a relation of impressions is requisite to these passions, and that because in the transition the one impression is so much confounded with the other, that they become in a manner undistinguishable. (THN II, 53/331)

He is talking of love and hatred, but he has to go on to say that they must be distinguishable. But, perhaps, the reason why one does not have to refer to the cause as a separate source of pleasure, in the case of love, is in no way connected with the difficulty of introspectively distinguishing between emotions.

One might want to say that the reason why the cause of pride must be an independent source of pleasure lies in the fact that a man who says he is proud of x, or in other ways displays pride in x, can always be called upon to justify his pride. The justification would consist in enumerating the valuable characteristics. With love, on the other hand, this is only sometimes the case, for we may claim to love x although we are not claiming x to be in any respects lovable. This is because love, when referring to people, usually stands for tender emotion (omitting any mention of sexual love) and does not mean 'thinking highly of'. Thus we claim to love our children without having to meet the challenge that there is nothing lovable or valuable about them; but we cannot claim to be proud of our children unless we are prepared to say that they have some valuable qualities. There is of course a sense in which I may be proud of my children considered as mere signs or indications or effects of a valuable quality in myself. Thus I might be proud of my family as showing my fruitfulness, irrespective of any quality they may possess. But this does not destroy the point I am making, that love differs from pride in that one may claim to love without in any sense implying the existence of any valuable quality at all.

If Hume had not been so convinced that the passions are simple

impressions, he might have seen that some of the difficulties he en-
counters are due to the fact that 'love' and 'hatred', 'pride' and 'humility' are complex concepts. He comes near to realizing this when he
says that 'esteem and contempt, indeed, arise on some occasions instead
of love and hatred; but these are, at the bottom, the same passions, only
diversified by some causes . . .' (THN II, 58/337). His confusion, however, is obvious in this passage, for if the causes of esteem and contempt
are different from the causes of love and hatred these passions are to
some extent different. It is only his associationist scheme, according to
which there can in the end be only four indirect passions, which dictates to him that love must 'at the bottom' be the same passion as
esteem, hatred the same as contempt. But it seems the neat scheme
of passions as simple impressions is threatened; esteem is only to be
differentiated from love in terms of the attendant circumstances, for
'at the bottom the same' could only refer to the impression or feeling,
if they are 'only diversified by some causes'. This almost looks as if
'some causes' refers to the attendant circumstances as part of the identifying characteristics of the passions, rather than causal conditions in
the ordinary sense.

It might be argued that this is too uncharitable. The identification
might only refer to the fact that the same associative principles explain
the origin of both. The sensation of these passions might still be different though the similarity might be close. It might even be difficult to
decide whether one was 'esteeming' or 'loving'. This, one might think,
could only be decided by a closer attention to the impression according
to Hume's principles; but we might also pay attention to the attendant
circumstances, for there must be some difference in these to indicate
whether 'love' or 'esteem' is the passion aroused. Hume would still
have to say that the two 'impressions' are slightly different, for although
they might be extremely similar their sensations must be specifically
different.

The meaning of the 'sensation' of a passion requires some clarifica-
tion. In describing two emotions as similar one may be referring to the
fact that the circumstances in which they occur have something in
common. For example, one might claim that there is a certain similarity between envy and jealousy, and back up this claim by pointing
out that both a jealous person and an envious person must think that
the object of the envy or the jealousy is in possession of (this must be
treated in a very wide sense) something it would be desirable to have.

When, however, two emotions are said to have a similar sensation, this indicates that, independently of knowledge of the circumstances, a person who has experienced both could detect a similarity – a medicine can taste like a certain fruit. Hume's view that the passions are simple impressions entails that each emotion has a special sensation to the person experiencing it. Jealousy and envy may be thought to have a similar sensation in addition to the similarity of circumstances already mentioned. Esteeming and loving may in a comparable way be thought similar. It must be remembered that I am attempting to explain my terminology, and not to justify the doctrine it presupposes.

In a discussion of the causes of love or hatred two circumstances must be taken into account: when we love or hate a person for something he has done, our feelings are aroused only if the action was intentional, and it is 'by the intention we judge of the actions; and, according as that is good or bad, they become causes of love or hatred' (THN II, 68/348). But this doctrine is soon modified, for when a characteristic belongs permanently to a person our love or hatred is likely to be aroused even though the person did not intend to do us harm or good. Even in the case of an intentional action, these emotions are aroused because the intention is a sign of a quality of character.

But there are also cases where an unintentional injury to us arouses our hatred, and it is only upon reflection that this may come to be modified. And even when a person's motives for injuring us are strictly honourable we may still feel antagonistic towards him, although here also our antagonism or hatred may be modified upon reflection. Hume, indeed, makes an explicit reference to reasonable hatred as opposed to unreasonable hatred. This can be understood only as a reference to the fact that when we look upon the source of our hatred objectively our feelings in the case may come to be modified.

> One that has a real design of harming us, proceeding not from hatred and ill-will, but from justice and equity, draws not upon him our anger, if we be in any degree reasonable; notwithstanding he is both the cause, and the knowing cause, of our sufferings. (THN II, 70/350)

But of course we are not always reasonable: our passions are not always modified by objective evaluations. Our approval of the character trait, which is the source of the injury done to us, may be too weak to destroy our hatred of the person. The reference here seems to be to what is vulgarly called a conflict between reason and the passions, which Hume considers to be misdescribed in these terms: 'We speak not strictly and philosophically, when we talk of the combat of passion and of reason. Reason is, and ought only to be, the slave of the passions, and can never pretend to any other office than to serve and obey them' (THN II, 127/415). This is not an exceptionally extreme statement in Hume's philosophy but a general statement of his main thesis. For not only is it the case that an 'objective judgment' can influence our attitudes only by arousing a passion, but reference must also be made to human passions in order to account for the fact that we take up an objective point of view at all. This can best be explained after a discussion of certain other features of Hume's theory, including the notion of sympathy and its function in his doctrine of evaluation.

3

SYMPATHY, COMPARISON, AND EGOISM

I

It can be most emphatically stated that it is impossible to give a satisfactory account of Hume's views on the nature of evaluation in the *Treatise* without introducing the principle of sympathy. An interpretation has, in actual fact, been given of Hume's ethical theory without the word 'sympathy' being used even once; I am referring to the chapter on Hume in C. D. Broad's *Five Types of Ethical Theory*. This can be explained by Broad's view that 'the best account of Hume's theory of ethics is to be found in his *Enquiry Concerning the Principles of Morals*' (FTET, 84). It is true that Broad mentions 'benevolence or humanity', but one of the things that must be emphasized in explaining the concept of sympathy in the *Treatise* is its difference from benevolence.

Those who do emphasize the importance of sympathy in Hume's account of morality often fail to explain its nature and its relation to moral value. Thus Richard B. Brandt, in his *Ethical Theory*, brackets together Adam Smith and Hume as thinkers who regarded 'moral values as almost entirely a matter of sympathetic responses, and moral judgments as almost entirely derived from these' (ET, 133). But this statement is misleading, for Adam Smith and Hume by no means agreed about the nature of sympathy nor did they hold the same view about its relation to moral value. Brandt's description of the concept of sympathy is also questionable. In this chapter I shall consider how far Hume's account of sympathy helps to elucidate or explain the various kinds of situation in which sympathy appears to be involved in one form or another. I shall also discuss certain passions and principles that stand in a special relation to sympathy or appear to be of importance for the correct understanding of Hume's views about evaluation. The most important of these is the principle of comparison. But this is only a preliminary discussion of sympathy; I do not at present propose to discuss the specific problems that arise in connection with the appeal Hume makes to sympathy in his explanation of moral valuation.

In a section of Book II of the *Treatise*, entitled 'Of the Love of Fame', Hume explicitly introduces the principle of sympathy and explains the way it works. He leaves us in no doubt about the importance he attributes to it and exclaims: 'No quality of human nature is more remarkable, both in itself and in its consequences, than that propensity we have to sympathize with others, and to receive by communication their inclinations and sentiments, however different from, or even contrary to, our own' (THN II, 40/316). He also includes opinions among those things communicated in accordance with the principle of sympathy, which he refers to as 'the principle of sympathy or communication' (THN II, 137/427). It is clear that a principle is not a special passion, although Hume, never very careful to remain consistent in his terminology, refers at least once to 'the communicated passion of sympathy'.

In explaining how sympathy operates, Hume argues that other people's passions are known to us only through their external effects; we cannot directly observe other persons' emotions but must infer them: an impression can only be known 'by its effects, and by those external signs in the countenance and conversation, which convey an idea of it' (THN II, 41/317). Thus it appears that the first step in the process is the movement from a person's behaviour, his words or involuntary signs of emotion, to the belief or knowledge that the person in fact has this emotion. According to Hume's views about the causal explanation of actions, there is no difference in principle between on the one hand the relation between the passion of anger and going pale with anger, and on the other hand the relation between the passion of anger and angry talk or angry behaviour. In each case there is a causal relationship that leads to our inferring one from the other. We may also come to infer the presence of a passion of anger from the words of another who tells us that he is angry.[1] But the thought of another's passions, which may

---

[1] I am not suggesting that Hume is not aware of the conventional nature of language. But natural motives explain the origination of the convention and once it is established the inference from words to emotion is of the causal kind.

start as only a thought and come to be a belief, if the signs are definite, is enlivened 'and acquires such a degree of force and vivacity, as to become the very passion itself, and to produce an equal emotion as an original affection' (THN II, 41/317). The enlivening of the idea is achieved through the operation of a related impression. This is one of the principles Hume appeals to when, in the first book of the *Treatise*, he is giving an account of the way in which, in causal inference, a belief comes to be engendered through the influence of a present impression. This obviously presupposes the view that the difference between an idea and an impression is a difference only in force and vivacity or liveliness: there is no difference in principle between the thought of pain and real pain; the thought of pain may become real pain if its force or liveliness is somehow increased. This curious doctrine is familiar to readers of Book I; but it is surprising to find that the impression which confers vivacity upon the idea of, or belief in, another's passion is the impression of the self, for in Book I Hume appears to deny the existence of such an impression.

Hume thought that sympathy worked in the following way:

The idea of ourselves is always intimately present to us, and conveys a sensible degree of vivacity to the idea of any other subject to which we are related. This lively idea changes by degrees into a real impression; these two kinds of perception being in a great measure the same, and differing only in their degree of force and vivacity. (THN II, 73/354)

Earlier on Hume had talked of 'the idea, or rather impression of ourselves' which he claims to be 'always intimately present with us' (THN II, 41/317). It appears that the perception of the self must be an impression if it is to have the enlivening influence already mentioned. It seems reasonable to suggest that something less vivid than an impression could not have the power of raising an idea to the vivacity of an impression. One could say that sympathy operates as follows: we have an idea of, or we think of, a passion in the mind of another being that has some relation to us. This idea or thought is raised to the status of an impression because of the enlivening influence of the impression of self. Since it is possible for the emotions of a human being to affect any other human being, by means of sympathy, there must be some relation that holds between all persons. The only relation of those recognized by Hume that meets the case is similarity. We can, though less powerfully, be affected by the emotions of animals. This is because they resemble us in some respects although they do not resemble us as closely as other human beings do. There is thus always a relation of similarity between the being whose emotions, feelings or opinions are transferred and the creature to whom they are transferred. Hume could have explained this aspect of his doctrine more carefully. Surely some similarities are much more important than others. The fact that animals resemble us in that they can experience pleasures and pains is much more important than resemblance in physical form. This is not to deny that we do take resemblance in physical form as some evidence for similarity of experience in the absence of knowledge of behavioural characteristics. But similarity in behaviour is more important than similarity in form. This is because behaviour, rather than form, is thought to indicate the quality of an individual's experience.

It is not entirely clear that sympathy always involves belief, but it may seem to be a necessary condition in the simple case when we are affected by signs of emotion in another. Does the effect not cease when we disbelieve the signs and think the person is shamming? It is not altogether unreasonable to suggest that the tears of another person have an emotionally disturbing effect upon the onlooker only as long as he takes them to be an indication of a genuine pain or sorrow. But the fact that disbelief tends to destroy sympathy does not entail that belief is a necessary condition for the operation of sympathy in each and every case. More will be said about this question later.

I do not propose to discuss in any detail whether Hume's appeal to an impression of self is consistent with his denial in Book I that any such impression can be found nor do I want to defend the way he appeals to an impression of the self in explaining sympathy; but this much must be said: in Book I he is concerned with the question of personal identity. What entitles me to say that I am the same person now as I was a short while ago? It is in this connection that he denies any impression of a self remaining uniformly identical and underlying our various interrupted and changing experiences. The fact that we remain the same person throughout a lifetime cannot be derived from an impression of a self, for there is no such impression that remains numerically and qualitatively the same during a person's lifetime.

But Hume does not deny that we can, at any time, identify a complex set of impressions which constitutes what we call our *self* at that particular time. A number of our desires and passions are non-representative and belong to ourselves. They form part of what we refer to as our person, as distinct from what is not our person. Our impressions of sense, of course, also belong to ourselves; but we do take them to represent an external reality, although it may be impossible to find arguments that would justify our belief in the independent and un-interrupted existence of an external world if this belief were called in question. Yet we have this belief, and thus must in fact have a concep-tion of ourselves as opposed to what is not to be counted as part of our person. All that Hume needs in his account of sympathy is that at any particular time, when we are conscious, there should be a complex impression we can identify as the impression of our own person. This impression need not remain unchanging, although at all times during our conscious existence there is something we can call 'self, or that individual person, of whose actions and sentiments each of us is inti-mately conscious' (THN II, 13/286).[1]

The whole process of sympathizing is conceived of by Hume in very mechanical terms, and the impression of the self enters into the picture only as a source of vivacity or liveliness. There is no suggestion that in sympathizing one imaginatively puts oneself into the other person's place, which is characteristic of Adam Smith's account: 'By the imagin-ation we place ourselves in his situation, we conceive ourselves en-during all the same torments [as the person with whom we sympathize], we enter as it were into his body, and become in some measure the same person with him, and thence form some idea of his sensations, and even feel something which, though weaker in degree, is not alto-gether unlike them' (TMS, 9). But common to Smith and Hume is the view that one can sympathize only with experiences that one has had oneself. One cannot, on Hume's account, form the idea of another person's emotion unless one has had the corresponding impression. This follows from the claim that the passions are simple impressions and that all simple ideas are copies of simple impressions.

Hume uses the models of (1) a mirror, and (2) an echo in illustrating the way in which sympathy functions. Thus he says: 'In general we may remark, that the minds of men are mirrors to one another, not only because they reflect each other's emotions, but also because those rays of passions, sentiments, and opinions, may be often reverberated,

---

[1] It is obvious that Hume is not referring to a special unalterable impression of a unique ego when he describes the impression of oneself as 'that connected succession of perceptions, which we call *self*' (THN II, 5/277). It is this self that is the object of pride and humility.

and may decay away by insensible degrees' (THN II, 82-83/365). He illustrates this by pointing out that people are pleased with riches. The principal source of our esteem of rich people is sympathy with this initial pleasure. The rich person in turn becomes even more pleased with his riches because of a sympathy with the esteem of others. This 'secondary' pleasure or satisfaction in wealth comes to raise in people a still greater desire of wealth, they come to value it still more. And Hume concludes: 'Here then is a third rebound of the original pleasure, after which it is difficult to distinguish the images and reflections, by reason of their faintness and confusion' (THN II, 83/365). The model Hume uses shows how mechanically he thinks about the way in which emotions and opinions are transferred from one person to another; and it is to be noted that the model fits only when there is an initial emotion to be communicated. A mirror image must be in the end traceable to a real thing other than an image. An echo similarly presupposes an original sound that is not an echo.

The following features of the operation of sympathy must be stressed:

(1) To sympathize with x is to have x's 'opinions and sentiments' communicated to us. It is to have x's opinions or sentiments because of a communication according to the principles of operation laid down.

(2) To sympathize with x is not as such to be motivated in any way unless I am sympathizing with x's motive. Thus to sympathize with x's desire for brandy is to desire brandy.

(3) The being with whose sentiments or opinions we sympathize must have some relation to us. We, furthermore, sympathize more easily and more completely with those who are closely related to us.

It is obvious that 'sympathy' is, for Hume, a technical term referring to a special psychological principle. The criteria for its use seem to be (a) that a person has the same feeling or opinions as x, and (b) that this feeling or opinion has come to be that person's feeling or opinion in a certain way, namely through the special enlivening of an idea into an impression through the influence of the impression of the self. This condition is absolutely necessary, for the bare fact that I and a farm worker in China both feel angry in no way indicates that sympathy is involved.

It is worth special mention that Hume says we may sympathize with another's opinions as well as with his sentiments, emotions (in fact his passions in the wide sense Hume gives to that term), and his bodily pleasures and pains. It seems strange to suggest that I may come to agree with another's opinion by the process of an idea being enlivened so as to become a belief. But there is no reason to suppose that Hume does not mean his words to be taken to refer to people's opinions as to matters of fact as well as to their moral opinions.[1] The influence of sympathy 'is not only conspicuous in children, who implicitly embrace every opinion proposed to them; but also in men of the greatest judgment and understanding, who find it very difficult to follow their own reason or inclination, in opposition to that of their friends and daily companions' (THN II, 40/316). The expression 'every opinion' makes it clear that the term is not being used in a restricted sense. And, on reflection, the view that the influence of sympathy stretches to opinions about matters of fact is quite natural. We know that certain opinions may be widely accepted in a community in such a way as to make it extremely difficult to convince a member of that community of their falsity. Let us take as an example the opinion that horsemeat is poisonous. This is to be distinguished from the disapproval of the eating of horsemeat, although the belief that horsemeat is poisonous would almost certainly lead to the general disapproval of eating it. It is natural to expect that a person brought up to the belief that horsemeat is poisonous would adhere to this view, in face of considerable evidence to the contrary, unless the opinion came to be questioned by other members of the community. The knowledge that the other members of his community were somewhat shaken in their opinion would tend to decrease the tenacity with which any one of the members would adhere to it. This we might ascribe to the influence of sympathy. Let us now apply Hume's analysis of the working of sympathy to the case: x, y, and z each say to w, 'Horsemeat is poisonous'. x, y, and z have a relation to w, and each time he is told this w has the thought that horsemeat has poisonous qualities. According to a Humean doctrine, a belief is a lively or vivid thought. Why should the conception in this case not tend to be enlivened into a belief, if the thought is closely enough related to the person? This relation is established by his repeatedly thinking of the poisonous qualities of horsemeat. He thinks of these every time he reflects upon the beliefs of others in regard to the edibility of horsemeat. The thought of their belief that horsemeat is

---

[1] There are grounds for thinking that Hume considered moral opinions to be emotions. The transference of such opinions would not be specifically different from the transference of passions.

poisonous is repeatedly raised in his mind by their talk and by their actions. His thought that the people belong to his own community further strengthens his belief. This recurrence of the thought in his mind may in time lead him to share the belief of others that horsemeat is, indeed, poisonous. This would be in perfect harmony with Hume's contention that frequent repetition tends to engender belief. And Hume, in fact, stresses the enlivening effect of repetition '. . . we may feel sickness and pain from the mere force of imagination, and make a malady real by often thinking of it' (THN II, 42/319).

We must also bear in mind that sympathy may be at work, even though it does not lead to an identity of sentiment or opinion, for it may have the effect only of making it difficult for men 'to follow their own reason or inclination, in opposition to that of their friends and daily companions' (THN II, 40/316). Sympathy, in fact, admits of degrees and may succeed in creating in our minds only a certain tension. The most conspicuous example of this and perhaps the most important, would be a conflict of motives engendered in this manner.

Let us now consider Hume's account of sympathy in relation to various situations where sympathy may be said to be involved.

There is a sense of 'sympathize' that I want to mention only to rule it out of our considerations. The term, on occasion, means 'to express sympathy'. This meaning is given in the Shorter Oxford Dictionary and the example quoted is 'A clergyman and his wife went to sympathize with a neighbour'. They might or might not have sympathized by using the terms 'sympathy' or 'sympathize'. One can express one's sympathy by just saying 'you have my sympathy'; but in a great many cases, perhaps in a majority, this does not happen. The clergyman and his wife may only have looked sympathetic, and perhaps laid a sympathetic hand on the neighbour's shoulder. Merely being in a certain place at a certain time may be taken as an expression of sympathy: a man who marches in a torchlight procession to protest about the imprisonment of certain people for political 'crimes' may want his action to be taken both as a protest and as an expression of sympathy with the victims of injustice and their families.

But Hume is not primarily concerned with the expression of sympathy nor with the use of the terms 'sympathy' and 'sympathize'. He is concerned with sympathizing as a kind of transference of emotions, feelings and opinions, rather than with the deliberate expression of sympathy, which must be clearly distinguished from any involuntary symptoms or signs that might reveal a person's sympathy or give away a sympathizing person. Both behaviour and involuntary signs may, of course, lead one to infer the presence of an emotion·in another person, which in turn may be the first step in sympathizing, according to Hume's account, already delineated. In the concept of behaviour we can here include what some psychologists now would call 'verbal behaviour'. Thus Hume says: 'When any affection is infused by sympathy, it is at first known only by its effects, and by those external signs in the countenance and conversation, which convey an idea of it' (THN II, 41/317). Conversation may lead us to infer a man's anger because he uses angry words and perhaps indulges in threats and recriminations. But we might also think a man was annoyed, simply because he tells us this. We have come to realize that people's testimony is generally trustworthy, and in cases where there is no reason for distrust, we therefore tend to accept their word when they inform us about their feelings. If there are also involuntary signs, our faith in the person's word is strengthened. If the girl blushes we are more inclined to believe her when she tells us she is embarrassed by a compliment. We thus have (1) involuntary signs of emotion, for example blushing; (2) expression of emotion, for example angry talk, deliberate expression of sympathy, angry or sympathetic behaviour; and (3) statement of emotion, for example, a report by someone of their annoyance with someone else. In each of these cases we have a phenomenon that can be important as the first step in the process of sympathizing.

'Sympathy' is often very close in meaning to 'compassion' or 'pity'. This meaning is given prominence in the Shorter Oxford English Dictionary. To sympathize with someone would correspondingly be much akin to pitying him. Confining ourselves for the moment to this sense of 'sympathy' and 'sympathize', we might note the following: sympathy refers to a motive that can help to explain actions of a certain sort. It may be given as an explanation of why a man helps someone who is in difficulties. This is not, of course, to say that one cannot sympathize and yet not act as a result of the sympathy. It would clearly be possible to claim truly to sympathize with the plight of the coloured people in South Africa, and yet not have done anything to ameliorate their suffering. The practical commitment of sympathy is there, but one might fail to act for other reasons, such as fear or lack of opportunity. It is true that the strength of the sympathy may be to a large extent determined by the person's readiness to act in conformity with it when conflicting tendencies, such as fear, are present. Yet one must allow weakness of will: a person may suffer, if he fails, because of weakness of will, to act in accordance with his sympathies. The pangs of conscience for failing to help a needy person may, at times, be correctly taken as an indication of sympathy. But in cases of actions performed where sympathy is given as the motive, only certain sorts of reasons can be adduced for the sympathy. 'Why did you visit the old lady every week?' 'Because she had recently lost her only friend and was lonely.' This is a perfectly possible reason for sympathizing. But if the answer had not pointed out something that could be thought of as a misfortune, it would be logically impossible to sympathize. We would think it ludicrous, for logical reasons, if it were suggested that the old lady's happiness was the reason for the sympathy; and 'I sympathized with her because she was rich' suggests that the visits may have had another motive than sympathy, since 'being rich' is not, on the whole, considered a misfortune in our community.

It is clear that one might sympathize with people because of physically induced pains as well as emotions such as sorrow. I might feel a strong sympathy with a man who is in severe physical pain. He has, for example, broken his leg while we were enjoying a skiing holiday together. It may seem rather odd to apply Hume's analysis to this kind of case, for it may be impossible for me to know what it feels like to have a broken leg, unless I, in the past, have suffered that calamity. But I may have suffered similar pains; it is the ideas of these that come to be enlivened into a real feeling. Even so it appears that our state of mind need not necessarily involve any feeling localized in the way the person's pain is localized in his leg. To sympathize with a man who has rheumatic pains does not consist in having this pain oneself. It may be rather difficult to imagine if one has never suffered from rheumatism. Rheumatic pains may have a special character of their own and yet there is no reason to believe that someone who has never experienced such pains is incapable of sympathizing with a rheumatic sufferer. One must insist that to sympathize in the sense of 'to pity' does not consist necessarily in having the same sort of feeling as the person with whose suffering one is sympathizing. One must not be confused by 'I certainly sympathize with you. I have had rheumatism myself' when this is said to a man suffering from rheumatism. The reference to the speaker's own rheumatism helps to emphasize that the sympathizer knows how much a man can suffer from this affliction. It certainly must not be taken to entail that the speaker could not have sympathized if he had not suffered from rheumatism.

It may seem less difficult to consider sympathizing with sorrow as the communication of sorrow; but even in this case it would be odd to talk of a communicated feeling or emotion. I might sympathize with a man who has lost someone dear to him, such as his father, although I might have thought privately that the father was a scoundrel and therefore I would not have the sense of loss the son has; but I may *understand* his feeling, and consequently have sympathy for him.

If taken as a criticism of Hume these considerations would miss the mark, for Hume is not committed to holding that sympathy, in the sense we are now considering, could be conceived of as a communication of feelings or emotions. It was made perfectly clear by him that pity and compassion were different from his principle of communication: they were passions, and although sympathy may (according to Hume) help to explain why pity or compassion occur, they cannot, any more than the other passions, be equated with a principle of communication of any kind.

In the section of the *Treatise* entitled 'Of Compassion', Hume claims that the principle of sympathy can explain the occurrence of pity, although, as we shall see, the facts force him to introduce considerations that involve special difficulties for him. Pity, he says, 'is a concern for . . . the misery of others' (THN II, 86/369). But he seems not to be adequately alive to the need to explain why a communication of sorrow or unhappiness from another should occasion in us a concern about the person. In the following passage he appears too ready to take this for granted:

> It will be easy to explain the passion of *pity* from the preceding reasoning concerning sympathy. We have a lively idea of everything related to us. All human creatures are related to us by resemblance. Their persons, therefore, their interests, their passions, their pains and pleasures must strike upon us in a lively manner, and produce an emotion similar to the original one, since a lively idea is easily converted into an impression. If this be true in general, it must be more so of affliction and sorrow. These have always a stronger and more lasting influence than any pleasure or enjoyment. (THN II, 86/369)

But why, even if I am affected through the process of communication, should I be concerned about the other person's suffering or sorrow?

This, it seems, needs explanation, and it is not given. Why could we not hate the other person, because we are made uncomfortable by the presence of his sorrow? Why, furthermore, do we feel concerned on many occasions, rather than turn away from the source of our discomfort?

Hume stresses the dependence of pity upon the imagination rather than reason. Women are more susceptible to it, and to be very prone to pity is supposed to be due to the same weakness as leads a person to faint at the mere sight of a sword, even though he is in no danger. The sword might be in the hand of a close friend who is merely showing it off as a choice possession. It is thus not the likelihood of danger that affects him but the 'images' suggested by the object. Likewise, in the theatre we are affected by sympathy, though we know that the people on the stage do not necessarily have the feelings they portray in their acting. Here, it seems, sympathy operates even though one does not believe in the existence of the emotions that supposedly affect us through sympathy. In the case of the sword they are non-existent, and they may also be absent in the actors on the stage; for I am assuming that an actor portraying an emotion on the stage need not necessarily feel the emotion he portrays. The account of sympathy as a principle of communication is already rather strained, for in the cases of sympathy just mentioned there is no emotion to be communicated. It is made clear, in the following passage, that sympathy cannot be described as involving communication in any ordinary sense of that term. 'There remains only to take notice of a pretty remarkable phenomenon of this passion, which is, that the communicated passion of sympathy sometimes acquires strength from the weakness of its original, and even arises by a transition from affections which have no existence' (THN II, 87/370).

It is strange enough for Hume to admit that the weakness of the original passion might make stronger the communicated one. This flies in the face of his contention elsewhere that in order to explain an increase in liveliness of a perception, we need to appeal either to closer connections or to the influence of a perception that has a force or liveliness that affects a related idea. But Hume has to admit the facts as he sees them. He describes these facts in the following way:

> Thus, when a person obtains an honourable office, or inherits a great fortune, we are always the more rejoiced for his prosperity, the less sense he seems to have of it, and the greater equanimity and indifference he shows in its enjoyment. In like manner, a

man who is not dejected by misfortunes is the more lamented on
account of his patience; and if that virtue extends so far as utterly
to remove all sense of uneasiness, it still further increases our
compassion. (THN II, 87/370)

In accounting for the apparent exception to his principles Hume here
appeals to the influence of general rules. We come to think of the idea
of the passion that generally arises in a certain situation 'and though
there be an exception in the present case, yet the imagination is affected
by the *general rule*, and makes us conceive a lively idea of the passion,
or rather feel the passion itself in the same manner as if the person
were really actuated by it' (THN II, 88/371). The absence of the emotion may, indeed, be taken as an indication of 'greatness of mind', and
seeing it in this light may 'increase our admiration, love, and tenderness for him' (THN II, 88/370). In this case, it becomes obvious that
one need not believe the original passion to be real in order that the
principle of communication may operate. It is not only that we overlook the fact that the emotion is absent in a particular case. It seems
that sometimes our belief in its absence may tend to heighten the sympathetically induced emotion. This is quite clear in the other example
Hume takes: we tend to become more embarrassed for a person if he
seems to be unaware of the foolish behaviour that makes us embarrassed for him. And when Hume goes on to say that our concern for a
person such as an infant prince in a great misfortune is heightened the
more unaware he seems to be of it, one wonders how sympathy, as it is
understood by him, could be the source of this compassion or concern.
Hume writes:

It is an aggravation of a murder, that it was committed upon
persons asleep and in perfect security; as historians readily observe
of an infant prince, who is captive in the hands of his enemies,
that he is more worthy of compassion the less sensible he is of his
miserable condition. (THN II, 88/371)

It is interesting to notice the references to value in the above passage.
The murder is 'aggravated' when the victim is asleep and the infant
prince is made more 'worthy' of compassion by his unawareness of his
own misfortune. In considering these situations we are moved by the
emotion which as a general rule attends these situations, although we
know that the case in question is an exception. But an entirely new
principle also comes into operation: the principle of contrast or comparison. This principle has an opposite effect to the effect of sympathy.

PV E

We conceive of the misfortune of the young prince in the liveliest of terms. This contrasts most sharply with his feelings of security. The contrast heightens our sympathetically induced distress, and increases our concern. This principle is supposed to have a powerful effect upon the imagination.

Let us at this point summarize our main conclusions:

(1) Hume initially defines sympathy as a principle of communication of passions and opinions. It is not a special passion. He initially uses the model of a mirror or an echo to show how, through sympathizing, passions and opinions are communicated from one person to another.

(2) Sympathy must thus be clearly distinguished from benevolence, which, on Hume's account, is not to be equated with love.

(3) One common use of the term 'sympathy' is close in meaning to 'compassion' or 'pity'. Hume gives the term a different meaning. Painful and pleasant emotions may equally well be communicated through sympathy, and it seems indefensible to claim that pity is the communication of an opinion or a passion.

(4) Although Hume clearly distinguishes compassion and pity from sympathy he hardly makes out a wholly satisfactory case for his claim that sympathy is a source of pity or compassion.

(5) The model of communication does not appear to fit all the phenomena where sympathy seems to be involved. In order to account for facts that seem to conflict with his theory Hume appeals to general rules and a principle of contrast or comparison. Since this principle has effects opposite to those of sympathy it is obviously important to explain why one or other of these principles should operate in any particular case.

When we come to discuss Hume's views about moral evaluation we shall see that only a principle that allows the possibility of sympathy with non-existent emotions will help towards the explanation of moral evaluation, and that there is a special difficulty connected with the admission of a principle of comparison.

In considering Hume's account of sympathy we have compared it only with one basic kind of sympathy, that in which it comes close in meaning to pity. We saw that neither in the case of sympathy with bodily feelings *nor* in the case of sympathy with emotions, can we treat that kind of sympathy as consisting in a communicated emotion. We may pity a man with a toothache without having toothache and, indeed, without ever having had toothache. We may pity a justifiably jealous husband, without being ourselves jealous. But there are many other kinds of phenomena that might be said to involve sympathy and it may be helpful to consider some of them:

(1) One can say that there is close sympathy between two people who share a common sorrow. Perhaps they have both lost a mutual friend and are conscious of each other's sorrow. A similar, though not an identical, situation is that in which two people have had a similar loss, although the source of the sorrow is not the same. In the one case we might have a family losing one of its members, in the other we might have two young widows each of whom has lost her husband. It would obviously be misleading to talk here of mutual pity. But the people involved might, indeed, gain a certain measure of emotional support and consolation from the consciousness that their sorrow is shared. This kind of sympathy is similar to Hume's sympathy, in that it need not be confined to the sharing of unhappy experiences or sorrow. One could say that the joy of a cup-winning football team, or any other group rejoicing in a common achievement, exemplifies a phenomenon of the same kind. Although there is here an emotional influence through the awareness of the emotion of another or others, the emotion has an independent common source, and does not, in any of the participants, arise only as a result of a communication. Hume, however, would consider this phenomenon to exemplify sympathy. In this he is justified for there is here a mutual heightening of the emotion through the awareness of the emotional state of the other. But, on his principles, sympathy with joy ought to increase the joy; sympathy with sorrow ought to increase the sorrow; yet one finds that sharing a sorrow makes it easier to bear. But it does not follow from this that the sorrow is not as strongly felt, or even increased. Sympathy with sorrow may thus make it more bearable although the emotion remains unabated. One may draw an analogy with pain to illustrate the point: people suffering similar pains may give each other mutual support, so that each finds his pain more bearable. The doctor may make this condition more tolerable by an injection that reduces the pain. To reduce a pain and to make it more bearable are thus two different things. To diminish sorrow and to make it more bearable may likewise be distinguished. Hume, in many places, emphasizes the great importance sharing emotions may have for human beings. He expresses this dramatically as follows:

Let all the powers and elements of nature conspire to serve and obey one man; let the sun rise and set at his command; the sea and rivers roll as he pleases, and the earth furnish spontaneously whatever may be useful or agreeable to him; he will still be miserable, till you give him some one person at least with whom he may share his happiness, and whose esteem and friendship he may enjoy. (THN II, 81/363)

(2) Similar to shared emotion is what Max Scheler has called 'emotional infection' (N of S, 14ff.) This kind of sympathy appears to have been uppermost in Hume's mind. A typical example would be the way in which one may be caught up in the atmosphere of gaiety or sadness on entering a room. In a letter of 28 July 1759 Hume writes:

An ill-humord Fellow; a man tir'd and disgusted with every thing, always *ennuié*; sickly, complaining, embarass'd; such a one throws an evident Damp on Company, which I suppose wou'd be accounted for by Sympathy. (LDH I, 169, 313)

Similarly a person's good humour tends to spread. Laughter is catching, and one tends to be saddened by the appearance of grief and sorrow. Even though, following Scheler, I call this emotional infection, it is quite different from the kind of infection you have in the case of an infectious disease. In emotional infection you are affected by the appearance of the emotion; the person that affects you need not have it. There is here no necessity for an emotion to be communicated. It may not exist in the person whose appearance of an emotion affects you. But a man who infects another with a disease must have the infection, although, admittedly, he need not suffer from the disease.

(3) There is a sympathy with emotions that cannot be accounted for as pity, nor does it necessarily involve the sharing of an emotion or emotional infection. When I say of a man, who is angry because he has just been dismissed from his job, that I sympathize with him, I need not be angry myself. All that is necessary for this kind of sympathy is that I consider the anger justified. In some cases the sympathy implies less than wholehearted approval of the person's emotion. Our sympathy with a person who becomes angry might indicate only that we think that he had a certain excuse for becoming angry, that there were extenuating circumstances. In cases where the anger sympathized with involves a strong evaluative element, as in righteous indignation, complete sympathy may, with some plausibility, be said to involve a communication to the sympathizer of the passion with which he sym-

pathizes. But this sort of sympathizing, as a kind of approval or evaluation, is foreign to Hume's thought on the subject. It is, however, to be found in the works of Adam Smith who writes:

> And if we consider all the different passions of human nature, we shall find that they are regarded as decent, or indecent, just in proportion as mankind are more or less disposed to sympathize with them. (TMS, 26)

We sometimes say that we sympathize with opinions and mean that we think them to a large extent justifiable. Thus it is not uncommon for people to say that they sympathize with the policies of the British Labour Party. It would be a little odd for a member of the party to claim to be a sympathizer; and if one were in complete agreement with all the views of the British Labour Party it would be too weak to claim to sympathize with these views. To sympathize one must share the opinions up to a point, but complete agreement would seem to be misnamed 'sympathy'.

(4) Some mention must be made of what may be called sympathetic imitation. When a man is watching 'a dancer on the slack-rope' (TMS, 10), he may sway and find a tension in his muscles, just as if he were himself performing the feat. Adam Smith explains this in terms of imaginatively putting yourself in the other person's place, and thus coming to feel as if you were that other person. But it may be suggested that a basic tendency to imitate may here be operative, and that the identity of feeling comes from the similarity in bodily state or posture. Dugald Stewart, in his *Elements of the Philosophy of the Human Mind*, places great stress upon our basic tendency to imitate and says[1]:

> This proneness to imitation, although (as was formerly observed) most conspicuous in childhood, continues, in all men, to manifest itself on particular occasions, through the whole of life; and, as far as I can judge, is the general law to which many of the phenomena, resolved by Mr Smith into the principle of sympathy, ought chiefly to be referred. If, indeed, by *sympathy* Mr Smith had meant only to express a fact, I should have thought it a term not more exceptionable than the phrase *sympathetic imitation*, which I have adopted in this chapter. But it must be remembered, that, in Mr Smith's writings, the word *sympathy* involves a theory or hypothesis peculiar to himself; for he tells us expressly, that where

[1] Dr George Davie drew my attention to the writings of Dugald Stewart on this subject.

this principle is concerned, the effect is produced by an illusion of the imagination, leading us to suppose that we ourselves are placed in a situation similar to that of our neighbour.

(EPHM III, 129)

This is no place to discuss Stewart's views in detail, but it may be suggested that when Hume explains, in terms of sympathy, the similarity in the emotions and 'turn of thinking' of people of the same nation, he perhaps underestimates the dependence of communication of emotions upon facial expressions and bodily postures. Perhaps a happy nature is, to some extent, acquired by imitating a smiling, happy expression, and the causal relationship is not always the other way round. This would seem to fit quite well the situations of emotional infection already mentioned: one enters a room where people are laughing. This tends to make one laugh and the laughter tends to make one feel happy. Not knowing the cause of the happiness, one begins by laughing in an embarrassed fashion, but this embarrassment disappears when real mirth has been engendered. Hume's account, though not involving 'putting yourself in the other person's shoes', does make the laughter the effect of the sympathetically induced emotion rather than its cause.

(5) Hume mentions a special kind of sympathy when discussing personal identity in Book I. He cites as an example the relation between parts of a whole as they serve 'some general purpose', and also have 'a mutual dependence on, and connexion with each other'. He mentions in this connection animals and vegetables as involving sympathy between their various parts. I mention this sense of 'sympathy' only in passing, for it plays no very distinctive part in Hume's moral theory.

We are, at this point, in a position to see how imprecise is R. B. Brandt's description of the sympathy from which Hume is supposed to derive moral judgments. 'Moral values are a matter of sympathetic responses' he says, and elucidating the concept of a sympathetic response he maintains that it covers

. . . such phenomena as the impulse to relieve a person or animal perceived to be in distress, being shaken emotionally by perception of a pain or distress situation, and experience of a thrill of joy at seeing another transported by joy on account of some good that has come to him. (ET, 133)

But there is a problem about the explanation of the relation between the 'sympathetic impulses' to which Brandt refers and Hume's principle of sympathy or communication. It is this principle of communication which is of basic importance in the account of moral evaluation given in Hume's *Treatise*. The elucidation Brandt gives of the meaning of sympathy also completely fails to give due weight to the importance of the imagination in Hume's account. If sympathy involved only the impulses and emotions Brandt mentions, it could hardly help to explain how we can make moral judgments about historical characters – and we do pass such judgments. In explaining this, Hume's account is much more complex than it would be if he simply appealed to 'general sympathetic tendencies in man'. He also, as we have seen, draws our attention to tendencies in human nature that have the opposite effect to the usual effect of sympathy; for example, the principle of comparison and the passions of malice and envy.

Let us now briefly turn our attention to the principle of comparison, and the passions which it helps to explain. This principle is of interest to us since it has an opposite effect to the effect of sympathy. Hume puts it thus:

> In general we may observe that, in all kinds of comparison, an object makes us always receive from another, to which it is compared, a sensation contrary to what arises from itself in its direct and immediate survey. (THN II, 92/375)

He draws an analogy with perception, and points out that the presence of a great object makes a small object look still smaller, and the great object looks greater by comparison with the small one. And, in the case of emotions, we find that considering the pleasure of another is immediately pleasing to us, but it pains us when we compare it with our own situation. The same principle is at work in the case of pains: 'His pain, considered in itself, is painful to us, but augments the idea of our own happiness, and gives us pleasure' (THN II, 92/376). Hume points out that we can even come to feel what he calls 'malice against ourselves'. Thus we may be pleased (by contrast) by reflecting upon our own past misfortune. We may similarly be pained at the thought of a past pleasure, by contrast with our present less fortunate situation. We may even go so far as to desire unpleasantness for ourselves. The principle of comparison is responsible for two different kinds of 'irregular appetite for evil'[1]: (1) We may feel uneasy about our own happiness when we think of a friend who is unhappy; and (2) we can feel remorse because of a crime we have committed, and want to be punished. The

---

[1] 'Evil' means pain in this connection.

happier we are the more we suffer from the feelings of remorse when reflecting upon our past crime: 'We even seek uneasiness, in order to avoid so disagreeable a contrast.' Hume seems quite right to draw our attention to the fact that desire for unhappiness or suffering, is very much an aspect of our consciousness of guilt. The person feels there is something improper about being both at once, happy and guilty. Part of the strong appeal of the retributive theory of punishment is no doubt derived from this. It is not so bad to be guilty if you suffer. The suffering is even sometimes thought of as purifying, as wiping out the guilt. There often is a moral element in the suffering that results from the comparison of our own happiness with the misfortune of a friend. One feels one has not merited such good luck, and that it is unjust that we should be happy when our good friend suffers. Hume does not give us an adequate analysis of these concepts, but the emotions to which he is drawing our attention are undoubtedly of interest to anyone who wants to understand 'the moral life'.

When we are envious, we have our own situation made to look less satisfactory by comparison with someone whom we think more fortunate. But envy arises only when there is some relation between the two persons: 'A common soldier bears no such envy to his general as to his sergeant or corporal' (THN II, 94/377). Some relation between the people is necessary to further the comparison. It would seem that sympathy and comparison are similar in this respect: both are furthered by relations; and in so far as all human beings do resemble, I suppose Hume would say they could envy each other. But in many cases this resemblance alone would be insufficient to further a comparison: 'A poet is not apt to envy a philosopher, or a poet of a different kind, of a different nation, or a different age' (THN II, 94/378). We find that we estimate size by comparison with other objects of the same species: an object like a mountain would have no effect upon our estimation of the size of a horse. When, however, we see together two horses, such as a Clydesdale and an Icelandic pony, then the small appears smaller and the large one larger; the objects here are similar enough for comparison to operate. Comparison can be seen at work in two different ways: (1) it determines the standard of comparison. This can be seen when we are explaining the origins of such passions as envy. We envy those that resemble us in a certain way, because resemblance furthers comparison. Similarly the standard of size for elephants is different from the standard of size for dogs. A large dog is smaller than a small elephant; (2) In the case of those things where the same standard of comparison is applied, one's estimate of them varies according to whether they are 'viewed together' or separately. When two horses of disparate size are seen together the larger horse appears larger and the small one smaller. Here there is a potential source of an erroneous estimate of size. In the same way one's conscious state may seem blissful when compared with the abject misery of some other person. The other person's misery may, by comparison, seem even greater than it would if viewed in isolation. We have here also a source of bias that may affect our emotions, for it affects our estimate of our own and other people's feelings.

II

It should be clear by now that Hume distinguishes between sympathy and benevolence in the *Treatise*. Sympathy is a principle of communication, but benevolence is defined by him as desire for the happiness, or aversion to the misery or unhappiness, of someone; anger is the opposite of this. These are passions that are naturally attached to love and hatred; in fact, one of the things that distinguish love and hatred from pride and humility is this connection with desire for the happiness or misery of the person loved or hated. But Hume resists the temptation to identify love with the desire for the happiness of others. This is not even a necessary condition of loving. We may, he thinks, love another without giving any thought to his happiness. If benevolence and anger are passions they are simple impressions and since Hume is treating a tendency to act as part of the character of these passions it seems that they are essentially complex and involve both an experience and a tendency to act. There is not the same difficulty about treating 'pure emotion in the soul' as simple impressions.

It is a familiar Humean doctrine that the difference between ideas and impressions is one of degree of force and liveliness only. But, in discussing benevolence and anger, Hume points out that impressions can mix with one another, whereas ideas are, as it were, impenetrable; they can form compounds and be joined, but they cannot mix. Ideas thus always retain some of their identity when conjoined with other ideas: they 'exclude' each other. But impressions, and in particular the 'reflective' impressions, are 'susceptible of an entire union' (THN II, 83/366). This quality of passions is important: 'Some of the most curious phenomena of the human mind are derived from this property of the passions' (THN II, 84/366). It must be noticed that a mixed passion is still a simple impression, for when two passions mix, each completely loses its identity. They are supposed only to 'vary that uniform impression which arises from the whole' (THN II, 84/366).

Hume introduces the concept of compound passions, and then goes on to discuss the relation between love and hatred on the one hand, and benevolence and anger on the other. But one must not conclude from this that he thinks any of these passions are compound. It is true that he claims that pride and humility are 'pure emotions in the soul', whereas love and hatred are not. But the purity of pride and humility consists in this only that they are 'unattended with any desire, and not immediately exciting us to action' (THN II, 84/367). From this one might expect Hume to make desire an essential part of the emotions of love and hatred; and he does, indeed, stress that they 'are not completed within themselves, nor rest in that emotion which they produce, but carry the mind to something further' (ibid.). But he soon makes it absolutely clear that the desires *attend* love and hatred, and are no part of the essential nature of these passions. Benevolence and anger 'are passions different from love and hatred, and only conjoined with them by the original constitution of the mind' (THN II, 85/368). It seems that love and hatred are just as pure as pride and humility, when we consider these passions as impressions. The only difference is that the two first mentioned are conjoined with certain desires – benevolence and anger; but the conjunction is a purely contingent one: 'I see no contradiction in supposing desire of producing misery annexed to love, and of happiness to hatred' (THN II, 85-86/368). The 'sensation' of the passion could be altered without any alteration in the desire that is conjoined with it.

The relations between love and benevolence, hatred and anger are due to an 'arbitrary and original instinct'. One must not, however, conclude from this that desires for people's happiness or unhappiness never arise except as a result of love and hatred. The effects of love and hatred can be counterfeited, and pity and malice are described as 'imitating' the effects of love and hatred. Thus one would expect Hume to describe pity and malice as more akin to benevolence and anger than to love and hatred. They must surely be active tendencies, rather than passive 'pure emotions in the soul'. Yet his first account of the nature of pity and malice has been taken to imply that these passions are passive: '*Pity* is a concern for, and *malice* a joy in, the misery of others, without any friendship or enmity to occasion this concern or joy' (THN II, 86/369). Elsewhere he describes joy as a pure emotion in the soul. How is this to be made compatible with the statement that 'malice is an unprovoked desire of producing evil to another, in order to reap a pleasure from comparison'? (THN II, 93/377). Hume's statements as to the nature of these passions are not very clear and there is some reason to agree with A. B. Glathe's charge of inconsistency (HTPM, 60). But let us consider the following points: (1) it is not clear that Hume means us to consider both pity and malice to be passive, even in the first quotation above; for although 'joy' is a pure emotion in the soul, 'concern' seems to involve a 'tendency to act'. Hume does not say 'concern at', but describes pity as a 'concern for the misery of others'. (2) There is a difference between pity and malice in one respect: pity presupposes that the pitied person has met with some misfortune, or is unhappy for some other reason. Malice may take one or other of two forms: it may be joy at the misery of another; but it likewise may take the form of wanting to make someone else unhappy. An unprovoked desire for another's unhappiness is malice, for 'if our ill-will to another proceed from any harm or injury, it is not, properly speaking, malice, but revenge' (THN II, 86/369). Hume here makes a valid point about the analysis of the concepts of malice and revenge, but what concerns us is this: a malicious person wants to make another unhappy or, to put it more precisely, desires the unhappiness of another person, for he may know that he is not in a position to do any harm to the person to whom he bears malice. But if the person who is the object of the malice is already unhappy, one would expect the malicious person to be pleased. Malice expresses itself in one or other of these two forms: the malicious person may want another person's unhappiness or he may be pleased because another person is unhappy. Hume does not stress this point but the unclarity of his account may be partly due to the dual aspect of malice.[1] Pity is not a parallel, because it logically presupposes that the pitying person believes in an unfortunate condition of the pitied person.

Although Hume brackets together pity and malice, we must not let it blind us to the fact that it is misleading to characterize these passions as merely opposites. Pity does not have the two aspects I have attributed

[1] The two aspects of malice can be seen if we look at the German language: *Schadenfreude* is joy at another's unhappiness, or gloating. A person who is *böswillig* wants the unhappiness of another.

to malice. It also appears that pity always is active: it involves a tendency to want the relief of the pitied person. Malice, when it takes the form of gloating or *Schadenfreude*, does not, it seems, have this active element; it does not involve a tendency to change the situation; the person who is the object of this kind of malice is already unhappy. But when one pities one wants to alter the situation of the object of the pity, or, if one has not the power to alter it, one at least wants it to be altered. Gloating presupposes the belief in the existence of the state of affairs that is wanted by the malicious person. Pity always presupposes a belief in the existence of a state of affairs that is not wanted by the pitying person. It thus, not unnaturally, always aims at, or involves a hope for, an alteration in that situation.

When I say that benevolence, pity and malice are passions, I am using the word 'passion' in Hume's sense. We must always bear in mind that 'passion' is used by Hume in a very extended sense when we compare it with its use in ordinary discourse today. He does not use this word even in the way it was used in ordinary language of the eighteenth century, but gives it a special technical sense. This we can clearly see by looking at the manner in which Thomas Reid attacked Hume for abusing language. But Reid was fond of appealing to common usage. Talking about 'natural desires and affections' he says: 'When they are so calm as neither to produce any sensible effects upon the body, nor to darken the understanding and weaken the power of self-command, they are not called passions. But the same principle, when it becomes so violent as to produce these effects upon the body and upon the mind, is a passion, or, as Cicero very properly calls it, a perturbation' (PWTR, 572). Thus it seems the eighteenth-century use of 'passion' was not very different from our own. But although Hume extends the use of the term greatly he does not mean it to include sympathy. There is, as we have seen, no room for the passion of sympathy in his scheme of the passions.

Section IX of Book II Part II of the *Treatise* has the title 'Of the Mixture of Benevolence and Anger with Love and Hatred'. Hume's pronouncements about this mixture are unfortunately not quite as clear as they might be. He begins by telling the reader that there are other passions 'confounded' with the passions of pity and malice: 'There is always a mixture of love or tenderness with pity, and of hatred or anger with malice' (THN II, 97/381). How can this be the case when pity is unpleasant and love pleasant, malice a pleasure and anger unpleasant? It is, first of all, not clear whether Hume thinks pity and malice are compound emotions, partly pleasant, partly painful or whether he is simply pointing out that pity gives rise to love and malice to anger. This would seem to contradict the principles that are supposed to explain the origination of the indirect passions: love would here arise from pain, and anger from pleasure. The use of 'produce' in the following quotation would seem to indicate that Hume is not so much analysing the nature of pity, as attempting to account for an apparent exception to the principles underlying the production of the indirect passions of love and hatred:

> For as pity is an uneasiness, and malice a joy, arising from the
> misery of others, pity should naturally, as in all other cases,
> *produce*[1] hatred, and malice, love. (THN II, 97/381)

In explaining the apparent anomaly that a painful experience can produce a pleasant indirect passion, and a pleasant experience a painful one, Hume introduces a new principle. In so doing he seems partly to abandon the notion that each of the passions *is* a simple impression. It must be remembered that some passions are not just pure emotions, but that they involve 'a tendency to act'. It seems that the tendency to act would in the case of these passions be an essential aspect of their nature. It must be admitted that if the passions are simple impressions this concept is somewhat stretched when Hume says:

> that it is not the present sensation alone or momentary pain or
> pleasure which determines the character of any passion, but the
> whole bent or tendency of it from the beginning to the end.
> (THN II, 97/381)

He points out that, in all cases hitherto considered, he has been supposing that the passions have been related by resemblance in their sensation; but now we must pay attention to the fact that their 'impulses or directions' may be 'similar and correspondent'. I do not think that Hume wants to go back on his previous contention that love and benevolence are connected in a purely contingent manner (although in the quotation above he seems to be doing this by implying that the 'tendency of the passion from beginning to end' determines its character); for Hume goes on to talk about benevolence as 'attending' love, and anger as 'attending' hatred. The direction of these desires may be similar when the sensation of the passions they attend differs. Thus, pity is a desire for a person's happiness and is in this way related to

[1] My italics.

love; malice is the desire for the unhappiness of another and therefore related to anger. But it now becomes a problem to explain why sympathy with pain produces other passions than 'good-will and kindness'. The solution Hume proposes is this: when we have a strong sympathy with pain, our interest is aroused in the whole welfare of the person, and thus the tendency of the passions aroused is similar to love, and arouses that passion. When, on the other hand, our sympathy is weak, it is not sufficient to arouse any concern about the person's welfare; what then comes to the fore is the similarity to unpleasantness, and hatred and contempt result:

> Benevolence, therefore, arises from a great degree of misery, or
> any degree strongly sympathized with: hatred or contempt from
> a small degree, or one weakly sympathized with. (THN II, 102/387)

Hume illustrates the application of this principle by pointing out that we tend to despise the poor, and pity beggars when their misery passes beyond a certain point. But there is a limit to this: when we witness an exceedingly horrible event the actual horror may be so great as to prevent the occurrence of love.

We have all along been confining our attention to the effect of sympathy upon our attitude to the person with whom we sympathize. When we sympathize with, or pity, a person who suffers some affliction, this may lead us to love that person; but whoever caused the calamity becomes an object of hatred, and the greater our compassion or pity, the more we detest the person that caused the suffering. Here we have the same passion, pity, giving rise to two opposite passions, love and hatred – love of the person pitied and hatred of the person who is the cause of his suffering. Hume explains this by a double comparison: the 'author' of the calamity has relation only to the calamity, and thus the similarity in the sensation of the passion operates and causes the unpleasant pains of hatred; in the case of the sufferer we become interested in his welfare because pity tends to lead to, or to involve, a desire for the happiness of the pitied person. This desire is similar to the natural attendant of love, that is, benevolence. When Hume defines pity as the desire for another's happiness he sometimes not only stresses its similarity to benevolence but suggests that they are the 'same desires':

> What wonder, then, that pity and benevolence, malice and anger,
> being the same desires arising from different principles, should so
> totally mix together as to be undistinguishable? (THN II, 98/382)

If they are the same desires, how then can they mix? Hume's pronouncements are not very clear at this point, perhaps because he talks in terms of the causal conditions that arouse the passions. Thus pity, if it is benevolence at all, cannot be just any sort of benevolence: it is logically impossible to pity a person unless one considers his condition undesirable. If benevolence is thought of as the desire for another person's happiness, it is not restricted in this way. One can have benevolent tendencies towards anybody, irrespective of whether he is suffering or not. Benevolence and pity are thus not just the same desire arising from different causal principles: there is a logical difference between them.

Hume ends the chapter we have been considering by pointing out that 'double sympathy' helps to explain the love we bear to close relatives. Their emotions are 'entered into' by us, 'as if they were our own'. This sharing of emotions usually accompanies love, and therefore helps to lead to the creation of love.

According to Hume respect and contempt are also 'mixed emotions'. There is, he says 'a mixture of pride in contempt, and of humility in respect'. The effect of comparison can be seen here:

> The same man may cause either respect, love, or contempt, according as the person who considers him, from his inferior, becomes
> his equal or superior. (THN II, 105/390)

Hume makes it clear that it is the comparison made by the respectful or contemptuous person that determines whether we feel one or other of these passions. He goes on to say that the element of pride in contempt is greater than the amount of humility in respect, and attributes this to the fact that people are generally much more prone to feel pride than humility. This raises a problem as to why qualities should ever produce any of the primary indirect passions. Why do they not always produce the 'mixed' ones? Any quality in another person, that directly considered, is fit to produce love, ought by comparison to produce humility, and thus one should expect *respect* always to result. Similarly any quality that directly produces hatred ought by comparison to produce pride and ought thus naturally to result in contempt. How then could pure love and hatred, pride or humility ever occur? In explaining this, Hume points out that there is a similarity between love and humility, although they are opposites when the hedonic quality of their sensation is considered. Both these qualities tend to 'enfeeble' the soul: 'Let us remember that pride and hatred invigorate the soul, and love and humility enfeeble it' (THN II, 106/391). This being so, there are certain qualities that are more suited by nature to the production of the enfeebling passions, and certain others that tend to produce the invigorating ones: 'Genius and learning are *pleasant* and *magnificient*' (THN II, 106/391). It is for this reason that these qualities tend to make a person proud, but they do not have the same tendency to produce love when we see them in someone else. They would therefore produce pride in the possessor but tend to lead to humility when they belong to another. Suppose that a quality is perfectly fitted to produce love, but imperfectly fitted to produce pride; in this case there would be hardly any humility produced by comparison, so love rather than respect would result. There are certain qualities specially fitted for love, but not so well suited to pride: 'This is the case with good-nature, good-humour, facility, generosity, beauty, and many other qualities' (THN II, 107/392). It is not clear at first that Hume is correct in including beauty in this list. Is consciousness of one's own beauty not one great source of pride? Hume himself strongly suggests that this is so, at least in animals. He considers it 'remarkable' that in the case of turkeys and peacocks ' . . . the pride always attends the beauty, and is discoverable in the male only' (THN II, 49/326). He does, however, draw our attention to a perfectly valid point: some valuable qualities are more easily compatible with pride than others. A kind-hearted person who is proud of being kind-hearted, is thought less well of for that reason alone. Generosity is also felt to be tainted if a generous person is proud of his generosity. One could suggest that a person's beauty is affected by pride: a beautiful person proud of being beautiful loses some beauty. In contrast, one might mention courage: to be proud of one's courage has no tendency to make a person appear less courageous. Pride, as a quality of character, is certainly quite often not unrelated to courage, since the 'proud man' has a tendency to reject assistance. Courage, one might feel, is more pride-inducing, and thus to be respected, than it is lovable.

It would be quite wrong to suggest that Hume is making a point about logical compatibility. He is simply claiming that some qualities more often cause pride than they do love, and vice versa.

In talking about love between the sexes, Hume makes a point that seems hardly compatible with the claim that passions are simple impressions and suggests, indeed, that he is consciously giving us an analysis of the passions, rather than a description of their causal conditions. He claims that three 'affections' 'compose' this passion. These are sense of beauty, carnal desire, or what he calls desire for generation, and benevolence or kindness. But Hume's language does not necessarily mean anything more than that 'love between the sexes' refers to a cluster of passions that normally go together in a certain way. He certainly thought love in general an emotion only contingently related to benevolence. But he here seems to realize that, at least sometimes, the names for passions may refer to a complex of conscious emotional states and tendencies to act.

To sum up: it is not at all obvious how sympathy, as Hume understands it, would overcome the natural bias of our passions. Its operation depends upon relations, and varies with the closeness of relations. We sympathize more with those closely related to us than with strangers. Since, however, these relations are irrelevant when we evaluate people's actions and characters, a simple appeal to man's sympathetic nature can hardly suffice to explain evaluation. It should, furthermore, now be clear that Hume thought that there were in man many anti-social tendencies; these are just as natural as the social tendencies. Thus, malice involves joy at other people's misfortune rather than concern about their welfare. Comparison is needed to account for this and some other features of the emotional life, such as envy. Since the principle of comparison has effects opposite to the effects of sympathy, it is obvious that there is here at least a prima facie problem. Why, in moral evaluation, is sympathy operative rather than comparison? Before I turn to a consideration of Hume's explanation of the development of objectivity in evaluating, I must first say something about the charge that he is committed to some form of egoism. I shall in particular consider whether his account of the nature of sympathy entails any form of egoism.

III

It has been a bone of contention among commentators whether Hume is or is not a psychological hedonist. T. H. Green attributes this doctrine to Hume in no uncertain terms (Introduction to the Moral part of the *Treatise*). F. C. Sharp (*Mind*, Vol. xxx, 1921), E. B. McGilvary (PR, Vol. 12, 1903)[1] and Kemp Smith (*The Philosophy of David Hume*) have been equally emphatic in denying the legitimacy of this interpretation of Hume's work. It must be obvious, to readers of Hume, that

[1] The discussion in this section owes something to these papers by F. C. Sharp and E. B. McGilvary.

an interpretation of him as a psychological hedonist must be primarily based on the *Treatise*. It is possible to take the view that this is one of the issues on which the two works differ. But we are not concerned with his views in the *Enquiry*; and if we can defend Hume against the charge that he is a psychological hedonist by consideration of his views in the *Treatise*, this will suffice for our purpose.

By 'psychological hedonism' will be understood the doctrine that all human actions are motivated by a desire for the agent's own future pleasure, or by a desire for the continuation of a pleasurable experience which the agent is already experiencing. Another form of hedonistic motivation would be the desire to get rid of an unpleasant experience.[1] In this case we could define the desire as an uneasiness and analyse the motive as the tendency to get rid of this unpleasant feeling. The ultimate end would, in the latter case, be the elimination of an unpleasant experience in the agent. If Hume can be shown to have held one or the other of these views he could be said to be a psychological hedonist.

A distinction must be drawn between the cause of a desire and the object of a desire. We have seen that psychological hedonism is a doctrine about the object of a desire. Although we may come to the conclusion that Hume believes that pleasure or pain are always the cause or the part-cause of a desire, we will not thereby have shown that he is a psychological hedonist. (The distinction drawn here is a well-known one; it is to be found in the works of Kemp Smith, McGilvary, G. E. Moore, and others.) Let us first consider whether Hume thinks pleasure, or the avoidance of pain, is always the ultimate object of a desire. The question can be put more simply: Are all objects desired merely as means to the agent's own pleasure or the avoidance of his pain?

At this point it would be useful to remind ourselves of some of the conclusions of earlier chapters: Hume's discussion of the passions is an attempt to account for their origin; he seeks a causal explanation and since each passion is a simple impression, there is a sense in which we cannot expect from him an analysis of it. Some passions arise from pleasure and pain in conjunction with other qualities, whereas others arise immediately from pleasure or pain. Since the first of these have a

[1] The name 'psychological hedonism' is sometimes used for the view that men always seek what they consider their own *greatest pleasure*. If Hume does not hold the doctrine of psychological hedonism as I understand it he cannot be a psychological hedonist in this other sense. For if men do not always seek what they think pleasant it follows that they do not always seek what they think most pleasant.

more complex origin Hume naturally devotes more attention to them. The length of the treatment accorded to different passions in Book II of the *Treatise* varies, not so much according to their importance in the explanation of morality, as according to the difficulty of accounting for their origin. This can be admitted without abandoning the view stressed later that the indirect passions are far from irrelevant to the explanation of morality. We have already seen that 'I am proud of x' may be construed as a form of self valuing, and that it may be suggested that there is a close connection between the indirect passions and evaluations.

It need not, therefore, occasion any surprise that so much space is allotted to pride and humility, although these passions are not, properly speaking, motives, but 'pure emotions in the soul'. Even love and hatred are strictly speaking not motives, for one of Hume's reasons for distinguishing these passions from pride and humility as 'pure emotions' is the fact that

> The passions of love and hatred are always followed by, or rather conjoined with, benevolence and anger. It is this conjunction which chiefly distinguishes these affections from pride and humility. (THN II, 84/367)

Hume in fact criticizes those who consider:

> that love and hatred have not only a *cause* which excites them, viz. pleasure and pain, and an *object* to which they are directed, viz. a person or thinking being, but likewise an *end* which they endeavour to attain, viz. the happiness or misery of the person beloved or hated; all which views, mixing together, make only one passion. According to this system, love is nothing but the desire of happiness to another person, and hatred that of misery. The desire and aversion constitute the very nature of love and hatred. They are not only inseparable, but the same. (THN II, 85/367)

Hume thinks that this view is 'contrary to experience'. We may love or hate persons, without thinking of their happiness or unhappiness. Although in most cases we do desire the happiness of those we love and the unhappiness of those we hate, the passion and the desire are not inseparable, and there is no logical connection between them, only a de facto connection.

> We may therefore infer, that benevolence and anger are passions different from love and hatred, and only conjoined with them by the original constitution of the mind. (THN II, 85/368)

These impressions are loose and separable, and we are told:

Love and hatred might have been unattended with any such
desires, or their particular connection might have been entirely
reversed. (ibid.)

Thus the emotion of love might have been connected with a desire for
the misery of the person loved. We here again see a result of the
tendency in Hume to treat each of the passions as simple impressions
and to think of it as a contingent fact that certain desires tend to follow
any particular passion.

It is fairly obvious that this is contrary to our normal way of looking
at these emotions. Let us imagine we found people sincerely claiming
to love someone and yet having, on this and other occasions when they
made such a claim, shown a propensity to harm the people they love.
Let us further assume that the contrary is the case when they claim to
hate someone. Whenever they say they hate someone, they have the
same tendency to be kind to them as we have now to be kind to those
we love. I think in a case of this kind we should feel inclined to say
that these people were using 'love' and 'hate' in a different way from
the way we use these terms. Hume, however, is using the terms 'love'
and 'hate' in such a way as to make it impossible to decide, by consideration of any behavioural signs, whether the emotion which is followed
by benevolence is really 'love' or not. Only the presumption that human
nature is more or less the same makes us infer that other people are
really having the emotion we should have if we claimed to love someone. There is thus a sense in which we cannot, in the nature of the
case, know whether some people are not constituted in such a way that
their benevolence follows upon their hatred.

Hume thus treats it as a purely contingent fact that benevolence is
conjoined with love. This is in complete conformity with his general
account of the emotions as simple impressions of reflection. Emotions
are thus contingently related not only to behaviour, but also to each
other. I am suggesting that although Hume talks about a natural connection between passions such as love and benevolence the connection
is in fact a logical one. Thus there logically could not have been a
general natural connection between love and desire for the unhappiness
of the loved object. That this is so may not be obvious if 'loving' is
treated as almost equivalent to 'thinking highly of'. But in so far as
'love' is the name for 'a tender emotion', it could not, it seems, have a
general natural connection with a desire for the unhappiness of its

object. This is not, of course, to claim that love cannot, in isolated cases, be combined with such a desire; only that this cannot be the general rule. And it must furthermore be admitted that in cases of love with a strong sexual element it may be quite common for this to be combined with a desire to hurt. When such love turns to hatred the hatred may in fact be increased by the passionate love for the person. In such cases it does not seem at all strange to suggest that love (a passion with a strong sexual element) and hatred are conjoined: the two might serve to fan each other. They are thus not opposites in Hume's sense; for opposite passions in Hume's scheme would tend to cancel each other out and leave an equilibrium.

Confining our attention to love and benevolence, we might perhaps notice the following points in the account given above:

(1) Hume differentiates between the object of a passion and the end of a desire. Only the latter is something we endeavour to attain.

(2) The end of benevolence is said to be the happiness of another person.

(3) The desire arises from love, but there is no suggestion that the end of this desire is not the ultimate end of the desire, or that it can be further analysed.

The account gives us no reason to believe that the desire for the happiness of another is not ultimate, that it can be shown to be desired only as a means to the agent's own happiness or pleasure. We can only say that human nature is such that desire for another's happiness is on most occasions the accompaniment of love.

It is clear that Hume distinguishes quite clearly between the cause of a passion and the end of a desire. Let us now inquire whether the causes of a passion are such that Hume is committed to saying that only the agent's own pleasure is ever desired as an ultimate end.

In tackling this question we may perhaps be allowed to refer to the interpretation given by D. G. C. MacNabb, one of the best modern commentators on Hume's philosophy, who seems to accept the view that the mechanism of sympathy is such that it makes Hume's account egoistic. It is true that MacNabb is dealing with Hume's account of the origin of approval and disapproval, but it seems plain that he is guilty of a confusion between the end of a desire and the cause of a desire:

My second criticism is that Hume is unnecessarily egoistic. Let us allow that pleasure and pain form 'the chief spring or actuating principle of the human mind'. Very well, then it must be pleasure and pain, or the thought of pleasure and pain, which produce moral approval and disapproval, just as they produce desire and aversion, hope and joy, grief and fear. But why should it be only my own pleasure or the thought of it which can arouse a direct passion? Why should not Hume say that pleasure and pain when thought of, not as our own, but as anybody's, arouse direct feelings of approbation and disapprobation? Plainly he thought that this was not true. It seems to him self-evident that only what is pleasant or painful to me can arouse in me a passion for or against it. Therefore it seemed to him that the thought of another's pleasure or pain must be converted in my mind by the mechanism of sympathy into an actual pleasure or pain of mine, before it can move my passions and actuate my will. (DHTK and M, 187-8)

MacNabb appears to think that Hume's view, which is that desire and aversion, approval and disapproval are aroused through the conversion of another's pain or pleasure into our own, is egoistic. This would be true only if the aversion was made an aversion to one's own pain, the desire a desire for one's own pleasure, the approval not *justified* unless one's own pleasure was aroused, and *justified* in direct proportion to the pleasure involved. MacNabb's statement suffers from the fact that he does not make it clear whether Hume is being charged with psychological or ethical egoism. It seems that in so far as the causal explanation of approval and disapproval through sympathy is thereby made egoistic, the charge is one of ethical egoism. On the other hand, the reference to the necessity of one's own pleasure being *aroused* in order to determine the will at all, seems to be an indication that Hume is a psychological egoist.

It is possible that MacNabb may have thought that we could, by one and the same argument, decide both that sympathy is 'egoistic' in that pain and pleasure must be aroused in us to determine approval and disapproval, and also that there is no disinterested benevolence. One is led to believe this by the fact that he writes as if benevolence (a passion which has an end) and sympathy are the same. But we must remember that when sympathy arouses approval and disapproval, these passions are not motives as such, although naturally attached to benevolence and anger.

Let us assume that A and B both want to alleviate the suffering of C; but whereas A sympathizes with C in the sense that he is brought to feel with him, and that C's sadness is communicated to him, B only knows that C is suffering, but is in no way distressed. Could one say that A's desire to help C was more egoistic than B's? This would only be the case if A wanted to alleviate C's suffering in order to alleviate his own. The fact of the matter is that it is only in so far as the end of the desire is changed by the mechanism which brings it about that this mechanism is relevant in deciding whether the desire is egoistic or not. MacNabb is simply assuming that the causal conditions laid down by Hume do have such an effect, although he does not support this interpretation by any quotation from the text. It seems rather that Hume believes people's capacity for feeling with one another to be much greater than MacNabb thinks; but to say that he is committed to any form of egoism on that account seems unjustifiable.

Although I am not convinced that MacNabb has shown Hume's account to imply some sort of egoistic doctrine, there is real point in his criticism. Hume depends upon his doctrine that ideas – as opposed to impressions – never determine the will directly, and that moral distinctions are derived from impressions. He therefore considers it incomprehensible that a man should be determined to act by having simply the idea of another's misery: the idea is too faint, has too little force to affect the will. But what if the idea amounts to a belief? If one accepts his doctrine that belief is merely a more lively or powerful idea or an impression, why should we not be determined by the belief that another is in pain, although the belief has not achieved the vividness of a real pain?

But there is a problem here which would still make reference to the self necessary. I could never experience the conjunction of the outward signs of pain and the pain of another. These two impressions cannot, in the nature of the case, succeed each other in my experience. The idea I have of the pain of another must be derived from the impression of my own pain. There must, therefore, be some impression in me that gives the mere thought, or conception, of another's pain the added liveliness that raises it to the status of belief. There does not seem to be any reason why Hume, with his mechanical conception of the origination of belief, should not have conceived it to be possible to be determined by belief, if the difference between this and an impression is one of degree only. But when Hume describes belief as involving an attitude of mind to future events, he tends to think of it as an acquired expectation. An expectation is different from a practical determination. Thus, simply expecting something to occur as a result of our actions would not suffice to determine our will; it would not as such suffice to furnish us with a motive. If, as Hume tends to think, practical determination to act is causal determination, it is naturally thought of as a determination by antecedents, and the expectation must lead to some further occurrence which will, so to speak, push us into action, since expectation is entirely consistent with passively waiting for something to occur. We should still have to account for the step between belief and the practical determination. If this must be a passion, one has to see how the less lively (belief) comes to raise in us a real impression. It is in order to account for this that Hume postulates a principle of sympathy.

One might want to admit that nothing could convince us that pain was bad if we have never experienced pain, simply because we could not understand what pain was; but admitting this, one still finds it paradoxical to argue that on no occasion may one abstain from something, simply because one believes that doing it would involve pain for another. The belief and the practical attitude are distinguished, but for Hume they must be distinguished as two experiences because of his tendency to think of all passions and all motives as occurrences, in a similar way to the occurrence of a particular pain. No passions, approval and disapproval included, are therefore to be thought of as merely attitudes: to approve is neither to *have* nor to *express* an attitude.

It must further be remembered that sympathetic pleasure and pain, in Hume's account, are efficient causes in arousing certain passions, but are never referred to as the objects or the ends of the passions aroused. Let us see how sympathetic pleasure and pain may function in the causal account of benevolence – the desire for the happiness of another. John possesses certain qualities that please me through sympathy with the pleasures of those affected by these qualities. This arouses in me love which has John as its object. But so far is it from being the case that any motive which may arise from this love would be conditioned by the continuation of my pleasure as its ultimate end, that it leads me to feel benevolence towards John, a desire to make him happy. Similarly, we must remember that the enlivening by the impression of the self which accounts for the thought of John's pleasure being converted into the pleasure itself, in no way changes its content. The thought of John's pleasure is merely enlivened; it becomes no more closely connected with me than was the thought. Thus there is no suggestion that sympathy with John is the conversion of the thought of his pleasure into *the thought of his pleasure as a means to my own*, and a consequent approval, or love or benevolence, arising therefrom. The causal conditions of love or benevolence neither determine the object of love, which itself is determined by an inexplicable natural connection, nor the end of benevolence, which is equally ultimate as far as Hume is concerned.

It must be emphasized once again that Hume considers himself to be primarily giving an account of the *causes* of passions. He does not claim to be able to explain why pride has self as its object, or why love leads to a desire which has the happiness of another as its end. These, for him, are just ultimate facts inexplicable by the principles of association.

There is little reason to believe that the influence of sympathy upon approval and disapproval commits Hume to ethical egoism, for Hume appeals to this principle in order to account for the fact that we approve of valuable qualities in others, even though we *know* that we shall never benefit from them.

In taking up an objective point of view, we are looking upon a situation as if we were any other human being. In such a situation, our approval would be determined only through sympathy with the pleasant or painful tendencies of the qualities of character determining our approval or disapproval, as the case may be. Hume thinks that unless, in this case, we were pleasantly or painfully affected, we should not take up any special attitude; but any change this may involve in our emotional state does not involve that the resultant benevolence or anger is directed at the object of this only as a means to the continuation of our pleasant consciousness (approval) or avoidance of the painful consciousness (disapproval). It seems that if we genuinely take up an objective point of view, our being pleased (approving) and our being pained (disapproving) are both purely disinterested.

But one might feel inclined to say: How then are we to understand Hume's view that pleasure and pain are 'the chief actuating principles of the mind'? The first thing to notice is that Hume's statement is a qualified one, and as far as I have been able to ascertain, the *Treatise* contains no passages which lead one to believe that the qualification was not intended. In dealing with the direct passions that arise immediately from pleasure or pain, according to Hume's classification in the introduction to Book II, Hume makes the following statement:

Besides good and evil, or, in other words, pain and pleasure, the direct passions frequently arise from a natural impulse or instinct, which is perfectly unaccountable. Of this kind is the desire of punishment to our enemies, and of happiness to our friends; hunger, lust, and a few other bodily appetites. These passions, properly speaking, produce good and evil, and proceed not from them, like the other affections. (THN II, 148-9/439)

This statement seems at first a little curious; for Hume has already said that the desire of happiness to our friends, and of unhappiness to our enemies, is connected with love and hatred in the shape of anger and benevolence. Do not love and hatred proceed from pleasure and pain like the other indirect passions? This is, I consider, perfectly correct. Why then does Hume single out these particular passions as productive of pleasure and pain, although they do not proceed from them? One can see that the bodily appetites have, as their ends, specific activities, the satisfaction of which may prove pleasing, and that the natural instincts are not for pleasures. But why does Hume include with these 'desire of punishment of our enemies, and of happiness to our friends'? These are not bodily appetites or instincts. The answer is as follows: each of the desires in question can be pleasant or painful, whereas love, he considers, is always pleasant and hatred always painful. The association of passions takes place only through resemblance, and therefore Hume can only notice the coincidence of love with benevolence and hatred with anger. There is no general principle of association to which we can appeal to account for this coincidence.

It is a mistake to quote this passage in order to show that these passions are disinterested in a way in which the passions arising from pleasure and pain are not. It is not the question of the disinterestedness of passions or otherwise which is at issue here, but their psychological or causal explanation. We can still appeal to Hume's account in support of our interpretation of him as an opponent of psychological egoism. Hume's statement shows, it is true, that there are motives to action that do not depend in any way for their occurrence upon the thought or occurrence of pleasure and pain. But it does not follow that the direct passions that depend upon the thought or impression of pleasure and pain for their occurrence are necessarily interested or selfish. Hume's words could give this impression only if we forget all he has said about sympathy. Describing the object of the direct passions in the chapter we are considering he says:

The mind, by an *original* instinct, tends to unite itself with the good, and to avoid the evil, though they be conceived merely in idea, and be considered as to exist in any future period of time. (THN II, 148/438)

The direct passions Hume mentions are not all motives directed to a future object. Desire, aversion, hope, fear, and volition might be thus considered, but grief and joy do not seem to have a reference to a future pleasure. They are in no sense desires. Joy may arise from the anticipation of a certain pleasure, but grief seems to be caused by a present or a past misfortune. Notice the very general way in which Hume states the object of direct passions, and the complete absence of any specific reference to the pleasure or pain of the person who is actuated by one or the other of these passions. The reason for this is that any other human being's pleasure or pain may arouse in us these passions through the operation of sympathy. Another's pain may arouse my sorrow, his pleasure my joy.

Although all the direct passions which have as their object an anticipated pleasure may be said to imply the obvious fact that we may desire pleasure, sympathy makes it possible for this pleasure to be that of any other human being. The object or end of those passions that proceed not from good or evil is not necessarily essentially different from the object or end of the direct passions that proceed from pleasure and pain, since private benevolence and anger are a desire for pain and a desire for pleasure respectively. But they produce, rather than proceed from, pleasure, in this sense: that sympathy is not needed to account for the fact that it is not the agent's own pleasure but someone else's which is the object. The agent's own pleasure is produced by their satisfaction, but cannot in the nature of the case be their original object.

As regards hunger, lust and a few other bodily appetites, it need only be stressed that the existence of these makes it quite obvious that Hume already in the *Treatise*, would have accepted Butler's refutation of psychological hedonism as a general theory of motivation.

4

LIBERTY

It has often been maintained that it is *in principle* impossible to give a satisfactory causal explanation of all human actions. Some human actions, at least, are free, and to say that they are free entails that they are not causally determined. In so far, therefore, as a science of human nature seeks causal explanations, it cannot give a satisfactory account of free human behaviour. Since it is, in particular, this aspect of man's life with which moral theory is preoccupied, the whole of Hume's attempt to establish a science of man must be doomed to failure, unless he can show that freedom and the causal necessity presupposed by this science are compatible, that the same actions can at once be free and causally determined.

Another great eighteenth-century scientific optimist, Immanuel Kant, agreed with Hume that one could not divide actions into two mutually exclusive classes, the free and the determined. He too thought all actions must be causally determined, that the problem was to see how any action could at the same time be causally determined and free. To classify either of these thinkers as determinists is more misleading than helpful. Although all actions have causes, both Hume and Kant thought that there was a perfectly good sense in which some human actions are free and others are not free. I do not want to stress too much the similarity between the views of Hume and Kant on this issue. There are vast differences between the solutions they offer to the problem of freedom. But both these thinkers are, for different reasons, committed to the view that the actions of human beings have causes.

Thus Hume attempts to show that the freedom possessed by human beings is in no way incompatible with the causal necessity presupposed by science.

Hume does not deny that the word 'will' has a meaning: There certainly is such an idea. As in the case of all other ideas, he hunts for the impression from which it is derived.

> I desire it may be observed, that, by the *will*, I mean nothing but *the internal impression we feel, and are conscious of, when we knowingly give rise to any new motion of our body, or new perception of our mind.* (THN II, 113/399)

He adds that this impression is, like pride and humility, indefinable. He also seems to think that any further description of this impression is unnecessary: the reader is supposed to be capable of identifying this 'internal impression' easily enough. In picking up a book in front of me, I have an experience which enables me to understand what the will is. There is supposed to be something common to all those actions we describe as knowingly doing something, whether this is performing an overt action, thinking of something, or, for example, looking, sniffing or listening. It would seem that the decisive factor is whether one *thinks* one is doing something.[1] The truth of what one thinks would seem to be irrelevant. If I think I am moving my leg, although it is paralysed, I have an impression of volition. Here my *freedom* is restricted, but it seems I could quite frequently have an impression of volition when this is the case.

It is fairly obvious why Hume should, on the whole, not wish to call the will a passion, although he classifies it, on at least one occasion, as a direct passion. The direct passions arise immediately from pleasure and pain: we knowingly seek what promises pleasure and avoid what threatens pain. Since the will is present whenever we knowingly exert ourselves, one can see the temptation to think of it as a direct passion. But the slightest reflection will suffice to convince us that there is something odd about this, for we may knowingly do this, that and the other

---

[1] One may knowingly give rise to thoughts as well as to overt actions. I do not, of course, want to suggest that *all* thoughts are voluntary. Thoughts pop into our heads. We cannot help the conclusions we reach when considering a problem, and some people cannot sleep because they cannot get rid of their thoughts. But these considerations should not lead us to conclude that we can never turn our thoughts to a thing or away from something. All that Hume's contention requires is that we should *sometimes* knowingly give rise to thoughts.

from a number of *different* motives. Thus hatred may lead me to cause deliberate harm to an enemy and love make me help a friend.[1] There is no emotion, no one passion that seems to be present, in these two cases, yet in both cases we have the impression we refer to in talking about the will.

According to the definition of 'will' given above, we must conclude that 'will' does not name a passion. If there is a will there must be an impression of volition to which the word refers. To talk of the will as a faculty, a hidden power in man to choose to do or not to do an action, is to indulge in the meaningless talk of mystics. Yet Hume himself sometimes talks of the will as a faculty: it 'exerts itself when either the good or the absence of the evil may be attained by any action of the mind or body' (THN II, 148/439).

How is this passage to be interpreted? May we not take it as a further elucidation of the situation in which we have the impression of volition? We desire many things that we see no chance of obtaining, and desire to avoid things that we know no effort of ours will enable us to get rid of. In other cases, our desires can be fulfilled by our own effort, and when, as a result of the desire, this effort is made, we have a case of volition. Expressions implying the existence of faculties are misleading. Yet we find this passage illuminating in that we normally identify the will with the effort, or rather the power to make the effort, to attain what we desire. By power we do not mean physical power, but rather the mental power to keep to a set course, in spite of hindrances in the shape of temptations and the opposition of others.

Readers of Book I of the *Treatise* will not be surprised to find Hume attempting to avoid explaining actions in terms of faculties. His account of the self as a bundle of impressions and ideas would seem inconsistent with a faculty psychology. We should be able to experience only the effects of such a faculty. What right could we have to infer its existence? A causal inference is impossible unless both the cause and the effect can be perceived. The appeal to a faculty would not be an explanation, for we should only be using a meaningless word in an attempt to hide our ignorance. In the absence of experience of a cause, any effect could have absolutely anything as its cause. Thus in spite of the fact that Hume sometimes talks of the will as a power of choice, of a faculty that enables us to make choices, we must bear in mind that he is anxious to

[1] Although not, strictly speaking, themselves motives, these passions are naturally attached to the motives of benevolence and anger.

account for the facts without an appeal to hidden faculties or powers. He even goes so far as to deny that we have any idea of power. Attacking the view that there is real power in matter, which does not lie in any of its discoverable qualities, he says:

> All ideas are derived from and represent impressions. We never have any impression that contains any power or efficacy. We never, therefore, have any idea of power. (THN I, 159/161)

Hume is, in this passage, concerned with refuting the belief that there is a necessary connection discoverable between objects. One object is said to have a native power to *produce* another. All we discover is an invariable succession; this also holds good for the relation between mental events and actions in the physical world:

> The motions of our body, and the thoughts and sentiments of our mind, (say they) obey the will; nor do we seek any further to acquire a just notion of force or power. (THN I, 159/Appendix 632)

But the relation between what we call a volition and the action is no more intelligible than any other causal succession.

Hume could hardly deny that the word 'power' has real use, and a proper use. What he in fact does is to give an analysis of it which would fit in with his notion of causal necessity:

> . . . there is but one kind of *necessity*, as there is but one kind of cause, and the common distinction betwixt *moral* and *physical* necessity is without any foundation in nature. (THN I, 168/171)

and he adds:

> The distinction which we often make betwixt *power* and the *exercise* of it, is equally without foundation. (THN I, 169/171)

Hume, indeed, appears to be denying an obvious distinction, for do we not often, with justification, say that one man makes an improper use of his power and that another, although he has the power to do something, refrains from using his? Hume insists that, if we speak philosophically, the fact that a man does not harm me shows that he had no power to do so. There must have been some motive determining his conduct, and this motive must have been more powerful than any faint desire the person may have had to harm me. On this interpretation, it is impossible to draw a distinction between having power and exerting it. Hume emphasizes that ' . . . the person never had any power of harming me, since he did not exert any' (THN II, 38/313).

It would be a mistake to conclude from the account of power so far given that Hume does not realize that there is a sense in which we may be scared of, or pleased with, a power which has not been exercised. It is true that

> the distinction we sometimes make betwixt a *power* and the *exercise* of it, is entirely frivolous, and that neither man nor any other being ought ever to be thought possessed of any ability, unless it be exerted and put in action. But though this be strictly true in a just and *philosophical* way of thinking, it is certain it is not the *philosophy* of our passions, but that many things operate upon them by means of the idea and suppositions of power, independent of its actual exercise. (THN II, 36/311-12)

This passage leads one to wonder how, according to Hume's doctrine, one could have an idea of power as opposed to the exercise of it. It is not entirely surprising to find him attempting an analysis of power in terms of probability and possibility. We deem an action possible when there is no very strong motive hindering the man from doing the action, and probable when, on the basis of experience, we conclude the occurrence of the action is likely.

The significant feature of this analysis of power is the absence of any reference to the power of choice. There are choices open to a rich man that a poor man does not have. Most ordinary people would, I think, insist, when pressed, that this is what they mean when they say that someone has power to do something. In having this power he also has the power to refrain from doing the actions.

Hume, indeed, moves very far from common conceptions in his account of power. This is well shown in the following passage:

> I do not think I have fallen into my enemy's power, when I see him pass me in the streets with a sword by his side, while I am unprovided of any weapon. I know that the fear of the civil magistrate is as strong a restraint as any of iron, and that I am in as perfect safety as if he were chained or imprison'd.
> (THN II, 36/312)

It is perfectly true that we would not think we had fallen into our enemy's power in this situation, if we think he is not going to attack us because of his fear of the civil magistrates; but the important point is that we think he *can* kill us if he so chooses. He could act in spite of his fear of the magistrates, whereas if he were chained or imprisoned there is no sense at all in which he can do us harm.

To this Hume would no doubt have retorted – but can he choose? Choices are determined by motives and, in the example given, the fear of the magistrates makes it impossible for the enemy to harm the other person. There is but one kind of necessity relevant in these situations: causal necessity; and this operates as much in the case of the actions of the mind, as in determining the movements of material bodies. This conception is at the very heart of Hume's philosophy and it is upon this presupposition that a science of man must be founded.

Let us now look more closely at the arguments in the first two sections of Book II, Part III. Hume recalls his own analysis of causal necessity:

Here then are two particulars, which we are to consider as essential to necessity, viz. the constant *union* and the *inference* of the mind; and wherever we discover these we must acknowledge necessity. (THN II, 114/400)

He then sets out to 'prove from experience, that our actions have a constant union with our motives, tempers, and circumstances...' (THN II, 114/401). Hume, needless to say, does not prove any such thing. It would, indeed, be a tall order to do so. It may be the case that the two sexes differ in their emotional make-up, but such a difference is surely not a clear-cut one. There will be men close in emotional character to women and vice versa. The same applies to all the other examples. Hume would find it difficult to point to a constant conjunction. He himself modifies his claim:

Necessity is regular and certain. Human conduct is irregular and uncertain. The one, therefore, proceeds not from the other.
(THN II, 117/403)

In answer to this objection Hume appeals to the fact that evidence may make a conclusion probable even though it may be based upon a sequence that is less than one hundred per cent regular. Here, he stresses that the sciences concerned with the study of material objects are in no better position than the science of man. We must acknowledge that many of the inferences we make about material objects are not based upon a sequence which is one hundred per cent regular.

In answer to the charge that human actions are irregular and uncertain Hume says:

To this I reply, that in judging of the actions of men we must proceed upon the same maxims, as when we reason concerning external objects. When any phenomena are constantly and invariably conjoined together, they acquire such a connection in the imagination, that it passes from one to the other without any doubt or hesitation. But below this there are many inferior degrees of evidence and probability, nor does one single contrariety of experiment entirely destroy all our reasoning. The mind balances the contrary experiments, and, deducting the inferior from the superior, proceeds with that degree of assurance or evidence which remains. (THN II, 117/403)

Hume thus claims only that we make inferences about human behaviour on the basis of past regularities. Although the regularity may not be perfect, this is no objection to the view that human actions are causally determined, for precisely the same applies in the case of many of our inferences about the behaviour of inanimate objects. He even goes so far as to emphasize that we do not abandon the belief that events or actions are causally determined, although the evidence for and against an occurrence is equal:

> Even when these contrary experiments are entirely equal, we remove not the notion of causes and necessity; but, supposing that the usual contrariety proceeds from the operation of contrary and concealed causes, we conclude that the chance or indifference lies only in our judgment on account of our imperfect knowledge, not in the things themselves, which are in every case equally necessary, though to appearance, not equally constant or certain.
> (THN II, 117/403-4)

It is not possible, here, to examine Hume's account of causality in detail. It will be sufficient to point out that he is insisting that we proceed as if there are causes even when we do not know what they are, and that this is the case whether we are dealing with human actions or inanimate objects. The regularity of sequence is all that is required and it turns out that this regularity need not be perfect. He stresses the non-human irregularities:

> But are the products of Guienne and of Champagne more regularly different than the sentiments, actions, and passions of the two sexes, of which the one are distinguished by their force and maturity, the other by their delicacy and softness?
> (THN II, 115/401)

It can be seen that, in both cases, we are likely to meet with exceptions; too many variables are ignored in these generalizations. Yet his point is made, if the same type of reasoning is involved, and if evidence of an inferior kind is accepted in our arguments both about human actions and non-human irregularity.

If regularity is the essence of necessity, and if we exclude the feelings of an observer, then it seems irregularity would be the essence of liberty. Yet this is not so: we do not think an action free just because it is unexpected on the basis of past experience. Some madmen, Hume points out, behave in the most surprising and erratic fashion. Yet we do not ascribe to them more freedom than we attribute to a man who consistently acts in a perfectly rational, and thus relatively predictable, manner.

We constantly make use of moral evidence:

Now moral evidence is nothing but a conclusion concerning the actions of men, derived from the consideration of their motives, temper and situation. (THN II, 118/404)

All our inferences from books on history are based on our faith in human veracity, and whenever we give orders to a waiter we have no doubt that he will carry them out:

Now, I assert that whoever reasons after this manner, does *ipso facto* believe the actions of the will to arise from necessity, and that he knows not what he means when he denies it. (THN II, 118/405)

All our insight into the operations of mind as well as of matter is simply derived from observed regularities. To drive home the point that the evidence is of precisely the same kind, Hume mentions that we 'cement together' *natural* and *moral* evidence in many chains of arguments. He takes the example of a prisoner who infers the impossibility of escape from the thickness of the walls, and the stubborness and incorruptibility of the gaoler. His death he foresees from the operations of the guillotine as a mechanism, and from the 'constancy and fidelity of the guards'.

We may conclude that Hume's kind of determinism is of the methodological kind, and that it is based on the contention that we make causal inferences about human actions no less than about inanimate objects. When we remember that all the necessity involved in the causal relation belongs to the mind thinking about or observing sequences, one may see that, to Hume, causal necessity would not, in any sense, restrict human freedom. It is because people have held erroneous views about necessity that they have failed to realize this. The error stems from confusing liberty of spontaneity and liberty of indifference. The first has as its opposite *violence*, the second has as its opposite necessity and causes.

Hume does not explain the liberty of spontaneity very adequately in the *Treatise*. A better statement is furnished in the *Enquiry Concerning Human Understanding*, where the arguments on Liberty and Necessity in the second book of the *Treatise* are reproduced with minor alterations. In the *Enquiry* Hume says:

> By liberty, then, we can only mean *a power of acting or not acting, according to the determinations of the will*; that is, if we choose to remain at rest, we may; if we choose to move, we also may. Now this hypothetical liberty is universally allowed to belong to everyone who is not a prisoner and in chains. Here, then, is no subject of dispute. (EHU, 95)

Although the statement in the *Enquiry* is fuller than the account given in the *Treatise*, it still does not make explicit whether the only violence which could destroy the liberty of spontaneity is external force. The last sentence of the quotation above would seem to imply that this is Hume's meaning. Yet he also defines liberty in such a way as to allow for the fact that a kleptomaniac would not have the liberty of spontaneity; we would normally say that he is to be distinguished from the common thief by the fact that his actions do not follow the determination of his will. If this is allowed, the freedom of spontaneity does not merely refer to the feeling we have when we consider ourselves free to do something. We may furthermore remind ourselves that Hume insists, in the *Treatise*, that a person who refrains from an action through fear has no power to perform that action. Psychological causes restrict freedom just as much as physical causes.

We may now be in a position to understand his reference to a false sensation or experience, even of the liberty of indifference, which is sometimes regarded as an argument for its real existence. We only need to remind ourselves that necessity does not refer to a quality in the agent, but to a feeling in an observer, to see why one could not possibly prove the independence of causal necessity from one's feelings when doing something. The similarity between Hume and Kant on this point is obvious. Kant is equally derisive of the argument that we are free because we feel free.

One of the main reasons why we consider that we were free to do what we did in fact not do, is that we can easily imagine ourselves doing it. We may, indeed, attempt to prove that we could have done it by now proceeding to do it; but this does not prove the point. The situation has altered: there is now a new motive, a desire to show our liberty.

A spectator could just as easily have predicted this action from knowledge of its motives and circumstances as he could have any other. This is all that is meant by necessity.

MacNabb is right in saying that Hume is here touching upon a point that has been made use of since to show that human actions are 'unpredictable in principle in a way that physical events are not, and dependent on human thoughts in a way that physical events are not' (DHTK and M, 201). He adds, however, that 'these facts do nothing to show that our actions and our thoughts do not take place according to causal laws' (ibid.). Hume, of course, could not accept the view that human actions are unpredictable in principle. His claim is that there is no difference in principle between human actions and other events in this respect: since human actions are affected by thoughts, the thought that *my* action has been predicted may affect my behaviour. I may *deliberately* decide to falsify the prediction. This may be granted. If one wants to predict someone's behaviour, it may be relevant to know whether that person does or does not know that the prediction is made. This, however, does not show that the action is not predictable, for one may know the person's character. He might be someone who is always inclined to be difficult, always trying to prove people wrong. One might, in fact, make him aware of the prediction in order to modify his behaviour. One thinks he will falsify the prediction one has made him aware of, and for this reason one is confident in making another prediction. The father says to his son 'I am sure you will fail your exam.' This he says in order to put the boy's back up, and his knowledge of the boy's character and ability may make him confident that the boy will pass. It may be argued that the statement made to the boy is not a prediction, since the father does not expect it to come true. Yet it may plausibly be said that it is a conditional prediction (it will certainly fail in its effect unless it is taken to be a genuine prediction by the boy). In some cases, the curious situation may arise that the condition necessary to falsify the prediction may be the making of it, and the communication of it to the person about whose behaviour it is made. The reason why the behaviour of inanimate objects and animals differs in this respect from that of human beings lies in the simple fact that only human beings are able to understand a prediction. It follows, therefore, that the knowledge that a prediction has been made can, in the case of human beings alone, be a causal factor in determining behaviour. It may be difficult to predict what effect this will have, although it is not impossible. But it may still be true that when we are unsuccessful, this is simply due to the fact that we do not know enough about the character, abilities, and the situation of the agent. Remembering the very weak form of determinism held by Hume, one may see why he would not be unduly concerned by the peculiarity of the case we are considering. Those who emphasize the difference between causal determination and determination by reasons may think that he ought to have been more concerned. For Hume the latter is just a special case of the former. Speaking entirely from the point of view of a spectator it is easy to see why this should be so: any conditions that lead to a prediction on the basis of previous experience of regularities are causal conditions.

> We may imagine we feel a liberty within ourselves; but a spectator can commonly infer our actions from our motives and character; and even where he cannot, he concludes in general that he might, were he perfectly acquainted with every circumstance of our situation and temper, and the most secret springs of our complexion and disposition. Now this is the very essence of necessity, according to the foregoing doctrine. (THN II, 121/408-9)

It is obvious, then, that the actions which we attribute to reasons are, in Hume's sense, as causally determined as any others.

Hume quite properly rejects the criticism that his views are dangerous to religion and morality; the only question should be whether they are true or not. Yet he thinks that this criticism is based on a mistaken doctrine, and maintains that his own doctrine is 'advantageous to religion and morality' (THN II, 122/409). Are not all laws based upon the presupposition that hope of reward and fear of punishment influence people's conduct? This, according to Hume, would be enough to show that we presuppose that human actions are subject to causes. It must be remembered that he believes he has disposed of the idea of a mysterious power in matter that somehow brings about the resultant effect:

> I do not ascribe to the will that unintelligible necessity, which is supposed to lie in matter. But I ascribe to matter that intelligible quality, call it necessity or not, which the most rigorous orthodoxy does or must allow to belong to the will. I change, therefore, nothing in the received systems, with regard to the will, but only with regard to material objects. (THN II, 122-3/410)

Necessary connection is nothing but 'the constant union' and conjunction of like objects, and the inference of the mind from the one to the other.

There is a further reason why the doctrine of liberty is inconsistent with the religious hypothesis and our moral notions. Hume reiterates his previous doctrine that the object of love or hatred is always a person, or another being endowed with thought and consciousness. These passions are not aroused unless their cause is closely related to their object. Unless the cause of the actions were to be found in the character or disposition of the agent, the action would be no more closely related to the agent than to any other. That he did it would be, in a manner, accidental. Although the action be wrong, the agent would in no sense be to blame. Yet this last is a necessary condition for all our moral evaluations of character. In fact it seems that the action could not be morally wicked in this case. It would only be unfortunate in the same way as are natural catastrophes. The justification for rewards and punishment also presupposes that they follow from something relatively permanent in the agent:

> It is only upon the principle of necessity, that a person acquires
> any merit or demerit from his actions, however the common
> opinion may incline to the contrary. (THN II, 124/411)

When people do an evil deed in ignorance, we do not blame them. When we act hastily or unpremeditatedly, we are blamed less than when the same actions are deliberate. The reason for this is, according to Hume, that we only blame a man for his actions in so far as they seem to indicate something relatively permanent in his character. Thus

> actions render a person criminal, merely as they are proofs of
> criminal passions or principles in the mind; and when, by any
> alteration of these principles, they cease to be just proofs, they
> likewise cease to be criminal. But according to the doctrine of
> *liberty* or *chance*, they never were just proofs, and consequently
> never were criminal. (THN II, 124/412)

In this way Hume turns the charge against his opponents. To him, the libertarian must believe that free actions take place by chance. It would seem that this doctrine is open to the criticisms mentioned above and that Hume's own view is not.

The reference which Hume makes at this point to the indirect passions of love and hatred is striking. The necessary conditions for the arousal of love and hatred are appealed to in order to explain how people can become praiseworthy and culpable:

> The constant and universal object of hatred or anger is a person
> or creature endowed with thought and consciousness; and when

any criminal or injurious actions excite that passion it is only by their relation to the person or connection with him. But according to the doctrine of liberty or chance, this connection is reduced to nothing, nor are men more accountable for those actions, which are designed and premeditated, than for such as are the most casual and accidental. (THN II, 123/411)

Here we have a clear indication that the indirect passions have to Hume a special significance in the explanation of morals. The basic moral value is virtue or the value of character. When actions cannot be traced to the character of a thinking conscious being, they are not fit objects for praise or blame, approval or disapproval. A thinking, conscious being is the basic object of both moral praise and blame, and the object of the indirect passions; and it is not implausible to suggest, with Hume, that actions are only *morally* wrong in so far as they entail some measure of moral guilt in the agent.

Hume distinguishes, as we have seen, between the cases where an agent knowingly does something, and the cases where he is compelled or restrained by external forces. I have also pointed out that there are grounds for thinking that he would deny freedom of spontaneity to such actions as the actions of a kleptomaniac. His account of the freedom of spontaneity is not as clear as one could wish, but he does maintain that there is a sense of 'free' in which he thinks we are sometimes free, and he claims that this has been confused with 'uncaused'. It can thus be said, with some justification, that his position is best described as a way of reconciling freedom with determination. To say that he comes down on the side of determinism is misleading, because the only libertarians he refutes are those who equate freedom with chance. It should be clear that Basson's contention that Hume thinks 'the doctrine of free will is irrelevant to morals'[1] cannot be defended. Hume, on the contrary, emphasizes that the libertarian view is incompatible with moral notions.

[1] See Introduction, p. 3.

5

THE CALM PASSIONS

Only a brief reference has so far been made to calm passions. Although it is true that the concept of calmness as applied to passions is of considerable importance in the *Treatise*, I believe the point of the distinction between calm and violent passions has often been missed by commentators.

I have already drawn attention to the classification of passions contained in the first chapter of Book II of the *Treatise*. Let us now consider in more detail the distinction drawn between calm and violent passions, which Hume states as follows:

The reflective impressions may be divided into two kinds, viz. the *calm* and the *violent*. Of the first kind is the sense of beauty and deformity in action, composition, and external objects. Of the second are the passions of love and hatred, grief and joy, pride and humility. This division is far from being exact. The raptures of poetry and music frequently rise to the greatest height; while those other impressions, properly called *passions*, may decay into so soft an emotion, as to become in a manner imperceptible. But as, in general, the passions are more violent than the emotions arising from beauty and deformity, these impressions have been commonly distinguished from each other. The subject of the human mind being so copious and various, I shall here take advantage of this vulgar and specious division, that I may proceed with the greater order; and having said all I thought necessary concerning our ideas, shall now explain those violent emotions or

passions, their nature, origin, causes, and effects. (THN II, 4/276)
The first two points I want to make about this can perhaps be called
guesswork, but I hope not unreasonable guesswork: (1) The quotation
we are discussing occurs in an introductory chapter, where a short
statement of key concepts is given. Such chapters are likely to be written after the bulk of the book has been completed, or at least to be
carefully revised in the light of the main arguments in the book. If this
is a reasonable contention, one can assume that the *main* distinguishing
characteristic of a calm passion is correctly stated here: (2) in a sum-
mary, a list of the members of a class may be taken as a means of illustrating a distinction. If there is in the rest of the book a longer list, we
may therefore assume that the longer list is to be taken as a fuller, more
complete account of the author's meaning. This point is important because Hume gives a longer list in another place, and, in fact, makes a
distinction between two kinds of calm passions.

As regards the quotation itself, we might want to make the following
observations:
(1) The *fundamentum divisionis* seems to be emotional intensity, the
    'disturbance in the soul' as Hume sometimes puts it. The term is
    used to describe the conscious state involved. It is analogous to the
    concept of 'force and vivacity' in impressions and certain ideas.
(2) The division is not exact, in this sense: that a passion classified as
    calm can, upon occasion, be violent – witness the reference to the
    raptures of poetry and music. Although, upon occasion, a calm
    passion can be violent, this does not entail that it belongs to the
    class of violent passions. A calm passion is thus a passion which *on
    most occasions* involves low emotional intensity, in the sense ex-
    plained. Hume, indeed, emphasizes the distinction between the
    violence and strength of a passion, between calmness and weak-
    ness. Thus, in criticizing Hutcheson's *Philosophiae Moralis Insti-
    tutio Compendiaria* he writes to the author in November 1742:
    > These Instincts you mention seem not always to be violent
    > and impetuous, more than Self love or Benevolence. There is
    > a calm Ambition, a calm Anger or Hatred, which *tho' calm
    > may likewise be very strong*[1] and have the absolute command
    > over the Mind. (LDH I, 19, 46)
(3) Hume calls the distinction vulgar and specious, and indicates that
    he uses it as a methodological device merely. The distinction can,

[1] My italics.

indeed, be called 'vulgar and specious', in the sense that there is nothing very sophisticated about it as stated here, and a similar distinction might well occur to common sense. Hume probably also wants to emphasize the fact that this is a rough and ready distinction, since any passion may become violent, and the calm ones are those which are so on most occasions. The distinction, as such, appears not of any very great importance. We know well from experience the difference between calmly enjoying something and being completely carried away, becoming animated, excited, possessed by a passion.

(4.) The calm passions enumerated here seem to be evaluations, and according to the interpretation given by Kemp Smith they inevitably are such. He says:

> . . . they can be identified as being the passions which we experience *on the mere contemplation* of beauty and deformity in action and external forms, *and may accordingly be further described as being modes of approval and disapproval.*
>
> (PDH, 167)

In a schematic representation of the division of passions, he describes them 'as proceeding *from the contemplation* of actions and external objects, viz. the moral and aesthetic sentiments'.

Kemp Smith's characterization of the calm passions as modes of approval and disapproval seems to gain added support from Hume's statements in the *Treatise*, Book III, Part III, Section I: our sentiments of praise and blame are naturally biased, because we take a much livelier interest in things that are close to us than in those far removed in space or time. Experience teaches us that it is convenient to judge all objects from a common point of view, abstracting from the different locations in space and time, and from our personal interest. In this connection Hume says:

> Here we are contented with saying, that reason requires such an impartial conduct, but that it is seldom we can bring ourselves to it, and that our passions do not readily follow the determination of our judgment. This language will be easily understood, if we consider what we formerly said concerning that *reason* which is able to oppose our passion; and which we have found to be nothing but a general calm determination of our passions, founded on some distant view or reflection. (THN III, 279/583)

The 'reason' referred to here is a calm passion, and Hume is referring back to the chapter 'Of the Influencing Motives of the Will' in Book II. He seems to be indicating that approval or disapproval, the calm passions which arise from a distant view and reflection, can lead to action, and that this has led the rationalists to think there can be a conflict between reason and passion. It should be noticed, however, that on certain occasions the 'sense of beauty and deformity in action' can be violent. The reference to the 'raptures of poetry and music' shows this clearly. Hume also stresses that our approvals and disapprovals do not have as much influence upon our actions as might be supposed, and this would explain why our value judgments have, on the whole, more consistency and uniformity than our actual actions.

Kemp Smith's characterization is vague on one important point. Is he making the same distinction as Hume makes in the opening chapter of Book II? In this case, experiencing the raptures of music and poetry would be a calm passion. Or is he saying that the calm passions are those only which are objective modes of approval and disapproval, arising from a distant view and reflection? In that case the calm passions are those only which we express by an objective judgment, when, for example, we say 'this is a good piece of music', and when this passion arises from a consideration of the piece in question, discounting any special relationship which we might have to it. (I might, for example, find that I was biased in thinking the piece in question enjoyable because the composer happened to be my son.)

It would appear that Kemp Smith's view is represented by the second of the two alternatives given above, and I shall try to show that his account is unacceptable and misleading; for in the enumeration of calm passions in the chapter entitled 'Of the Influencing Motives of the Will', Hume includes passions which cannot be taken to be forms of approval and disapproval at all. People often fail to notice this. Thus Mrs Mary Warnock in a paper to the joint session of the Mind Association and the Aristotelian Society makes the following statement:

> In general it [a calm passion] is a feeling inspired by the rational and detached consideration of some object, a feeling either pleasant or painful. An early example, and indeed *the only example that Hume gives is*[1] 'the sense of beauty and deformity in action, composition, and external objects'. (PAS (SV) 1957, 44)

The following quotation from Hume shows her mistake:

> Now it is certain there are certain calm desires and tendencies,

[1] My italics.

which, *though they be real passions*,[1] produce little emotion in the mind, and are more known by their effects than by the immediate feeling or sensation. These desires are of two kinds; either certain instincts originally implanted in our natures, such as benevolence and resentment, the love of life, and kindness to children; or the general appetite to good, and aversion to evil, considered merely as such. (THN II, 129/417)

It seems fairly clear that the *fundamentum divisionis* is still the same as the one we started off with. The calm passions are those which, on the whole, involve low emotional intensity, and this factor is decisive. It seems obvious that when we are motivated by a calm benevolence to children this need not be a passion arising from a distant view or reflection, and is therefore not to be equated with approval or disapproval thus understood.

Kemp Smith notices the extension of the class of calm passions, but in classifying the passions schematically he puts those instinctive passions which do not arise from a previous experience of pleasure and pain into a separate class, which he calls primary passions. The secondary passions are then divided into direct and indirect, according to whether they arise directly from pleasure or pain, or from these and a conjunction of other qualities. The calm passions are then taken as a subdivision of the direct secondary passions. This is misleading because the division of passions into calm and violent cuts across Hume's distinction between primary and secondary passions. The calmness or violence of a passion, although determined by causes, is independent of the mechanism which brings it about, whether direct, indirect, primary or secondary; but the primary passions and some of the secondary direct passions can be classified as calm, since they, *on the whole*, involve little emotional disturbance.

As regards the 'general appetite to good and aversion to evil', the context seems to make it plain that 'good' and 'evil' are taken to mean pleasure and pain; for Hume points out how a violent passion may overcome a calm one by drawing our attention to the fact that we often prefer a lesser immediate good to a greater distant good, and are thus made to act against our own best interest. In this case, the conflict is not between an 'approval' and a passion, if approval is taken to be moral approval. It is not the moral sentiment which is involved here at all, but rather a conflict between what we conceive to be prudent and a

[1] My italics.

particular passion. This clearly shows that Kemp Smith's classification is misleading.

Hume is, in this chapter, concerned to show that the distinction between a calm and a violent passion is entirely different from the distinction between a weak and a strong passion. The latter is a distinction in terms of strength of motivating power, whereas the former refers to the intensity of the emotion considered as a feeling or a conscious state. In this sense a violent passion may prove weaker than a calm passion considered as a motive. This makes it initially plausible to think that reason may be in direct opposition to passions.

When Kemp Smith classifies volition as a violent passion we must bear in mind that on the occasion when a calm passion determines the will there does not seem to be any reason to believe that the volition is a violent passion. It must be taken to be violent in the sense that it is so on most occasions. Consider Hume's definition of volition as *'the internal impression we feel, and are conscious of, when we knowingly give rise to any new motion of our body, or new perception of our mind'* (THN II, 113/399). This impression seems to accompany all voluntary acts, however motivated, and if we are to call it a passion at all, volition seems on a different level from the other passions in question, since it does not appear to be a motive, but occurs whether our motive is a calm or a violent passion.

Although Kemp Smith has textual justification for classifying volition among the direct passions, it may be doubted whether this is strictly correct. Hume enumerates, as direct passions, 'desire and aversion, grief and joy, hope and fear' along with volition; but when he introduces the description of volition already quoted, he prefixes the description by saying that volition is not properly speaking a passion. It seems important to realize this, when we are talking of the passions as motives, for Hume thinks that the will is always determined by motives.

A similar mistake seems to be made by MacNabb with regard to sympathy, which he calls 'another calm, regular and general passion' (DHTK and M, 166). For Hume, sympathy is a principle which accounts for the fact that we come to feel pleasant or painful emotions at the thought of such emotions in others; it is not a separate passion on a level with the other passions. In fairness to MacNabb, it is only right to point out that he does not treat sympathy in this manner throughout his interpretation of Hume. Although the passage quoted may not represent MacNabb's considered opinion it is unfortunate that he should express himself in this way; for some readers of Hume have thought that Hume believed approval and disapproval to be 'a species of sympathy', and if approval and disapproval are passions it seems we must then consider sympathy a passion also.

Let us now confine our attention exclusively to the calm passions of the second type, that is 'the general appetite to good and aversion to evil, considered merely as such'. Hume makes repeated references to the fact that we sometimes have a conflict between a violent passion and what we consider to be (1) our true interest or (2) the nature of the object as a source of pleasure generally. The second principle sometimes prevails, especially when we have developed a firm unshakable disposition. Strength of character indicates that we are not swayed over much by particular violent passions.

In this connection it is not inappropriate to point out that Francis Hutcheson makes a distinction between calm desires and particular passions in his 'An Essay on the Nature and Conduct of the Passions and Affections':

> There is a Distinction to be observed on this Subject, between 'the calm Desire of Good and Aversion to Evil, either selfish or publick, as they appear to our Reason or Reflection; and the particular Passions towards Objects immediately presented to some Sense'. (BM, 399)

The similarity between this statement and the use Hume makes of the notion of 'calm passions' as motives is obvious, although he emphasizes that even a passion such as anger may often be calm. Anger, however, must be counted as a violent passion because on most occasions it involves 'emotional disturbance'. In both Hume and Hutcheson, there seems to be a denial of the doctrine which is apparently implied in Locke's Essay, Book II, Chapter XX:

> The uneasiness a man finds in himself upon the absence of anything whose present enjoyment carries the idea of delight with it, is what we call *desire*, which is greater or less as that uneasiness is more or less vehement. (LE, 161)

If 'greater or less' means 'stronger or weaker as a motive', this is the very point Hume, and presumably Hutcheson, is concerned to deny.

In Hutcheson's account of calm desires, there is a reference to them as arising from a reflection upon (1) what is to the interest of the agent, (2) what is in the public interest. He does not say that when a passion leads to actions that are prudent, or in the public interest, then the passion involved is calm. This is, however, the view attributed to Hume by Rachael Kydd in her book *Reason and Conduct in Hume's Treatise*. Her view can be shown to be mistaken, and to be based on a wrong reading of certain passages in Hume. The calm passions, she thinks, are of four kinds:

(1) Desires which accord with the real qualities of their objects independently of a special consideration of these objects. (2) Desires which accord with these qualities as the result of the agent forming an adequate conception of them. (3) Desires which accord with the real qualities of their objects as constitutive of or a means to happiness without the agent considering them as such. (4) Desires which accord with these qualities as constitutive of or a means to happiness as the result of the agent forming an adequate idea of them in this relation. (R and C, 149)

The criterion for deciding whether a desire is calm or violent is here taken to be not emotional intensity, but rather the consideration whether or not the desire is such that it would have arisen from an adequate consideration of the object giving rise to it. If we consider the first type of calm passions, such an interpretation leads to some paradoxical results. Let us imagine that a man falls passionately in love with a certain woman, and that his passionate desires lead him to propose marriage, although he has given no clear thought to whether or not she would be a suitable wife. It would be rash to deny that this sometimes occurs, and one has reason to believe that some marriages contracted in this way may be perfectly satisfactory. The man might later on decide that he had, indeed, acted in his own best interest and this might be the general opinion. But does this mean that the passionate desire which caused him to make a proposal of marriage was necessarily a calm passion? We do not decide whether a passion is calm or violent by considering whether the behaviour it leads to has fortunate or unfortunate consequences. Hume most certainly would not consider the sexually inspired love leading to this fortunate action a calm passion.

Love is, on the whole, considered to be a violent passion. An adequate conception of its object might have the result of increasing it, of making it rise to a higher pitch; and this does not entitle us to say that it is therefore calm on this occasion. Kydd's mistake is to think that a calm passion is always preferable to a violent one, and that this is so by definition. She is right in thinking that a violent emotional disturbance often leads to rash behaviour, because it hinders us in apprehending the real nature of the object arousing our passion; this point is, indeed, emphasized by Hume. What she fails to realize is that Hume thinks also that our passions may become too calm; this is brought out in the section of the *Treatise* where Hume discusses the causes of the violent passions:

> There is not, in my opinion, any other natural cause why security diminishes the passions, than because it removes that uncertainty which increases them. The mind, when left to itself, immediately languishes, and, in order to preserve its ardour, must be every moment supported by a new flow of passion. For the same reason, despair, though contrary to security, has a like influence.
> (THN II, 133/421-2)

It seems probable that Hume is suggesting that it is sometimes desirable that the mind should 'preserve its ardour'.

In the cases where the passion based on a calm consideration of self-interest opposes a violent passion, it is certainly a false interpretation to suggest that the passion is not really calm unless a person has formed an adequate idea of his own interest – unless, in fact, his judgment is correct. In either case the motive would be a calm passion opposed to a violent one. Although violent passions may hinder true judgment we may be led astray for other reasons: we might, for example, have been given wrong information. This important fact is overlooked by Kydd because she is misled by the fact that Hume seems to emphasize, in this chapter, the cases where a calm passion is dependent upon correct judgments. He is showing in what precise way there can be a conflict of motives such as to mislead people into thinking that there is a real opposition between reason and passion. Consider the following passage:

> Men often act knowingly against their interest; for which reason, the view of the greatest possible good does not always influence them. Men often counteract a violent passion in prosecution of their interests and designs; it is not, therefore, the present uneasiness alone which determines them. (THN II, 129/418)

The expression 'the view of the greatest possible good' may be read in two ways according to whether you emphasize the word 'view' or 'greatest possible good'. Kydd would emphasize the latter, and thus considers that the calm passions should be based upon correct judgment. I should want to emphasize 'view'. Consider the conclusion drawn from the premiss that men 'counteract a violent passion in prosecution of their interests and designs': this is taken to show that the 'present un-easiness' does not always determine the direction of our will. Hume's inference is justified, even though the designs in question might be based upon a false estimate of the object.

But, one might now feel inclined to ask, does Hume not say strength of mind indicates a prevalence of calm passions over the violent? Does he not further say that this is a virtue, and deplore that people succumb too easily to 'the solicitations of passion and desire'? This is easily explained by the obvious facts (1) that great emotional disturbance often hinders us in forming an unbiased view of the objects of our desire; and (2) we often find that violent desires are due to a biased view of the object. This can be admitted without making it a defining characteristic of a calm passion that it arises from adequate knowledge, or is in harmony with adequate knowledge of the objects desired. Such an interpretation gives an unduly rationalist bias to Hume's doctrine.

Kydd appreciates that Hume is serious when he distinguishes the calm from the violent passions in terms of emotional disturbance or intensity, and she tries to show how this can be made to fit in with her own interpretation:

> ... it is evident that when passions are calm in the sense that they are either conducive to or directed towards our greatest possible good they are co-ordinated with one another and cannot come into conflict. Such passions, since they do not conflict, cause no dis-order in the soul, for it is only when our passions are not so co-ordinated by a single principle that they can cause a 'sensible emotion'. (R and C, 147)

Kydd gives no textual reference to substantiate this interpretation, but it seems palpably false. It is true that a conflict of passions is taken by Hume to increase, on the whole, the predominant passion; but a calm passion may be turned into a violent one by the simple expedient of bringing the object closer to the person. 'The same good, when near, will cause a violent passion, which, when remote, produces only a calm one' (THN II, 131/419). ('Calm' and 'violent' here refer to emotional intensity on particular occasions. This must not be confused with the sense of 'calm' in which moral approval is a calm passion.) Hume further points out that if we want to change a man's attitude it is by working on his violent passions that we are more likely to meet with success. It seems clear that we might often succeed in changing a man's attitude in this way for his own good, that is, in such a way as to increase his true welfare. The desire might be fully in harmony with the real qualities of the object, considered as a factor contributing to the agent's welfare, though he does not himself view it in this light. According to Kydd's interpretation, this could happen only if the passion was a calm one. The mere fact that the object in question is the object I ought to desire more than anything else at this point of my life, would be a sufficient condition for saying the passion motivating me was a calm one. One could give many exceptions, such as passionate sexual love, to show the absurdity of saying that a 'sensible emotion' is produced only when there is a conflict of passions.

In criticizing the treatment of the so-called 'doctrine of calm passions' by other commentators, my main point is that they have failed to take seriously Hume's own words in the first section of Book II. When he there draws the distinction between calm and violent passions in terms of emotional intensity, and calls this distinction vulgar and specious, he means what he is saying. Kemp Smith makes the mistake of thinking he is referring exclusively to approval and disapproval; Kydd makes a different error. In dealing with the rationalists' claim that reason can be a motive to the will, Hume indicates that this is simply a failure to appreciate that the passion associated with a firm disposition may be a stronger motive than a violent passion; and further, that when we reflect upon a situation objectively, this arouses in us a passion directed towards this object. This passion on the whole involves little emotional disturbance, although it may hinder a particular violent passion in leading to action. The rationalists think that Reason is the motive here, because there is hardly any felt emotion; but they are wrong: we may be in possession of all the facts, know the whole truth about the situation, and the conflict might still remain. Whether the calm passion or the violent one will determine our conduct depends entirely upon our situation and the habits we have developed. But it should be remembered that it is possible to acquire a habit based upon a mistaken view of our own interest, and that in this case a calm passion would be in conflict with a violent one. Kydd mistakenly thinks that Hume has a special doctrine of calm passions, designed to replace the rationalist doctrine, but essentially based upon rationalist premises. Hume, in fact, uses his distinction between calm and violent passions to explain the rationalists' mistake, but in so doing he was well aware of the fact that he was merely making use of a 'vulgar and specious' distinction.

It must be emphasized that it is no part of my intention to belittle the importance of the concept of calm passions in understanding Hume's views on evaluation. I merely want to stress the point that calmness is, in one sense, not the defining characteristic of approval or disapproval.

We must distinguish between 'calm passions' as a class name, and as the characterization of a passion occurring on a particular occasion. If we take the first interpretation, the class includes more than approval and disapproval. If we take the second interpretation, many passions, even those that are commonly the most violent, may be calm on particular occasions, although they do not arise from 'a distant view and reflection'.

Hume realizes that there must be some evidence that appears to support the description of moral conflict as a conflict between reason on the one hand and passions on the other. Unless there was an *apparent* difference in kind between the two 'parties' to the conflict it would be hard to explain why the mistake was so widespread, and why it even seemed plausible to the unsophisticated. When one tries to control an incidental desire for something, the emotion tending to oppose the desire appears to be almost indistinguishable from a mere opinion or belief. Hume accepts this as an undeniable fact, and that there must be passions involving so little emotional disturbance as to be hardly discernible, if it is true, as he contends, that a passion can only oppose another passion or desire in determining behaviour.

It is also possible to maintain that Hume thinks one of the causes of the widespread belief in free will is derived from the same source. A violent desire may seem to necessitate action. If all our actions were thus motivated, one would not be inclined to believe in freedom of the will. It is because we often act contrary to violent desires that we think of the actions as having no cause. Furthermore, when the desire has abated, and we reflect upon the situation, we can imagine ourselves as having taken the one course of action as easily as the other. We tend not to see the alternatives while the violent desire is determining our conduct.

There is the further important point that, although approval and disapproval are emotions or passions for Hume, he sees that when we calmly evaluate, and are not ourselves vitally involved in the issue, our state of mind seems often to involve little detectable emotion. When we look at the facts, the calmness of our mind may lead us to think of our evaluation as a conclusion inferred from the facts, whereas an evaluation is determined *by* and not inferred *from* the facts as we see them. The following quotation states clearly the main point of Hume's distinction between calm and violent passions:

> What we commonly understand by *passion* is a violent and sensible emotion of mind, when any good or evil is presented, or any object, which, by the original formation of our faculties, is fitted to excite an appetite. By *reason* we mean affections of the very same kind with the former, but such as operate more calmly, and cause no disorder in the temper: which tranquillity leads us into a mistake concerning them, and causes us to regard them as conclusions only of our intellectual faculties. (THN II, 147/437)

Although the fact that a calm passion often arises when we do reflect may further persuade us that reason is our motive, reflection is not a necessary condition for the passion to be calm:

> Generally speaking, the violent passions have a more powerful influence on the will; though it is often found that the calm ones, *when corroborated by reflection, and seconded by resolution*,[1] are able to control them in their most furious movements.
> (THN II, 147/437-8)

Thus it appears that reflection may add strength to a passion already calm, without making it violent. But violence must not be equated with strength, for then 'reason' would always be the loser. A calm passion can be made violent either by a change of temper, a change in the situation of the object, or a change in strength of an *attendant* passion. Hume implies by this that a particular passion can be altered without changing its identity; for he talks of the 'borrowing of force from any attendant passion, by custom, or by exciting the imagination' (THN II, 147/438).

He also emphasizes that what we wrongly take to be the dictate of reason as opposed to passions may vary between people, according to their dispositions and tempers and in the case of the same man at different times. He therefore concludes the chapter by saying:

> Philosophy can only account for a few of the greater and more sensible events of this war; but must leave all the smaller and more delicate revolutions, as dependent on principles too fine and minute for her comprehension. (THN II, 147/438)

Passions that are evaluations are distinguished by their qualitative character which is due to the fact that they arise from special causes and have peculiar objects. They may vary in calmness or violence, in

[1] My italics.

the same way as an idea may vary in force and vivacity. These ways of characterizing experiences (the term 'experience' being used to include ideas) are parallel. We shall later see that approval and disapproval arise largely from the imagination, and the ideas of the imagination are relatively faint. This should make us less surprised that approval and disapproval are classified as calm passions.

No passage from the *Treatise* is more often quoted than the following:

> Reason is, and ought only to be, the slave of the passions, and can never pretend to any other office than to serve and obey them.
> (THN II, 127/415)

It is tempting to interpret this passage to mean that Hume is advocating a reversal of the roles of reason and passion.[1] He makes an explicit reference to the traditional doctrine that reason ought to guide our actions in preference to the passions. In explaining the traditional view he says:

> The eternity, invariableness, and divine origin of the former, have been displayed to the best advantage: the blindness, inconstancy, and deceitfulness of the latter, have been as strongly insisted on.
> (THN II, 125/413)

The people Hume wants to criticize have, it seems, claimed that reason is a better guide than passion. The passions are a poor guide, reason is a good guide. This may easily lead one to believe that Hume is going to argue that it is passion we ought to follow rather than reason, because reason is an inferior guide. But the way Hume attempts to combat the traditional rationalist view is inconsistent with this interpretation; for he argues not that reason is a poor guide, but rather that there is a sense in which it cannot be a guide at all. Its capacity for guiding us is limited in such a way that it can only affect our conduct as subservient to passions. He argues 'that reason alone can never be a motive to any action of the will' (THN II, 125/413), and draws from this the conclusion 'that it can never oppose passion in the direction of the will' (THN II, 125/413).

The question now arises as to why Hume should say that reason ought to be a slave, when he backs this up by maintaining that it can be nothing but a slave. I do not want to argue that Hume's way of expressing himself is unambiguously clear, but the following consider-

---

[1] I am greatly influenced by A. B. Glathe's *Hume's Theory of the Passions and of Morals* in the interpretation of this passage.

ations may help to make sense of his view about the relation of reason to the passions. That, according to him, it *is* the slave of the passions involves little difficulty. It is the 'ought' that is puzzling; but the puzzle vanishes if one takes Hume to be making a terminological recommendation. To say that reason ought only to be the slave of the passions would then mean that we should use the word 'reason' only in a certain way. This is not because ordinary usage dictates it, for the word is used also for a 'certain calm passion'. But Hume thinks it may be confusing to use the term in this way, and wants us to amend our language, so as to make it plain that when people criticize conduct on the ground that it is unreasonable, the criticism is not always of the same kind. The restriction of the terms 'reasonable', 'unreasonable', 'contrary to reason' 'in conformity with reason' will make us more conscious of a valuable distinction too easily overlooked.

What then is this distinction? Let us confine our attention to unreasonableness for the sake of simplicity. When we criticize conduct as unreasonable we may be doing one or other of two things. Consider Hume's apparently scandalous and paradoxical statements in the following passage:

> It is not contrary to reason to prefer the destruction of the whole world to the scratching of my finger. It is not contrary to reason for me to choose my total ruin, to prevent the least uneasiness of an Indian, or person wholly unknown to me. It is as little contrary to reason to prefer even my own acknowledged lesser good to my greater, and have a more ardent affection for the former than the latter. (THN II, 128/416)

All these actions would normally be described as eminently unreasonable. Hume would agree. But when you charge a man with unreasonableness, on the grounds that his preferences are as described in the quotation from the *Treatise*, you are in effect attacking his character; you are disapproving of him. Hume wants us to see that this disapproval is different from criticism of a person for holding a false belief about a matter of fact. To criticize actions on the ground that they are based upon a false belief about the nature of a situation, or a false judgment about causal relationships, involves no necessary *disapproval* of the person. The two different ways of using terms such as 'unreasonable' might as well be kept distinct. It is no doubt partly because Hume equates thinking a person unreasonable with having an emotion of disapproval with regard to him that he proposes we confine expressions such as 'contrary to reason', 'reasonable', to cases where the criticism refers to the truth or falsity of a belief. In doing this he is departing quite widely from ordinary usage because an action based upon a *false belief* would not normally be described as unreasonable for that reason alone. A man may be said to behave in a perfectly reasonable manner when he has acted in conformity with the evidence at his disposal, although the belief accompanying his action, and upon which it is based, is in fact false. Thus it is reasonable for a person to take a train in preference to using his car, if the A.A. has warned against the danger of black ice. Even if the A.A. message was incorrect the man still acted reasonably, assuming that A.A. warnings are usually reliable.

When we describe conduct as reasonable or in conformity with reason, we normally do not want to indicate that the beliefs upon which the conduct is based are true. Hume, in making his linguistic recommendation, is indeed departing widely from ordinary usage. He cannot appeal to ordinary usage to show that the sense he gives to 'reason' and allied terms is the *proper* sense. It is the proper 'philosophical' sense, if you accept Hume's account of evaluation as an emotion of a certain sort. But, as we shall see in Chapter 9, there are special reasons why Hume should, upon occasion, express himself in such a way as to fail to make it clear whether evaluations consist in true or false thoughts or in certain calm passions or emotions.

6

MORAL SENTIMENTS

I

We can now turn our attention to the moral sentiments, and to the function that Hume allots to sympathy in explaining the occurrence of approval and disapproval.

Before we can enter into a discussion of the origin of the sentiments of morality, we must say a few words about their nature. It is important to distinguish the account given of the definition or analysis of approval and disapproval, from the causal explanation of the emergence in human consciousness of these passions. Some commentators have failed to appreciate that Hume appeals to sympathy in accounting for the origin of the sentiments of morality and does not define these sentiments in terms of 'sympathetic consciousness'. He never thinks that approval and disapproval are a species of sympathy. Approval and disapproval are passions, and I shall argue hereafter that there is in the *Treatise* a close relation between the indirect passions and the moral sentiments.

I have already stressed the fact that Hume looks upon the passions as simple impressions, which are indefinable and unique, although they may resemble one another; and I have also said something about the criticism that what resembles cannot be simple. There is no need, therefore, to enter further into this controversy at this point, and it will be sufficient to remind ourselves that Hume thought that resemblance between simple impressions was consistent with their simplicity. We need not be surprised that Hume insists upon the unique nature of the sentiments of morality, when specifically dealing with this topic in Chapter II, Book III of the *Treatise*.

The sentiments of morality are either pleasant or painful. When we are satisfied that 'morality . . . is more properly felt than judged of' (THN III, 178/470), it is not unreasonable to go on to ask ' . . . of what nature are these impressions, and after what manner do they operate upon us?' (THN III, 178/470), and Hume appeals to our experience in support of the view that we 'must pronounce the impression arising from virtue to be agreeable, and that proceeding from vice to be uneasy' (THN III, 178/470). We have now concluded that 'the distinguishing impressions by which moral good or evil is known, are nothing but *particular* pains or pleasures' (THN III, 179/471).

But there are many pains and pleasures that are not of the peculiar nature which distinguishes the sentiments of approval and disapproval: 'An action, or sentiment, or character, is virtuous or vicious; why? because its view causes a pleasure or uneasiness of *a particular kind*'[1] (THN III, 179/471). In the same paragraph, Hume again stresses that here we are dealing with 'a particular kind' of pleasure: 'To have the sense of virtue is nothing but to *feel* a satisfaction of a particular kind from the contemplation of a character' (THN III, 179/471). It must be strongly emphasized that Hume is referring to the sentiments as impressions, as they appear in consciousness, although we can also differentiate this peculiar kind of pleasure from other pleasures, in terms of the causes or attendant circumstances that arouse it.

Hume goes on to say that people might object that, since pleasure and pain determine approval and disapproval, then any object that arouses pleasure could thereby be deemed virtuous. To this he gives an answer which is of the utmost importance:

For, *first*, it is evident that, under the term *pleasure*, we comprehend sensations, which are very different from each other, and which have only such a distant resemblance as is requisite to make them be expressed by the same abstract term.

(THN III, 179-80/472)

The pleasure aroused by the contemplation of character is intrinsically different from the pleasure aroused by drinking good wine; and the pleasure derived from listening to good music differs from both. But this is not all, for Hume goes on to say:

Nor is every sentiment of pleasure or pain, which arises from

---

[1] My italics.

characters and actions, of that *peculiar* kind *which makes us praise or condemn*.[1] (THN III, 180/472)

I have quoted extensively from the text, in order to show that it would be most unreasonable to suppose that Hume is guilty of gross careless-ness in insisting upon the peculiar character of the pleasure or pain which constitute the moral sentiments. It is important to remember that approval is a form of pleasure and disapproval a kind of pain; but it is equally important to bear in mind that they are simple impressions, and consequently unanalysable, although we may describe those cir-cumstances which occasion their occurrence and point out their simi-larity to other impressions.

In this same chapter Hume goes on to point out 'a still more con-siderable difference among our pains and pleasures' (THN III, 180/473). The passage is difficult to interpret, but it refers to the close relation between the sense of virtue and vice and the indirect passions. I shall have occasion to stress this relation, and may therefore be excused for quoting the passage in full:

> Pride and humility, love and hatred, are excited, when there is anything presented to us that both bears a relation to the object of the passion, and produces a separate sensation, related to the sensation of the passion. Now, virtue and vice are attended with these circumstances. They must necessarily be placed either in ourselves or others, and excite either pleasure or uneasiness; and therefore must give rise to one of these four passions, which clearly distinguishes them from the pleasure and pain arising from inanimate objects, that often bear no relation to us; and this is, perhaps, the most considerable effect that virtue and vice have upon the human mind. (THN III, 180-1/473)

One can see from this why the sentiment aroused by virtue must be pleasant, and the sentiment aroused by vice unpleasant, for, unless this were so, Hume could not explain why virtue gives rise to pride and love, and vice to the contrary. The resemblance, which is necessary for the association of impressions to work, would otherwise be missing.

But perhaps the close relation between the moral sense and the indirect passions has not yet been fully appreciated. Again I must emphasize that Hume's statement here is no momentary aberration. The same point is repeated at the beginning of Book III, Part III, even more forcefully:

[1] My italics.

We have already observed, that moral distinctions depend entirely on certain peculiar sentiments of pain and pleasure, and that whatever mental quality in ourselves or others gives us a satisfaction, by the survey or reflection, is of course virtuous; as everything of this nature that gives uneasiness is vicious. Now, since every quality in ourselves or others which gives pleasure, always causes pride or love, as every one that produces uneasiness excites humility or hatred, it follows that these two particulars are to be considered as equivalent, with regard to our mental qualities, *virtue* and the power of producing love or pride, *vice* and the power of producing humility or hatred. In every case, therefore, we must judge the one by the other, and may pronounce any *quality* of the mind virtuous which causes love or pride, and any one vicious which causes hatred or humility. (THN III, 271-2/574-5)

A little later Hume writes: 'Actions themselves, not proceeding from any constant principle, have no influence on love or hatred, pride or humility; and consequently are never considered in morality' (THN III, 272/575). Here again it is stressed that the causes of the indirect passions and sentiments of morality (pleasure and pain of the peculiar kind which makes us praise and blame) are the same. Perhaps the connection between the accounts of the origins of the indirect passions on the one hand and approval and disapproval on the other is more important for the understanding of Hume's moral theory than some commentators have maintained (see p. 17).

If Hume's account of the indirect passions has as little bearing upon his moral philosophy, as Kemp Smith appears to think, it seems strange that Hume should take such pains to emphasize, in Book III of the *Treatise*, that, as regards mental qualities, the causes of the indirect passions are virtue and vice, and that he should give as the reason why certain qualities are not taken account of in morality their failure to arouse the indirect passions. Hume's statements make sense only if there is a strict parallel between the principles accounting for the origin of the indirect passions and those accounting for the origin of approval and disapproval of persons. If we can show that this is the case, by a direct appeal to Hume's own pronouncements, we shall cease to think of his preoccupation with the indirect passions in Book II as a useless game, instigated by his fondness for the principles of association, but of no importance for his moral theory.

Is there any justification for thinking that Hume considers reference to the indirect passions absolutely necessary in accounting for morality? The answer to this question is put beyond doubt by the following:

> The pain or pleasure which arises from the general survey or view of any action or quality of the *mind*, constitutes its vice or virtue, and gives rise to our approbation or blame, *which is nothing but a fainter and more imperceptible love or hatred.*[1]
>
> (THN III, 306-7/614)

This passage, occurring towards the end of Book III, furnishes us with a key to the understanding of Hume's moral theory.

The first observation that springs to mind at this point is that approval and disapproval (approbation and blame) are indirect passions; but Hume does not include approval and disapproval among the indirect passions when he discusses this topic in Book II. Is he then saying that we are mistaken when we take approval and disapproval to be special, simple, unanalysable passions? Is he saying that 'love' and 'hatred' on the one hand, 'approval' and 'disapproval' on the other, are just two pairs of words used to refer to precisely the same two opposite passions? Such an interpretation would be mistaken; for Hume puts great emphasis upon the variety of those feelings we include in the concept 'pleasure'; they are related by resemblance only to a sufficient extent to justify the use of the same abstract term. This in no way indicates that these feelings are not simple impressions, the full, intrinsic nature of which is immediately revealed to an individual's consciousness. In a similar way, Hume emphasizes that an indirect passion, such as love,

> may show itself in the shape of *tenderness, friendship, intimacy, esteem, good will*, and in many other appearances; which at the bottom are the same affections, and arise from the same causes, though with a small variation, which it is not necessary to give any particular account of. It is for this reason I have all along confined myself to the principal passion. (THN II, 156/448)

Hume realizes that it may be misleading to suggest that there are only four indirect passions: this number is dictated by the kinds of association which could give rise to such passions. Still, some differences in the causes may be noticed, although the associative principles are the same: 'love' may be used to cover all those passions produced according to one general scheme of association, and we can therefore say that although there is variety among these passions, they are at bottom the same. They are also related by resemblance; their sensations are similar,

[1] My italics.

although not identical. The minor differences in the causes may lead to a difference in the sentiment: 'It is easy to imagine how a different situation of the object, or a different turn of thought, may change even the sensation of a passion; and this may in general account for all the particular subdivisions of the other affections, as well as of fear' (THN II, 156/448). The name of a passion may sometimes be a generic name. 'Love' and 'hatred' here appear to be thus conceived. The 'sensation' of a passion could only be altered if we are thinking in generic terms. An alteration in a simple individual impression would result in a different impression, unless we were dealing with a change in vivacity. Hume's view, therefore, is in perfect conformity with the doctrine that the pleasure, or displeasure, aroused by the contemplation of character from an 'objective' point of view may cause in us special kinds of pleasure or pain, which will also affect the resultant love or hatred, approval or disapproval, when considered as impressions.

We are now in a position to see one important reason why Hume should have adhered to the apparently strange doctrine that approval is always pleasant, and disapproval unpleasant: the indirect passions operate through a double association, and the association of impressions involved always refers to a similarity in pleasantness in the one case and unpleasantness in the other. It would be impossible to make this scheme work unless the pairs of opposite passions involve pleasure and pain respectively. In so far as approval and disapproval are treated as a species of indirect passions, they must consequently be opposites in precisely this hedonic sense.

Hume seems too open to the charge that his fondness for his associationist scheme clouds his view of the facts. We know perfectly well that some people dote on disapprovals. At social gatherings the time is sometimes thought to be most pleasantly passed in malicious gossip, dwelling on the less fortunate characteristics of colleagues and acquaintances. Furthermore, approval is not always pleasant. Is it not often painful when we find ourselves forced to approve grudgingly of the deeds and character of a person we intensely dislike? When Hume emphasizes how difficult it is for us to allow justice to prevail in our estimate of enemies, he ought to have become more suspicious about the influence of the similarity in hedonic quality on the origination of the indirect passions, approval and disapproval.

It may be suggested with some plausibility that a person who grudgingly approves of his enemy's qualities is experiencing both pleasure and pain, and that it is because of the experience of pleasure in contemplating the character of an enemy that the pain results. But can it be denied that disapproval is sometimes, at least, extremely pleasant?[1] Are a man's feelings unpleasant when, for example, he gloats over the discovery of vice in his enemy? Hume's answer to this would be that gloating is neither moral approval nor disapproval but simply malice; the man has not achieved the objectivity which alone results in approvals and disapprovals. But, on the other hand, it is hard to see what is felt, if not approval, when a man grudgingly admits virtue in someone else whom, for personal reasons, he dislikes.

Even when we confine our view to love and hatred, and pride and humility, it is not obvious that these passions are necessarily pairs of opposites as regards their hedonic character. What is more painful than the love of an undeserving person, or unrequited love? It is only when we think of a man as 'glowing with pride' that pride is obviously pleasant. One may also, with some justification, point out that a person who is proud of something can be described as pleased with himself, or as pleased with whatever it is that makes him proud. When, however, 'pride' is used as a description of a character trait, little is implied about the pleasantness or unpleasantness of the proud man's life. One can, of course, answer that Hume is not concerned with the latter sense of the term, but his account would undoubtedly have been more interesting if he had been less obsessed with the notion that terms such as 'pride' and 'love' could be treated as names of simple impressions. It also makes it difficult to understand how these passions, thus understood, can have an object. But at the same time as he thinks of them as simple impressions, he treats them as forms of valuing and, as such, they must have an object, for to value must be to value something.

Approval and disapproval cannot be defined any more than the other indirect passions; we can only point out those circumstances from which they arise. Hume does not bother to do this with *all* the different species of indirect passions, deeming it 'not necessary to give any particular account of them'. But approval and disapproval are of such central importance in accounting for the nature of evaluation, that a special

---

[1] It may be suggested that a man's state of mind is mixed in these cases. There is no impossibility in finding a pain pleasant. Thus, in dwelling on one's disapprovals of people's morals over a cup of tea, the disapproval might *be* a pain that in this case one happens to enjoy. It would normally be a very faint pain because in this kind of situation, when people are indulging in malicious gossip, the disapprovals expressed are generally not very strongly felt.

examination of these passions is necessary. It is only when we take up an 'objective' point of view that they are aroused, although, on other occasions we sometimes mistake the love and hatred aroused, because of a close relation of their object to ourselves, for the 'calmer' variety of these passions.

Some evidence has already been drawn from the *Treatise* to show that Hume thought there was a close analogy between those approvals and disapprovals that make us call a person virtuous or vicious, and the indirect passions of love and hatred. Sympathy may be appealed to in accounting for the origins of both, but Hume must somehow characterize those approvals and disapprovals, properly described as evaluations of character, in order to distinguish them from love and hatred in the ordinary sense of these terms.

We are told that approval and disapproval are love and hatred, 'which arise from mental qualities', and a warning is given that the enquiry will take us 'pretty deep', and that we shall have to compare some principles which have been already examined and explained. We must appeal to these principles in order to discover 'the true origin of morals'. The discovery of the 'origin of morals' is the main topic of the third book of the *Treatise*. It is, therefore, reasonable to presume that a discussion specially concerned with this topic is of central importance in understanding the principles in terms of which the origin and nature of morals are to be explained.

Hume begins by emphasizing that sympathy is a principle which can be seen to operate universally in human nature. It is, not unexpectedly, described as essentially a principle of communication of passions between human beings:

> As in strings equally wound up, the motion of one communicates itself to the rest, so all the affections readily pass from one person to another, and beget correspondent movements in every human creature. (THN III, 272/576)

Sympathy, a principle of communication, is appealed to in order to explain the origin of approvals and disapprovals; but it is the *cause* of what is sympathized with that is approved or disapproved of. The feeling sympathized with, and the object of the passion, are different, and this is important when we come to consider the view that Hume thinks of approval and disapproval as a species of 'sympathetic consciousness'.

Talking of the causes that lead us to call objects beautiful or ugly, he emphasizes that it is, to a considerable extent, the tendency of objects to produce pleasures and pains that determines the aesthetic valuing of them. It is sympathy with the effects that leads to the valuing of the cause.[1] The principles involved are the same in moral evaluation. This is perhaps most conspicuously true of our approval of the artificial virtues, since they derive all their value from utility. The sympathy, however, in no way constitutes the evaluation, but ' . . . produces our sentiment of morals' (THN III, 274/577). Since we find that sympathy with the effects of justice upon happiness or misery is the sole productive agency in giving rise to our approval of justice and other artificial virtues, we may presume it to have some effect in the case of the other virtues. We find, indeed, that a great number of the natural virtues have a tendency to increase the happiness of society. This tendency would have no effect on our passions, if it were not for the influence of sympathy. The difference between the natural and the artificial virtues lies in this: that the pleasures with which we may come to sympathize, arise immediately from each individual act in the case of a natural virtue. The artificial virtues on the other hand have pleasant results only when a conventional system of behaviour is presupposed, and, even when the system has been established, we may find that an action, considered in isolation, may have no beneficial consequences at all.[2]

But it soon appears that sympathy is not sufficient to account for the origin of morality, although it is indeed a necessary condition, without which our sentiments of morals would be impossible. Sympathy, as has already been emphasized, may be a universal principle in human nature, but it varies with the closeness of relations: 'We sympathize more with persons contiguous to us, than with persons remote from us; with our acquaintance, than with strangers; with our countrymen, than with foreigners' (THN III, 277/581). As a result of this, our love or hatred is strengthened or weakened according to the closeness of the relations. In fact, we find that our love is much more lively and intense when the qualities arousing it belong to someone closely related to us than when they belong to a person living in a distant time or age. The important point is that this variation in our passions is to a considerable

---

[1] It will appear later in this chapter that this view needs modification.
[2] The way in which the difference between artificial and natural virtues is described here overlooks the important fact that there is no natural *motive* to an artificial virtue. This will be discussed later.

extent accentuated by sympathy. It is not only love that tends to be increased by close relations, the same can be said of hatred. One tends, in general, to feel more strongly about close relations and associates than about complete strangers and people far removed in space and time. Since, however, the closeness of relations is deemed irrelevant in pronouncing about the virtuous or vicious nature of a character, how on earth can we claim that a principle which contributes to a biased view of qualities of character can be said to be the foundation of morality? It is Hume's answer to this question which determines the fundamental nature of his moral theory and the precise way in which sympathy operates in helping to produce approval and disapproval.

'Judgments of value' appear to be objective in some important sense in which love and hatred are not. Objectivity consists in taking into account only those features of a situation which would be common to any spectator. Hume's answer to the rationalists consists in his attempt to show how the adoption of this objective point of view can be accounted for in terms of well-known human motives, which operate in our understanding as well as in practical affairs. There is no need to appeal to a special intuitive faculty of reason to account for this. In fact the motive behind objective judgment can be seen to belong to our passions as much as any other motive: 'Reason is and ought only to be the slave of the passions.' Even if the 'ought' is taken to be rhetorical, the 'is' must be taken perfectly seriously.[1]

To judge situations objectively is an acquired habit. Let us now see how it is acquired. We find that our situation in regard to objects varies from time to time, and our moods may also change the effect the same object has upon us at different times. We soon learn that changes in our situation alter the appearances of things. Hume could perhaps have said that an object looks small at a distance, but appears to become larger as we approach it. It is fairly obvious that if we tried to base our actions upon the momentary appearances of things we should be more often thwarted in seeking the satisfaction of our needs and wants. A golfer, deciding upon a club to play his shot to the green, will take a stronger club when his caddie tells him that there is a dip in the fairway between his position and the flag, a dip he does not see. I might have had a drink of stagnant water when plagued with extreme thirst, and yet I would not be inclined to claim that such water was delicious. I realize that the unusual condition of my extreme thirst may have had

[1] An interpretation of this passage is attempted at the end of Chapter 5.

something to do with the way the water tasted to me at the time.

The appearances of objects vary according to our situation in regard to them and our own condition. Some changes in appearances seem to be most naturally explained by attributing the variation to a change in us or in our position. Differences in the apparent colours of objects come to be attributed to changes in the light, or, as in jaundice, to a change in our sense-organs. Thus, with wide experience, we begin to draw a distinction between changes due to a change of qualities in the object, and changes due to our special situation or condition which is perhaps not shared by others. The motive for judging of things from a special point of view, distinguishing the subjective appearance from the objective reality, is simply convenience.

The argument gains added force when we consider the advantages of language, the value of which depends largely upon the ease with which it allows us to communicate with our fellow men. In order that communication may be achieved, a general rule of usage must be observed by people speaking the language. It must be objective in the sense that the various people using the language must apply the rule more or less in the same way. This applies to all language, even the language used to describe appearances and purely personal likes and dislikes. But it may also be found convenient to abstract from all cases the most variable conditions that govern appearances. We can then apply some more or less definite intersubjective standard or general rule. An object is red if it appears so to any spectator, given normal conditions of light and the normal state of a man's sense-organs. In judging size, we have standards of comparison that may be applied by those using the language; a conventional system of weights and measures is adopted. But there is no suggestion that anyone has invented and deliberately laid down a standard for the use of all words. As in the case of the artificial virtues, experience teaches us the advantages of language, and a tacit agreement to abide by the rules of language grows up. It is, indeed, natural to say that in Hume's view a correct use of language is one of the artificial virtues. Successful communication in individual cases depends upon a general adherence to the conventions that govern the rules of the language.

The case is precisely parallel in 'moral judgments'. We form the habit of looking upon a person's situation in such a way as to take into consideration only those characteristics that are independent of the special situation in which any one spectator may find himself. The acquisition of this habit of objectivity is also convenient, because it tends to eliminate the friction which arises in our arguments about the value of qualities of character, and which is due to our talking at cross purposes about them. The people arguing might have their attention focused upon different aspects of the person they are evaluating, because he is differently related to them and they might not be fully aware of this. One might be influenced by personal gratitude, the other might be harbouring an old grudge. The habit of disregarding your personal relation to the object does not necessarily eliminate all disagreement about the value of the object; but it will tend to decrease friction, because we are all more or less alike in being affected by the pleasure or pain of others through sympathy, although in somewhat unequal degrees. In many cases our habit of objectively judging a character may not determine our love or hatred, but it may still have an effect in modifying our conduct; for the objective view will make us realize the causes of the violent love or hatred we bear to a person. The objective judgment will arouse in us a calm passion, approval or disapproval, which may counteract the violent passions of love or hatred. If nothing else it may serve to regulate our language.

Thus Hume's theory has the merit of both explaining how we come to form 'objective moral judgments' or, indeed, judgments of value generally, and at the same time accounting for the fact that our actions very often go against our judgments. In some cases, this happens even though we have looked at the situation objectively: we may not be able to control our bias to favour unduly our children or friends although we know others to be more deserving.

There is also the case where our moral valuation is still biased although we may be quite sincere in pronouncing a person vicious or virtuous. We may have tried to be impartial, but owing to the similarity between the love and the hatred which arise from objective reflection and the biased variety, we may mistake the one for the other. We may think we really approve or disapprove, when in fact we only like or dislike, love or hate. Hume quite often mentions how we may mistake one passion for another which is similar, although a passion is a simple impression and thus revealed in consciousness just as it is. The mistake in a case like this consists only in the association of the wrong verbal expression with the impression we have. Approval and disapproval can be distinguished from other kinds of love and hatred by describing the circumstances in which they arise, and in this case it would seem that the special circumstance is that they arise from objective reflection on the object in question. That they are still a species of the class of passions we generally call love or hatred, helps to explain how it is possible to mistake ordinary love for approval and ordinary hate for disapproval. One can hardly doubt that in many cases we may genuinely think our feelings towards someone are righteous indignation, when in fact we detest him for different reasons. I think it would be misleading to say that, in all such cases, we know our feelings but do not know how to describe them.

Hume does not deny that there is something special about approval and disapproval considered as experiences – quite the contrary; for, as we have seen, he seems to insist upon this. I should like to quote a passage towards the end of the chapter on the Natural Virtues:

Now, in judging of characters, the only interest or pleasure which appears the same to every spectator, is that of the person himself whose character is examined, or that of persons who have a connection with him. And, though such interests and pleasures touch us more faintly than our own, yet, being more constant and universal, they counterbalance the latter even in practice, and are alone admitted in speculation as the standard of virtue and morality. They alone produce that particular feeling or sentiment on which moral distinctions depend.

As to the good or ill desert of virtue or vice, it is an evident consequence of the sentiments of pleasure or uneasiness. These sentiments produce love or hatred; and love or hatred, by the original constitution of human passion, is attended with benevolence or anger; that is, with a desire of making happy the person we love, and miserable the person we hate. We have treated of this more fully on another occasion. (THN III, 286/591)[1]

The other occasion referred to is, of course, the discussion of the passions in Book II, particularly the discussion of love and hatred, and their connection with benevolence or anger. This is by no means the only passage in Book III which shows the importance of the discussion of the passions.

One further point must be emphasized. When Hume refers to 'ex-

[1] It will be seen that Hume does not consistently adhere to the view that we always consider the interests of people affected by the character of the person whom we are evaluating. He has to admit that sometimes we do evaluate the character of someone when he, in fact, has no influence upon the interests of others. Here, as we shall soon see, the imagination must be appealed to.

tensive sympathy', and says that the sentiments of virtue depend upon it, he is not referring to any form of benevolence or desire for the happiness of another. He is simply referring to 'the principle of communication', which extends to all human beings, and which operates by resemblance, the one relation which has any force at all when we take up an objective point of view. It operates in virtue of the fact that all human beings resemble one another, even though the relation of causality (such as family relations), or that of contiguity in space or time, is absent. Hume can still hold, with absolute consistency, that there is no such passion as 'love of humanity merely as such', or desire for the happiness of every other human being. He is not making an appeal to altruism as an essential feature in human nature, if by this we mean a desire for the happiness of human kind, irrespective of their relation to us and their personal qualities. Extensive sympathy may serve to determine our approval or disapproval without determining our actions:

> Sentiments must touch the heart to make them control our passions: but they need not extend beyond the imagination, to make them influence our tastes. (THN III, 282/586)

Hume makes no sweeping assumptions as to the essentially egoistic or altruistic nature of man. He says only that the benevolent tendencies in man generally outweigh the egoistic. But when he says this he is not intimating any altruism in human nature. Many of the benevolent tendencies would be of essentially limited scope, and would involve, on the whole, a bias in favour of those closely related to us. If an altruist is a person who entirely devotes himself to the increase of happiness of human beings, other than himself, Hume would consider such a saintly being highly exceptional.

Hume always emphasizes the view that in so far as objects are valued for their utility, it is not the actual consequences but their 'seeming tendencies' that determine the mind to approve or disapprove. The reason for this is that in taking up an objective point of view, we approve or disapprove of the object because of its causal properties, and distinguish this from certain accidental circumstances which may prevent the effect from occurring on special occasions. This goes for all evaluation of the useful, and not only that peculiar evaluation we call moral. It is a misunderstanding of Hume's view to suggest that he holds that 'moral evaluation' is distinguished from other forms of valuation by being objective. Aesthetic valuation of inanimate objects is objective in exactly the same way: in distinguishing objective valuation from our subjective feeling, Hume takes, as an example, aesthetic 'judgment'.

It is worth while to point out that we must distinguish between admiration of an object, such as a work of art, and admiration for the artist as the originating cause of the work. It is possible that what we call approval may refer sometimes to a direct, and sometimes to an indirect, passion. In so far as this approval has people as its object, it is a special kind of love, an indirect passion. If the object were oneself, it would be a species of pride. In so far as we approve or disapprove of a work of art itself, the passions would arise immediately from pleasure or pain, communicated by sympathy, and would consequently be direct ones. Hume, we may remind ourselves, classifies 'the general appetite to good and aversion to evil' among the calm passions. It is possible he may be referring to the valuation of pleasant and painful results such as works of art; but, as we shall see more clearly when we come to discuss the artificial virtues, approval of results is not moral approval. Moral approval always has a person as its object. We can morally approve or disapprove of actions only as having their source in a person or a group of persons.

Let us now turn our attention to a 'remarkable circumstance' which is of the utmost importance for understanding the way in which sympathy helps to arouse the sentiments of morals. In describing the way sympathy operates, Hume initially wrote as if the thought of someone else's pain or pleasure comes, through sympathy, to be enlivened in such a way as to pain or please us. It would seem that we can only sympathize with actual pains and pleasures, or at least pains and pleasures *believed* to be actual. If, therefore, it is sympathy with the effects of qualities of mind that leads us to approve or disapprove, it would appear that our approval and disapproval must be determined by the actual consequences of actions, or at least by those consequences believed to be actual. But we saw, in an earlier chapter, how the principle of sympathy came to be modified. At first described as a principle of communication, it was seen to operate where there were no feelings to be communicated. This now becomes important, because virtue for Hume is a quality of mind or character. Surely this quality can remain unaltered, even though circumstances prevent the beneficial effects it would normally have.

Virtue in rags is still virtue; and the love which it procures attends a man into a dungeon or desert, where the virtue can no longer be exerted in action, and is lost to all the world. (THN III, 280/584)

Hume agrees that this is prima facie an objection to his system, for it
seems to be the case that

> if sympathy were the source of our esteem for virtue, that senti-
> ment of approbation could only take place where the virtue
> actually attained its end, and was beneficial to mankind.
> (THN III, 280/584)

But we approve of a dwelling house that is well adapted to its purpose,
and value a fertile soil and a good climate, even though the soil is
uncultivated and the climate belongs to an uninhabited island. We
approve of the generosity of a pauper, and the courage of an imprisoned
hero. We do so, because we judge character by reflection upon the
beneficial effects these qualities would have, if the normal effects of
these qualities were not hindered: 'It is sufficient if everything be
complete in the object itself' (THN III, 280/584). No changes in the
consequences, other than those that result from an alteration in the
object to be evaluated, will have any effect upon an evaluation. In
accounting for this, Hume has to have recourse to the imagination:

> The imagination has a set of passions belonging to it, upon which
> our sentiments of beauty much depend. These passions are moved
> by degrees of liveliness and strength, which are inferior to *belief*,
> and independent of the real existence of their objects.
> (THN III, 280/585)

It is, therefore, the *fittingness* of the object to have beneficial effects,
that determines our evaluation of it. We are, that is to say, determined
in our evaluation by the kinds of effects the quality in question would
have as a general rule, and not by the actual effects of the characteristic
in the particular case under consideration.

It is instructive to see that Hume here talks of the ideas that move
the passions as inferior to belief in strength and liveliness. He talks as
if no belief is involved in our actual evaluations according to general
rules. This is clearly not the case, and Hume's statement depends upon
a somewhat narrow conception of belief. What we believe, when our
approval is determined by a general rule, is that certain beneficial
effects would follow *if certain specifiable conditions were absent*, such as
a man's imprisonment or his poverty. It clearly has nothing to do with
whether we think the beneficial effects will, in fact, occur; for our
approval is not determined by whether we think the man will be re-
leased from prison, or will meet with financial success. This important
point is not made clearly by Hume, and is obscured by his mention of

the imagination as 'inferior' to belief, by his claim that we are here only dealing with a 'species of probability' as opposed to belief. The fact is that the belief in this hypothetical proposition is not merely a weaker form of conviction as to the likely occurrence of something. Perhaps Hume wants to convey this by saying that the ideas of the imagination which affect our passions are, in this case, 'independent of the real existence of their objects'; but he does not make the point clearly. When our evaluation is determined by the imagination it is still a belief that determines it and not something inferior to belief; our belief is in the truth of a conditional statement. Thus, if we believed that the absence of the restricting conditions would not tend to make a man behave in a way which would have beneficial effects, we should no longer approve of him. If the imprisonment, for example, kills the hero's spirit we might pity him, and he would now no longer be a courageous man in our eyes.

But Hume is right in emphasizing that, by judging a man as virtuous or vicious, we are talking about his character and discounting the accidental circumstances that may affect his actions. We might count as equally generous the pauper who gives a cigarette to a friend, and the wealthy man who gives hundreds of pounds to charities. It is perfectly true that Hume writes at some length about our esteem for the rich and the powerful; he certainly thinks the rich are valued more highly because of their riches. Yet I doubt if even Hume, who extends the notion of virtue more than most writers, would count 'being rich' a *moral* characteristic. It is, after all, not a 'quality of mind'.

Remembering our discussion of sympathy in an earlier chapter, it should not surprise us that, in so far as it operates in accounting for approval and disapproval, sympathy is misleadingly described as a principle of *communication*, for we are affected by sympathy in cases where the pain or pleasure sympathized with is not actual:

When I run over a book with my eye, I imagine I hear it all; and also, by the force of imagination, enter into the uneasiness which the delivery of it *would give the speaker*.[1] The uneasiness is not real. (THN III, 281/585-6)

We may be pained by the reading of the book because the expressions used have a tendency to cause pain, and we consequently talk of the style as 'harsh and disagreeable'. These terms express disapproval, and are a condemnation of the style and not just an expression of personal

[1] My italics.

preference, for we are being determined in our evaluation by the effect the book would have as a general rule.

We can see that sympathy is involved in these evaluations, but it is once again clear that we cannot identify this principle with 'limited generosity' or benevolence; these are motives in man that need not determine our actions, even though sympathy has made us approve or disapprove of a particular object:

> My sympathy with another may give me the sentiment of pain and disapprobation, when any object is presented that has a tendency to give him uneasiness; though I may not be willing to sacrifice anything of my own interest, or cross any of my passions, for his satisfaction. A house may displease me by being ill contrived for the convenience of the owner; and yet I may refuse to give a shilling towards the rebuilding of it. Sentiments must touch the heart, to make them control our passions: but they need not extend beyond the imagination, to make them influence our taste. (THN III, 281-2/586)

This quotation may also serve to show why I think that the following statement by Mrs Warnock is misleading:

> One of the differences between attitudes and even the calm passions seems to me to be that we do not necessarily *act* as a result of adopting some attitude. (PAS 1957 (SV) 48)

She goes on to emphasize that Hume thinks of the passions as motives. This is odd, in view of the fact that none of the four indirect passions – pride, humility, love, hatred – is for Hume a motive.

The distinction drawn between taste and passions in this last quotation from Hume may be thought to go against my view that approval and disapproval are passions. But one can hardly take this objection seriously when one remembers that Hume has a little earlier, in talking about approval and disapproval, made reference to 'a set of passions' belonging to the imagination. He obviously means us to understand 'approval' and 'disapproval' as naming passions; and, indeed he has told us that they are nothing but a species of love and hatred. We may also remind ourselves that love and hatred are not motives as such. We may love someone, as we may approve of him, without giving any thought to his happiness. This also makes it clear that Hume could not give an analysis of approval and disapproval in terms of a disposition to act in a particular way. Approval and disapproval do not necessarily involve any disposition to behave in one way rather than another. All behaviour is only contingently connected with the passions. The point is, in some ways, important for its bearing upon the problem of testing sincerity.

If a man disapproves of a government's racial policies one has a certain uneasiness about the view that he cannot *really* disapprove unless he is willing to do something to ameliorate the lot of a persecuted minority. Would this be conclusive evidence that he was insincere? One may hesitate to accept this view, because a man may, through weakness of will fail to live up to his standards of value. The problem is complicated by the fact that we recognize that a man both may deceive himself as to what he values and may act against his 'better judgment'.

It thus seems we have deliberate deceit, self-deception and weakness of will. A way of detecting the presence of the first is by the inconsistency between a man's avowed evaluations and his actual behaviour. If a man has a great deal to gain by evaluating in one way and behaving in another, and tries to hide the inconsistency, one would tend to suspect deliberate deceit. Yet in some such cases it is possible the man may be deceiving himself: he may believe that there are good grounds for his apparently inconsistent behaviour; but one suspects that such rationalization of behaviour indicates only a limited self-deception. The situation is very similar to that involving weakness of will, except that, when suspecting weakness of will, one would look for some evidence of effort on the part of the man to live up to his ideals.

To convict a man of insincerity is difficult, and one would tend to say that only fairly consistent behaviour, incompatible with the avowed evaluation, would be conclusive. We need less behavioural evidence if a man acts against his evaluations when under no temptation to do so. If a man, in what he believed to be a secret ballot were known to vote against a government on a specific issue, one would, it seems, have fairly conclusive evidence that he does not approve of the government's policy on this issue. This presumes that the man does not suspect that his vote may come to be known, and that, in other respects, he knows what he is doing.

I would not deny that a man's behaviour is generally a better guide to what he values than his verbal pronouncements. It would be absurd to make such a denial, for the simple reason that a man is not always the best judge himself as to how strongly he approves or disapproves. He cannot decide this by a simple introspection; he may have to be put to the test. He may even put himself to the test. He may genuinely believe that he would be willing to make considerable sacrifices for the sake of his convictions; yet other people may know his character better than he himself does, and realize that his approval or disapproval is only half-hearted.

These considerations show, I think, the weakness of construing approval and disapproval as occurrent feelings, whose nature and strength a man can determine by attending to his conscious state of mind. It is not, of course, obvious that Hume is committed to this view. The strength of our approval might be determined by the tendency of the 'calm passions' to regulate conduct rather than by the *violence* of the emotion involved, although the sensation of the passion is always decisive in deciding its identity. I would, however, hesitate to say that a man disapproved *strongly* of any form of racial persecution, if he never got emotionally roused by glaring cases of injustice and racial murders, however consistently he worked for improved racial relations. There are other possible motives for such behaviour. The man who strongly disapproves of something is not just expected to behave in a certain way: he is also expected to feel in a certain way. For we must admit that we know what it feels like to approve or disapprove strongly of something in one sense, and yet when the question of the strength of our feelings arises we may accept behaviour as a test of this. If this is admitted, we see that neither analysis in purely behavioural terms, nor the construction of approval simply as a feeling, can be counted as wholly satisfactory. We may again think that Hume tends to over-simplify the issue by construing such passions as approval as simple impressions, and by thinking of the motives as only contingently connected with these passions; this would make it possible for genuine approval or disapproval to be consistent with *any* behaviour. But although the criteria based on behaviour may not always decide the issue, the fact that sometimes they are taken to be decisive would show this analysis to be mistaken.

I have already stressed that in so far as we approve or disapprove of people, these passions can be construed as species of love and hatred. Hume emphasizes that the peculiarly moral sentiments arise only from contemplation of tendencies of character, one's own special position being disregarded. Such approval and disapproval commonly involve less emotional intensity than love and hatred based on close connections with the agent. Yet the former may give rise to stronger motives.

This is one of the facts that lead him to talk a great deal about calm passions; we have seen how important he thinks it is to distinguish calmness from lack of motivating power.

When considering the notion of desert, Hume again stresses the close relation between the approval and disapproval of persons, and love and hatred. The pleasure or uneasiness that the contemplation of tendencies of actions produces leads us to love or hate (approve of or disapprove of) the agent. These passions are, by nature, closely allied to benevolence or anger, and this is why we think virtue deserves happiness, and vice deserves to be punished.

We may not be satisfied with this account of desert, for we may think that a crime deserves punishment or that a man deserves reward, without desiring ourselves to punish or reward. There is an obvious difference between thinking that a man deserves to be made happy and wanting to make him happy; but Hume clearly has in mind his discussion of the passions in the part of Book III we have been considering.

Hume's interpretation of approval and disapproval and the reasons he gives for their occurrence makes it more intelligible how sympathy helps to explain our approval of the useful virtues. It is curious that one of the accepted versions of Hume's view of the nature of approval and disapproval completely fails to give a satisfactory account of this.

The indirect passions have an object which is not an end to be achieved. The object is that which I am proud of, or that which I love, because of certain qualities belonging to or closely related to that object. In a similar way, I approve of a person possessed of certain qualities of character, when these please me in a special way. The pleasures thus derived may vary, and this variety gives rise to differences in my approval, indicated by the use of different terms, such as 'love', 'respect', 'esteem'. Though these arise according to the same principles, and may in a sense involve the approval of a character, yet their *feeling* is different. Sympathy accounts partly for the way in which qualities of character come to please us or displease us. My sympathy with the pleasure or pain of those affected by a quality of character is not the same as my approval or disapproval, but it does enter in as a causal element. In the same way my sympathy with the pleasure a rich man derives from his wealth is not my esteem of him; but some commentators seem to find it difficult to appreciate this fact because they think that Hume is reducing the moral sense to a species of sympathy, and they are troubled by the obvious fact that his account of the function of sympathy as a principle of communication, and his appeal to the imagination, make this reduction impossible. For the doctrine that approval is a sympathetic consciousness of pleasure appears to entail that we could only approve of pleasure. But Hume's doctrine in the *Treatise* is not that we approve of pleasure as good and think that other things are good only as a means to this. The experience of pleasure enters into the causal genesis of the passion which constitutes the evaluation. The process is conceived of in quite mechanical rather than teleological terms.

The Swedish philosopher Ingemar Hedenius insists that Hume's attempt to 'reduce the moral sense to a more general principle, that of sympathy, inevitably leads to an interpretation of all sympathy as moral approval or disapproval' (SHE, 461). This is repeated again and again as an indubitable Humean doctrine. We are told that 'he is not unfamiliar with the idea that sympathy is the same as moral consciousness, and that sympathy as such is moral approval or censure' (SHE, 460). And again we are told that not only is he committed to the view 'that consciousness of something as a virtue or a vice is a sympathetic consciousness of the pleasure or pain of others, but that the sympathetic consciousness also necessarily constitutes moral approval or censure' (SHE, 461). It is not to be wondered at that Hedenius goes on to complain 'that the moral valuation of the majority of virtues, and indeed the most important ones, cannot be a sympathetic consciousness at all'.

What is Hedenius' evidence for his view that Hume identifies approval and disapproval with 'sympathetic consciousness'? Needless to say, he draws all his evidence from passages in the *Enquiry Concerning the Principles of Morals*. This is unfortunate for several reasons. It could claim to be an authoritative account of Hume's view only in his later work, and it may well be that the term 'sympathy' does not always bear the same sense in the *Enquiry* as in the *Treatise*. In the *Enquiry* Hume omits to explain in any detail the causes of our passions, including approval and disapproval. I do not propose to consider whether Hedenius' interpretation is correct as far as the *Enquiry* is concerned; I want only to reject the notion that Hume teaches in the *Treatise* that moral consciousness is a form of sympathy. Although Hedenius *supports* his interpretation by reference to the *Enquiry*, he does not clearly suggest that Hume's view in the *Treatise* is totally different; but he does suggest in outline, although he does not accept, the interpretation of Hume's views on approval and disapproval that I have adopted:

Hume seems here to have combined two lines of thought that are incompatible. Moral approval is sympathy. The sympathy in which the approval here consists is explicitly defined as a sympathy with the happiness that is the effect of the useful virtues. But, on the other hand, the object of sympathetic approval cannot of course be anything but the useful virtue itself.

Hedenius continues:

From Hume's point of view the only possible solution of this problem would seem to be to assume that the moral valuation of useful virtues is not a simple sympathetic consciousness but a complex process in which sympathy merely enters as an element. It would then seem a fairly obvious method to interpret the approval of the social virtues on the analogy of the theory on which Hume explains 'love' and 'pride'. (SHE, 467)

It is only his conviction that Hume identifies approval with sympathy that prevents Hedenius from accepting the solution he suggests above and which in my view represents a correct interpretation of Hume's doctrine in the *Treatise*.

Hume maintains that 'we are never to consider any single action in our inquiries concerning the origin of morals, but only the quality of character from which the action proceeded'; but his reason for holding this view is not that it is the motive, occurring in consciousness as a desire or a passion, that we either approve of or sympathize with, but rather that the quality of character from which the action proceeded must be *durable* enough to affect our sentiments concerning the person. An action, considered merely as such, is not closely enough related to the person responsible for it unless it is seen to be a legitimate sign of a motive or quality of character in him. Motives and intentions make a person a candidate for moral appraisal. The character or qualities of mind of another person are known only from experience, and thus we would say of a person who had shown consistent benevolence in his past actions that an action which led to an increase in unhappiness performed by him did not justify the inference that malice was the motive. As a consequence of this, such incidental uncharacteristic actions do not determine our love or hatred, approval or disapproval of the person.

In showing why intentionality is important in determining love and hatred, Hume's arguments follow a similar course: 'By the intention we judge of the actions; and, according as that is good or bad, they become causes of love or hatred' (THN II, 68/348). Now it is not the intentionality as such which causes love or hatred, for in many cases, where the quality in a person which pleases or displeases us is very constant, love may be aroused although there is no intention. The intention becomes important in dealing with individual actions because 'an intention shows certain qualities, remaining after the action is performed'. It is as a sign of some qualities of character that the intentionality becomes important, for it shows a close relation between the agent and his actions. Motives are important for precisely the same reason.

Hume makes it quite clear that when an action is accidental the relation between it and the person as its 'immediate' cause is too loose. But he is equally clear that no conscious design or purpose need be present in the person's mind in order that love or hatred may be aroused as a result of an action. It is not sympathy with the agent's conscious state in acting which constitutes our approval or disapproval, whether this is conceived of as a motive or an intention, although this may contribute to the creation of love or hatred, approval or disapproval. In order to refute the notion that Hume believes approval to be 'sympathy with a motive', it is perhaps sufficient to mention that motives which are unpleasant may be approved of. 'Anger and hatred are passions inherent in our very frame and constitution. The want of them, on some occasions, may even be a proof of weakness and imbecility' (THN III, 299/605). It is clear from this that we may disapprove of a character because the absence of an essentially unpleasant motive may be an indication of a characteristic which tends not to have felicitous results. We are most certainly not committed to disapproving other people's disapproval, although this passion is an unpleasant one. This is easily intelligible when we remember that such disapproval may be a sign of a quality of mind or character which tends to have beneficial results.

Let us remind ourselves of the following points about my own interpretation: (1) In his *Treatise* Hume is not concerned to give a reductive analysis of the basic notions of moral evaluation, approval and disapproval. These are passions, simple impressions, that cannot be reductively analysed. (2) It is important to see that evaluations could not, on his principles, be reduced to species of sympathy. Approval and disapproval are passions; the sympathy that enters into the explanation of the occurrence of these passions is a principle and not a passion. (3) It is sympathy with the effects of qualities of mind or character (or what one thinks would in normal circumstances be their effect) that leads to the occurrence of a passion which is directed to a person as its object. The evaluation *consists* in this passion. What is sympathized with, and what is approved of, are thus always different, according to this account. (4) We must pay attention to motives because the motive gives us information about the character of the person. The object of the approval or disapproval, however, is not a motive but a person.

II

In Chapter 3, I mentioned that the account Hume gives of the function of sympathy in moral evaluation differs materially from the views of Adam Smith as expressed in his *Theory of Moral Sentiments*. Although Hume did not think that moral evaluation could be analysed as sympathy with people's motives, there are *some* grounds for attributing such a doctrine to Adam Smith. I shall make no attempt to do full justice to Smith's complex doctrines; I want to say only enough about his views to indicate how he differed from Hume, with regard to both the nature of sympathy, and the way it is related to moral evaluation. It is not altogether implausible to maintain that Smith held the view that moral consciousness can be 'reduced to a species of sympathy', although this is undoubtedly not Hume's doctrine in the *Treatise*.

In so far as we sympathize with people's sorrows Adam Smith claims that this involves putting ourselves in their shoes:

Neither can that faculty [the imagination] help us to this any
other way, than by representing to us what would be our own, if
we were in his case. It is the impressions of our own senses only,
not those of his, which our imaginations copy. (TMS, 9)

Smith appears to be making two points, both of which seem to agree with Hume's account of the operation of sympathy. In sympathizing, (1) we come to have the same feeling as the person with whom we sympathize, and (2) our imagination must depend upon copying our own previous sensations and emotions. As in the case of Hume's account, one feels like objecting that it cannot be a necessary condition for sympathizing that the sympathizer has had exactly the same experience as the person with whom he is sympathizing. One could at most demand, for example, that a sympathizer must have had some experience of suffering in order to be in a position to sympathize with others. One might want to make this a necessary condition for knowing what suffering is. To demand that the sympathizer must have experienced the same kind of emotion or feeling seems absurd. One may sympathize with a person suffering from toothache although one has never had toothache oneself. When thinking of sympathy simply as a principle of communication, one could say that in so far as toothache is a special kind of feeling, one has to have experienced it to know what toothache is. Smith, however, minimizes our tendency to sympathize with pain where it is not accompanied by danger. We have a much greater tendency to sympathize with fear than with bodily pain: 'The gout or the toothache, though exquisitely painful, excite very little sympathy; more dangerous diseases, though accompanied with very little pain, excite the highest' (TMS, 29. See also TMS, 125). If by 'sympathy' is meant pity, I see no reason for thinking that Smith is correct. If, however, sympathy involves corresponding experiences in the sympathizer and the person with whom he sympathizes, there is a difficulty about sympathy with physically caused experiences. 'The frame of my body can be but little affected by the alterations which are brought about upon that of my companion: but my imagination is more ductile, and more readily assumes, if I may say so, the shape and configuration of the imaginations of those with whom I am familiar' (TMS, 28). But Smith's account is strikingly different from Hume's doctrine in certain respects. The following quotation makes it clear that Smith thinks of 'pity' and 'compassion' as terms that stand for a special sort of sympathy:

> Pity and compassion are words appropriated to signify our fellow-feeling with the sorrow of others. Sympathy, though its meaning was, perhaps, originally the same, may now, however, without much impropriety, be made use of to denote our fellow-feeling with any passion whatever. (TMS, 11)

Smith's 'sympathy with sorrow' is the same as pity or compassion, whereas pity, or compassion, is, on Hume's account, a special passion not reducible to sympathy. Hume's own principle of sympathy or communication, however, involves coming to have the emotions of the person with whom one is sympathizing, and in this it resembles Smith's account of sympathy. But there is a material difference between the two accounts, for Hume's basic principle of sympathy does not work through an imaginary change of place with another person. An idea of another's suffering comes, according to Hume, to be real suffering, because of the influence of the impressions of the self. Smith, on the other hand, bids us consider what we should feel were we in the sufferer's place. But it might be possible to do this and conclude that we should not suffer at all—or very little. There may be a difference between the sufferer and myself that would help to explain this: I might be very insensitive to the kind of thing that makes him suffer intensely. Smith is aware of this, and it appears that he is maintaining that, in sympathizing, we imagine that we are just like the other person:

By the imagination we place ourselves in his situation, we conceive ourselves enduring all the same torments, we enter, as it were, into his body, and become in some measure the same person with him, and thence form some idea of his sensations, and even feel something which, though weaker in degree, is not altogether unlike them. (TMS, 9)

The following point is worth mentioning in this connection. Smith seems to be suggesting that the sympathy consists in the feelings you have, when you imagine yourself as enduring all the unpleasant experiences of the other person. The thought of what you would feel were you, so to speak, inside the other person's skin, leads to a feeling *now*. It is this feeling that constitutes the sympathy. The thought of the other's suffering makes us 'tremble and shudder'.

In support of the contention that compassion with suffering is explained by imaginary change of place, Smith mentions several phenomena, some of which appear to have little to do with compassion or pity. Among these may be mentioned the way in which people sway in sympathy with a dancer on a slack-rope. Although we may sway in sympathy with such a person, we are no more likely to pity him than we are to envy him; the fact is not in question: 'The mob, when they are gazing at a dancer on the slack-rope, naturally writhe and twist, and balance their own bodies, as they see him do, and as they feel they themselves must do, if in his situation' (TMS, 10). Other cases mentioned are sympathy with miserable 'beggars in the street', and the way in which we draw back our foot when we see a blow aimed at the leg of another. It is fairly obvious that only in the case of the beggars do we have something approaching pity. But does the sympathy in any of these cases consist in an imaginary change of place, which Smith calls an illusion of the imagination? Dugald Stewart had this interesting observation to make:

In the instance of the rope dancer, the most pertinent of all of them [the examples] to Mr Smith's purpose, the sympathy which accompanies the movements of the performers is extremely analogous to what is exhibited on various other occasions, where this theory cannot be supposed to apply. A person, for example, who

plays at bowls, and who is deeply interested in the game, while he
follows his bowl with the eye, naturally accompanies its deflections
from the rectilinear course, with correspondent motions of his
body; although it cannot well be imagined, that, in doing so, he
conceives himself to be projected from his own hand, and rolling
along the ground like the object about which his thoughts are too
strongly engrossed. (EPHM III, 130-1)

Yet it must be said that, in some way, the person here is identifying
himself with the bowl. When he thinks it is going off course, he leans
in the other direction to correct its movement. He does what he wants
the bowl to do. Of course, he does not imagine what it feels like to be a
bowl – it does not feel like anything. But Smith, presumably, would
want to say that he imagines what it would be like to be a bowl, and
retain his own consciousness, sensitivities and intelligence. I leave it
to the reader to make sense of this suggestion. Smith soon notes that
sympathy 'does not arise so much from the view of the passion, as from
that of the situation which excites it' (TMS, 12). Thus we are often
embarrassed by the rudeness of a person who is entirely unaware of
the impropriety of his conduct; this is also noted by Hume. But the
important point is that in a case like this we could not imagine that we
were the other person, with all his psychological characteristics, for
then we should presumably be as insensitive to the situation as he is.
But we do blush for him 'because we cannot help feeling with what
confusion we ourselves should be covered, had we behaved in so absurd
a manner' (TMS, 12). Thus it seems we must understand the imaginative substitution of place differently in different cases: in sympathizing
with sorrow we must imagine that we have the sensitivities of the
other person; our sympathy with the man for whom we are embarrassed, involves imagining ourselves in his place with our own sensitivities. But it is not altogether easy to see how we sympathize with the
dead, the mentally deranged, or young babies. In each case, we imagine
ourselves in the other individual's place, with all our own mental
powers and sensitivities. Thus the mother imagines all the great cala-
mities that might be in store for her child, who is in no position to
appreciate the possible significance of his suffering. Dealing with our
sympathy with the dead, Smith writes:

The idea of that dreary and endless melancholy, which the fancy
naturally ascribes to their condition, arises altogether from our
joining to the change which has been produced upon them, our

own consciousness of that change, from our putting ourselves in their situation, and from our lodging, if I may be allowed to say so, our own living souls in their inanimated bodies, and thence conceiving what would be our emotions in this case. (TMS, 13)

Smith describes this as an illusion of the imagination. It is an illusion, indeed, for one cannot easily see how one could use the method described, when the bodies of the dead have finally disintegrated. The model of a substitution of place does not seem to fit here at all. It would seem possible to sympathize with those that die and are cremated in just the same way as we might sympathize with those buried. Yet there is here no question of lodging 'our own living souls in their inanimated bodies'.

It may be said that the sympathizing consists in the work of the imagination and in no way depends upon the actual existence of dead bodies. And is it not simply that the horror of death is partly derived from images such as lying in the grave or being thrust into an oven in the crematorium? This may be so; yet one feels that whether or not one can sympathize with the dead, and that if one can what form the sympathy takes, depends very much upon one's beliefs about life hereafter. If one thinks that death involves total lack of consciousness, one pities the person for the deprivation, and this could not consist in imagining what one would feel or think were one devoid of consciousness. The suggestion involves a contradiction. If, on the other hand, one believes in life hereafter and considers that a dead person is suffering, then compassion with him would not seem to involve any imaginary substitution of place involving his dead body unless one thinks that his consciousness after death is somehow tied to the body. But one cannot make sense of the idea of a person's consciousness being tied to the particles of a disintegrated body. Personal consciousness is not divisible in the way in which particles of matter are.

We can now turn our attention to Smith's account of sympathy as approval. He suggests that we judge the propriety of a person's feelings or character by considering what we should feel if we were in his place. The following quotations illustrate the point: 'If we hear a person loudly lamenting his misfortunes, which however, upon bringing the case home to ourselves, we feel, can produce no such violent effect upon us, we are shocked at his grief; and, because we cannot enter into it, call it pusillanimity and weakness' (TMS, 15-16). And a little later he writes 'We are even put out of humour if our companion laughs louder or longer at a joke than we think it deserves; that is, than we feel that we ourselves could laugh at it' (TMS, 16).

It seems fairly clear that this analysis is untenable as it stands, although it may be true that there is a sense in which a person who laughs with me at a joke 'cannot well deny the propriety of my laughter'. He may see that the joke is a bad joke, although he laughs at it. He may believe that he has a somewhat unusual sense of humour and on that account refuse to take his own laughter as a standard of merit. It is, of course, very much more obvious that if you take propriety to mean 'what is socially proper', one's own laughter may be thought socially very improper by oneself. One may feel ashamed of laughing at a person whose ludicrous movements are due to a physical deformity. One often laughs in spite of one's better judgment.

Our sympathy varies in these cases according to the nature of the cause of the emotion, but not equally so in all cases. The fury of the angry man leads us to consider the feelings of those with whom he is angry. This tends to counteract our inclination to sympathize with his anger. In fact, it is doubtful whether we have any tendency at all to sympathize with a man's anger. When we imagine ourselves in his place, we may come to realize that the provocation *justified* his anger. Can we describe this as considering what we should feel if we were in his situation? If we think we should be angry, we might want to say that we cannot but sympathize with a man's anger. But here 'sympathize with' would be somewhat different from merely 'having a fellow-feeling'. It has come to mean something very much more like 'approve of'. We sometimes do say to someone else 'But would you not be angry?' in order to get agreement about the justification of a man's fury. But here, I think, one of two situations will in fact be found to obtain: (1) One may be implying a value judgment. One may, in fact, be using this form of words to ask whether the person would not feel justified in becoming angry. (2) On the other hand, this question may not be used in order to get the person to agree that the man did right to be angry. 'Would you not have been angry?' may be a plea for a certain indulgence: 'Don't you think you should be less hard on him? There was considerable provocation', etc. It is, as I have already mentioned, sometimes thought that a man is hardly in a position to disapprove if he would have shown the same characteristics he is condemning in another.

Even though we cannot sympathize with a man's anger unless we know what caused it, this does not mean that such emotions as grief and joy are entirely different. It is true that anger points beyond itself, and sympathy with the objects of our anger tends to oppose sympathy with the anger. There is no such opposition in the case of grief and joy, because these emotions are not aimed at an object in the way in which anger is. Yet unless we know the causes of grief and joy our sympathy is very *imperfect*. Here one must be careful to interpret 'imperfect' correctly. It is not that our grief is necessarily increased by knowing the cause. We may, in fact, find that we cannot sympathize with the grief if it arose from some trifling matter or was due to the man's own stupidity. What must be meant by the sympathy not being complete in these cases, is that we feel we are not in a position to judge the propriety of the emotion unless we know its cause. It is relevant to know the object as well as the cause; for we would not sympathize with the anger of a man towards someone who in no way seems to have been responsible for the cause of the anger. We would disapprove of a man who becomes angry with his children because, for example, his boss has reprimanded him. People are affected by the strength of the general tendency people have to sympathize with different emotions. What we consider the proper degree of an emotion is to a great extent determined by the general tendency people have to sympathize with that emotion. There is little tendency to sympathize with people's anger, and we therefore try to control our anger. We want the sympathy of others, which is a source of comfort, and we want to bring our emotions to a level others can sympathize with.

We have seen that sympathy may be equated with compassion or pity in some cases, but not in all. We further saw that sympathy, as it occurs when we feel embarrassed for a person, must involve a different kind of imaginary change of place from sympathy when it is equated with pity. But sympathy also sometimes comes close in nature to approval.

Approval and disapproval of emotions are described by Smith as involving a certain comparison of emotions, and an instructive analogy is drawn to approval and disapproval of opinions:

> To approve of another man's opinions is to adopt those opinions, and to adopt them is to approve of them. If the same arguments which convince you convince me likewise, I necessarily approve of your conviction; and if they do not, I necessarily disapprove of it: neither can I possibly conceive that I should do the one without

the other. To approve or disapprove, therefore, of the opinions of
others is acknowledged, by every body, to mean no more than to
observe their agreement or disagreement with our own. But this
is equally the case with regard to our approbation or disapprobation of the sentiments or passions of others. (TMS, 17)

Let us now consider this more closely. It is obvious that by 'approving
of a man's opinions' Smith does not mean 'approving of a man for
holding certain opinions'. I might admire a man for his stubborn
loyalty: I might admire him for refusing to believe me when I tell him
of his wife's infidelity. I admire him for remaining loyal to his conception of the fidelity of his wife. But, in this case, I do not agree with the
man's opinions of his wife, for I believe what I told him was true, and
yet approve of his refusal to believe it.

To adopt a man's opinions would normally be thought to consist in
believing or considering to be true what the other person believes or
considers to be true. My adoption of someone else's opinion need not
be taken here as equivalent to being persuaded by him; it is enough
that I should come to have them by being convinced by the same arguments that convinced him. In order to approve his opinion I must know
what his opinion is. For, although I may hold the same opinion as he
does, I cannot approve of it unless I perceive the identity, and it is in
this that the approval is supposed to consist.

It would seem from the above that sympathy simply consists in having certain opinions in common. It is certainly far removed from pity,
or rejoicing because of another's good fortune. I can sympathize with
the point of view of a political party, without thinking they are in either
a precarious or a strong position. If, therefore, approbation of sentiments is comparable, it amounts to noticing that I sympathize with the
sentiments of someone else, in that I have the same sentiments in
similar situations. If the man laughs when I laugh, I cannot withhold
my approval.

'The man whose sympathy keeps time to my grief cannot but admit
the reasonableness of my sorrow' (TMS, 16). Smith seems here to
vacillate between the notion of correspondence of actual emotions, and
consideration of what would be his emotion if he were in the person's
situation. When I consider this and try to imagine my reaction, it is
not necessary that any emotion need arise in my breast now with
which I can compare the emotion of the person who is the object of my
judgment. It is possible that when I compare the person's emotion

with what I think would be my emotion, this may arouse in myself an emotion of approval. Smith, in fact, sometimes talks as if there are always two passions involved in these cases. Referring to a letter from Hume written in July 1759 (LDH I, 313) Smith writes:

It has been objected to me that as I found the sentiment of approbation, which is always agreeable, upon sympathy, it is inconsistent with my system to admit any disagreeable sympathy. I answer that in the sentiment of approbation there are two things to be taken notice of; first, the sympathetic passion of the spectator; and, secondly, the emotion which arises from his observing the perfect coincidence between this sympathetic passion in himself, and the original passion in the person principally concerned. This last emotion, in which the sentiment of approbation properly consists, is always agreeable and delightful. The other may either be agreeable or disagreeable, according to the nature of the original passion, whose features it must always in some measure retain. (TMS, footnote 44)

Here it seems approval does not just consist in noting the coincidence of emotions: it consists in an emotion that arises when this coincidence is noted. Furthermore, it seems obvious that there must be a causal relation of some sort between the original passion and our sympathetically aroused passion. How else could the latter be said to retain some of the features of the former?

In this case, as in the former, the approval itself cannot be thought of as a species of sympathy, although in the one case the approval consists of a comparison, whereas in the other it is the emotion arising from the comparison that we call approval. I do not think 'spectator' here means 'impartial spectator': the context appears to indicate that it more probably refers to any person who is evaluating the actions or character of another agent. But it is more important to notice that Smith's view seems to be that approval is a sentiment arising from sympathy, but that it is not to be equated with sympathy.

But let us now consider whether Smith is right in classifying together approval of anger and approval of opinions in the way in which he does. In so far as we are committed to sharing a man's opinions if we approve of them, this is so only because we approve of opinions according to whether they are true or false. If I do not hold the opinion I obviously cannot approve of it for its truth. But in the case of anger, I may perfectly well approve of a person's anger without in any sense sharing it. It is true that if I do share it I may tend to approve of it; but this is so only because we tend to approve of our own anger – at least while we are angry. I might, on the other hand, notice that I become angered by the same thing as someone else and at the same time disapprove of both my own anger and his.

But Smith seemingly does not think that approval, in all cases, consists of considering the identity of one's own and another's feelings or emotions. I may not laugh at a joke because I happen to be in a particularly bad mood; but I still approve of it because 'We are sensible that upon most occasions we should very heartily join in it'. Approval here seems to consist of a comparison between someone's emotion and what we think we should feel upon most occasions. It still is the case that 'I judge of your sight by my sight, of your ear by my ear, of your reason by my reason, of your resentment by my resentment, of your love by my love. I neither have, nor can have, any other way of judging about them' (TMS, 18).

'Judging about' means considering the correctness of, for example, the visual judgment, or the appropriateness of the emotion. But, in fact, one does not take one's own vision as a standard of correctness in vision. I might know that my sight is faulty in various ways. It is not by considering what I should see upon specifiable occasions that I determine the standard for correct vision. This would be a plausible account of the situation only if there were, in fact, as many criteria as there are variations in the sharpness of the senses. The same would apply to emotions.

I cannot, therefore, agree with Smith's view when he says in criticizing the Utilitarian view: 'Originally . . . we approve of another man's judgment, not as something useful, but as right, as accurate, as agreeable to truth and reality: and it is evident we attribute these qualities to it for no other reason but because we find that it agrees with our own. Taste, in the same manner, is originally approved of, not as useful, but as just, as delicate, and as precisely suited to its object' (TMS, 20).

Spectators never have, in sympathizing with sorrow, precisely the same kind of feeling as the person principally concerned. The consciousness that the situation that gives rise to it is imaginary makes the sympathetic emotion different in kind and not only in degree.

Our sense of the propriety of actions arises, according to Smith, from what he calls 'a direct sympathy with the affections and motives of the person who acts . . .' (TMS, 68). The sense of the merit of an action arises from what he calls 'an indirect sympathy with the gratitude of the person who is . . . acted upon' (TMS, 68). It is, in fact, a 'compound' sentiment made up of two emotions; 'a direct sympathy with the sentiments of the agent, and an indirect sympathy with the gratitude of those who receive the benefit of his actions' (TMS, 68).

This statement is curious; for surely the merit of a man's actions cannot depend upon the gratitude of those whom he benefits. We soon find that this is realized by Smith. The question to ask becomes: Do I feel gratitude when I bring the case home to myself? It is enough then that the emotions of the beneficiary would correspond with this if he were grateful. This is, Smith says, a case of illusive sympathy.

But is it a case of sympathy at all? It seems that any emotion that arises from considering yourself in the situation of another is a case of sympathy, whatever the other person is feeling. Here I am not at all certain that Smith rightly describes the situation. I imagine myself in the situation of a man who has received a certain benefit. Can I, in such a situation, feel gratitude towards the person who has benefited him? It is true that I may believe that I would feel gratitude, if placed in that situation. But I do not think any sympathetically induced gratitude of mine gives rise to my approval of the person's benefactor. Would it be true, in any sense, if I said I am grateful to him? I can only be grateful to people who have benefited either myself or someone closely associated with me. I am grateful to him because he was kind to my son. Can I become grateful to him because he was kind to just anybody?

If the only sympathy involved here is that in which 'to sympathize' is almost, if not completely, synonymous with 'to approve of', it can hardly be used to throw any light on the latter. We are able to approve of a benefactor when no one at all is feeling any gratitude. This would seem to cast some doubt upon Smith's analysis.

Are we to say that sympathy is simply the name we give to the interest people take in the welfare of others? Hardly; for the appeal to the function of the imagination in this matter is meant to show us how we come to bring home to ourselves the situation in which others find themselves. It is not thought to need any explanation that we should consider it a reason against doing something that it threatens disaster for us. Our undoubted self-regard is supposed to explain why this counts as a reason. But why should *my* preferences be modified by consideration of the way in which other people may be affected?

'In the absence of sympathy', W. Kneale says in *Philosophy* (1950, 162), 'no consideration of the interests of other men could amount to a reason for adopting a policy; and although men might still be prudent, there would be no reason why onlookers should approve their prudence.

When we imaginatively suppose ourselves in the situation of another, we may indeed come to feel really pained; but this does not as such suffice to furnish us with any reason for trying to help him. This pain of ours can be equally well avoided by averting our gaze from the painful spectacle. It is furthermore pointed out by Hume that such imaginative realization of other people's suffering may, by comparison, come to lead us to congratulate ourselves on our luck. It may, however, lead us to feel more strongly than before how precarious our own position may be, and how important it is to take steps to avoid falling into the miserable position of the people with whom we are supposed to sympathize.

No mention has so far been made of the concept of an impartial, well-informed spectator. It is sometimes thought that Smith believed all approval to consist in sympathy with the feelings of such a creature. We have, however, already seen that he sometimes describes approval in such a way as to pay less regard to the need for objectivity than sympathy with an impartial, well-informed spectator would seem to involve.

We must distinguish between love of praise and love of being praiseworthy. The first is by no means always admirable: it only involves consideration of what, in fact, pleases other people, what their actual feelings are or would be. If, however, we are to consider whether we are praiseworthy, we must consider what would be the feelings of a well-informed and impartial spectator. In order to attain the satisfaction of thinking ourselves admirable 'we must become the impartial spectators of our own character and conduct' (TMS, 102). In being satisfied with one's own conduct a person '. . . views it in the light in which the impartial spectator would view it, he thoroughly enters into all the motives which influenced it' (TMS, 104). Smith goes on to equate this with what people would admire were they properly informed and impartial. The approval seems to consist in the pleasure one feels when, from the point of view of the impartial spectator, one can sympathize with one's own motives. Similarly a man may feel dissatisfied with himself, although he may think that his activities and motives will for ever remain unknown. This is because 'When he looks back upon it, and views it in the light in which the impartial spectator would view it, he finds that he can enter into none of the motives which influenced it' (TMS, 106). The voice of conscience is that of the impartial and well-informed spectator, also referred to as 'the man within the breast', and 'the great judge within'. Talking about the man of great constancy, firmness and justice, Smith says that he '. . . almost becomes himself that impartial spectator, and scarce even feels but as that great arbiter of his conduct directs him to feel' (TMS, 128). Smith, like Hume, thinks that we tend to be naturally biased in favour of ourselves. It is thus not only in connection with self-evaluation that we need reference to an impartial spectator: in comparing our interests with others, we must view the situation 'with the eyes of a third person, who has no particular connection with either, and who judges with impartiality between us' (TMS, 119). It is true, however, that it is with reference to evaluation of one's own conduct that most of Smith's references to the impartial spectator are made. This is most likely explained by the fact that it seems odd to suggest that self-approval could consist in considering whether one can sympathize with oneself. But Smith is not as clear with regard to this important point as one might wish. He insists, it is true, that the principles underlying approval of others, and those underlying self-approval, are the same; but with regard to approval and disapproval of others he makes no reference to the taking up of the position of an impartial spectator; he merely says: 'We either approve or disapprove of the conduct of another man according as we feel that, when we bring his case home to ourselves, we either can or cannot entirely sympathize with the sentiments and motives which directed it' (TMS, 99). In our own case, we view our own conduct from another's point of view. We must place our actions at a distance from ourselves. 'But we can do this in no other way than by endeavouring to view them with the eyes of other people, or as other people are likely to view them' (TMS, 99). In this quotation, there is again no reference to a well-informed or impartial spectator; but to consider whether other people are likely to praise our conduct or not, does not seem to be equivalent to considering whether it is praiseworthy. And, indeed, without warning that any different principles are involved, Smith, in the same paragraph, goes on to say: 'We endeavour to examine our own conduct as we imagine any other fair and impartial spectator would examine it. If, upon placing ourselves in his situation, we thoroughly enter into all the passions and motives which influenced it, we approve of it, by sympathy with the approbation of this supposed equitable judge. If otherwise we enter into his disapprobation, and condemn it' (TMS, 100). Here there is mention of the condition that the spectator must be equitable and later on, as we have seen, he adds that the judge must be well-informed.

This short outline of some of the main things Adam Smith has to say about sympathy and its relation to approval and disapproval suggests points of comparison with Hume's doctrine in the *Treatise*:

(1) Smith emphasizes that in considering the propriety of actions we consider whether we could sympathize with a person's motive. This consists in imagining what our motives would be in his situation. When evaluating our own conduct, we imagine whether or not an impartial and well informed spectator would sympathize with our motives. It seems that he ought to have held that all evaluation of actions consisted in this but on this point fails to make himself clear.

(2) Sometimes, as in his answer to Hume's letter, Smith describes approval as a sentiment or passion that arises from a sympathetic emotion. It is clear that this account comes closer to Hume's view as I understand it. Approbation is a separate sentiment or passion arising from sympathy. To approve, as such, is not the same as to sympathize; but the sympathizing is different, since for Smith it is primarily the motives we are evaluating that are also the objects of sympathy. It is not that he does not consider the tendency of the motives to lead to pleasure or pain important. He explicitly does mention this. One of the reasons we find it difficult to 'go along with' a man in his anger, derives from the fact that we tend to sympathize with the object of the anger as well as the angry person. It remains, however, a fact that Hume lays much more stress upon 'the tendencies of actions' than does Smith.

(3) As regards self-evaluation, my interpretation of this is that it consists in pride and humility that are aroused from an objective consideration of one's own character. Hume, however, would not describe what happens as considering whether an impartial judge would sympathize with one's motives. This is primarily because he does not conceive of sympathizing in terms of an imaginary change of place. But if one thinks that Hume considers approval to *be* sympathy, then self-approval could only amount to sympathy with other people's approval of one. If this view is taken, it appears natural to conclude with T. H.

Green that Hume is accounting not for a genuine moral self-valuing, but for 'the temper of the man who seeks to stand well with his neighbour' (see SHE, 406). To get others to approve of you is the only way to self-approval.

It must be granted that to equate self-approval and disapproval with special kinds of pride and humility seems less obviously justified by the text than the treatment of approval and disapproval as love and hatred that arise under special conditions. Hume, for example, nowhere explicitly says that all self-approval of a moral kind is pride. Yet I tried in Chapter 2 to show that the indirect passions are four basic but biased ways of valuing. If I am right in thinking that the problem for Hume is to account for the overcoming of this bias, then it seems natural to conclude with me that self-valuing *is* pride or humility that arises from impartially considering the tendencies of certain personal characteristics. This interpretation certainly removes the necessity for the unattractive conclusion that to value yourself is to sympathize with other people's opinion of you. We saw that even Adam Smith, who comes nearer to identifying approval and sympathy than does Hume, introduces here the notion of the impartial well-informed spectator in order to be able to draw the all-important distinction between love of praise and love of praiseworthiness.

We may, to finish, mention the fact that the analogy between the moral sentiments and the indirect passions helps to explain why we do not feel the same about a good man and a well-contrived machine. These passions, we may remember, have sensitive creatures as their natural objects. The nature of the cause of the pleasure that leads to an indirect passion affects the quality of the resulting emotion. Thus we do not feel the same way about a useful machine and a good person. Animals are important in that we can sympathize with their feelings; but since sympathy functions by similarity, the feelings of animals are less important than those of men. It is not clear to me whether there is, in principle, anything against attributing to animals some virtues, although none of the artificial virtues because of the inability of animals to understand certain concepts such as property, promise, etc. If animals are incapable of adopting an impartial objective point of view, they can have no conception of morality, and one could conclude from this that they cannot be moral.

7

THE NATURAL VIRTUES AND SYMPATHY

In our treatment of all virtues, natural and artificial, we must keep firmly in mind that 'the imagination adheres to the *general* views of things, and distinguishes the feelings they produce from those which arise from our particular and momentary situation' (THN III, 282/587).

When people sing the praises of 'great men', it is, Hume thinks, found that most of the virtuous qualities which they approve in these men are such that they benefit either society or the persons possessed of the virtues. To the first class belong generosity and humanity, and to the second prudence, temperance, frugality, industry, assiduity, enterprise, and dexterity. All these virtues are natural virtues; the concept of an artificial virtue will be discussed separately. Let us call the two classes of natural virtues *social* and *self-regarding* respectively. Hume also thinks characteristics of persons may be deemed virtues if they are immediately pleasing to the person himself, or immediately pleasing to others.

It must not be forgotten that Hume thinks the self-regarding virtues furnish him with the best evidence for his contention that sympathy is needed to explain evaluations. In the case of social virtues it can be argued that there is always a possibility that we approve of them because of the benefit *we* derive from society. When the person we are judging is the member of another society, or belongs to a past age, it might be said that we approve of him because of the benefit we imagine we should have received if we had belonged to that society. Although we may here have to appeal to the imagination, it is not absolutely clear that we need to appeal to a principle of sympathy; but Hume is confident that:

> were nothing esteemed virtue but what were beneficial to society, I am persuaded that the foregoing explication of the moral sense ought still to be received, and that upon sufficient evidence. (THN III, 283/588)

But when I approve of a person because he possesses qualities that 'have a tendency to promote *his* interest and satisfaction', it seems that the end these qualities are 'fit to produce' must somehow 'be agreeable to me'. How can this be the case if the man is to me 'a total stranger', to whom I am under no obligation, and who is not likely to be of any service to me because he possesses qualities that have a tendency to serve *his* interests? It seems obvious to Hume that only sympathy with the happiness of the person in question could explain why I approve of him because of his possession of self-regarding virtues. It is for this reason alone that the tendency these virtues have to serve the possessor of them 'have an agreeable effect upon my imagination, and command my love and esteem' (THN III, 284/589).

Without sympathy, cool self-love or enlightened self-interest would be unable to account for our approval of these self-regarding virtues. We are, with the aid of sympathy, also in a position to see why the same qualities of mind give rise to pride and love on the one hand, humility and hatred on the other. A man will have a high opinion of himself by reason of possessing the very *same* qualities that would lead him to have a high opinion of someone else, if they belonged to that other person. Without the appeal to sympathy, one might perhaps understand why a man could be proud of qualities that serve his own purposes, but it would be more difficult to see why others should love him because of them. Though the objects of love and pride are different, the qualities that determine our 'evaluation' are the same:

> This theory may serve to explain why the same qualities, in all cases, produce both pride and love, humility and hatred; and the same man is always virtuous or vicious, accomplished or despicable to others, who is so to himself. (THN III, 284/589)

It seems that Hume is making a false factual claim at this point. Surely a man may have a low opinion of himself, though others have a high opinion of him. Many a proud man is surely disapproved of by others. Hume certainly does not overlook this obvious fact, for the next section of the *Treatise*, 'Of Greatness of Mind', is, among other things, concerned with explaining how pride comes to be disapproved of by others. Pride is often a vice. There must, therefore, be another explanation for the way Hume expresses himself.

Hume is mainly concerned to show how the self-regarding virtues can be made intelligible only if we appeal to the principle of sympathy. When he talks of the indirect passions in this connection he is referring to the unbiased variety of these passions. This becomes clear when he maintains that a man 'whose character is only dangerous and disagreeable to others, can never be satisfied with himself, *as long as he is sensible of that disadvantage*'[1] (THN III, 284/589).

The trouble with the man whose pride is greater than his qualities merit lies just in this: that he is insensitive to the fact that his pride is disagreeable to others. When pride is a vice it comes under the heading of those qualities immediately disagreeable to others. The fact that qualities of mind are immediately disagreeable to others, when known to us, may make us 'displeased with a quality commodious to us, merely because it displeases others, and makes us disagreeable in their eyes; though perhaps we can never have any interest in rendering ourselves agreeable to them' (THN III, 284/589).

To be displeased with yourself because you cause others displeasure is one thing. To be displeased with yourself because other people's displeasure will hinder you in your own designs and purposes is another.

Hume insists, in the *Treatise*, that our approval of the qualities of mind immediately pleasing to the person himself or to others can only be explained if we appeal to sympathy. We tend to approve of a man who is prone to the pleasant rather than the unpleasant passions. This we could do only if we were not entirely unaffected by the man's pains and pleasures. Hume's distinction of four categories of virtues depends upon the fact that, in each case, we should approve of the virtue even though the three other sources of pleasure were absent. This is not meant to imply that if a man's pleasant passions had undesirable consequences we should still approve of him.

In the case of qualities immediately agreeable to others, we must appeal to sympathy because we judge these virtues by their seeming tendencies. The following quotation makes Hume's meaning perfectly clear:

But, however directly the distinction of vice and virtue may seem

[1] My italics.

to flow from the immediate pleasure and uneasiness, which particular qualities cause to ourselves and others, it is easy to observe
that it has also a considerable dependence on the principle of *sympathy* so often insisted on. We approve of a person who is possessed
of qualities *immediately agreeable* to those with whom he has any
commerce, though perhaps we ourselves never reaped any pleasure
from them. We also approve of one who is possessed of qualities
that are *immediately agreeable* to himself, though they be of no
service to any mortal. To account for this, we must have recourse
to the foregoing principles. (THN III, 285/590)

It is, as Hume points out, only those qualities that give pleasure and
pain 'from the mere survey' that are denominated virtues and vices,
and this we can explain only if we have recourse to the function of the
imagination, and that sympathy which is operative when men fix on
a 'common point of view, from which they might survey their object,
and which might cause it to appear the same to all of them' (THN III,
286/591).

It is very important to remind ourselves that approval and disapproval cannot be equated with just any pleasure and pain. The feelings or sentiments upon which moral distinctions depend are of a
particular kind. Only those interests and pleasures that arise from our
adopting the standpoint of an impartial spectator counterbalance those
that naturally arise in our particular situation in life:

And, though such interests and pleasures touch us more faintly
than our own, yet, being more constant and universal, they
counterbalance the latter even in practice, and are alone admitted
in speculation as the standard of virtue and morality. They alone
produce that particular feeling or sentiment on which moral distinctions depend. (THN III, 286/591)

Hume, therefore, clearly claims in the *Treatise* that the approval of
all virtues depends upon our taking up an objective standpoint, that
the imagination is involved, and thus sympathy with the effect the
quality of mind in question would tend to have.

It has been argued by Hedenius that one need refer to sympathy in
explaining only some of the virtues, and that this leads to a radical
incoherence in Hume's system. I shall attempt to defend Hume against
this charge.

Both in the *Treatise* and in the *Enquiry*, Hume distinguishes four
sources of the merit of qualities of mind. I have already mentioned

that such qualities may be deemed virtuous because they are immediately agreeable to the person himself, immediately agreeable to others, useful to the person himself, or useful to others. It must be remembered, however, that these four classes are not mutually exclusive. The same quality of mind may be both agreeable and useful, and an explanation of its virtue would in that case have to mention both these characteristics.

(1) *Qualities immediately agreeable to ourselves.* There are also certain passions which are inherently disagreeable: propensity to these would be a vice. Hume mentions the following in a footnote in the *Enquiry*: fear, anger, dejection, grief, melancholy, anxiety. These are all 'passions' which most human beings will have experienced from time to time. In concentrating upon immediately disagreeable qualities we must not forget that a propensity to agreeable passions is a virtue. A man is not vicious just because he is stricken with grief at the loss of a close friend, nor is an angry person necessarily bad. It is, in fact, not the disagreeable passions themselves which are vicious but rather the *propensity* to these passions. A person's character becomes disagreeable to us if he has a propensity to these passions, simply because these passions are communicated to us by sympathy. It is possible to suggest that the list of passions given above could be regarded as a list of motives: moods and emotions are sometimes regarded as motives; but the important point about this class of virtuous qualities is that they are not approved of as motives. The word 'motive' belongs to the vocabulary of explanation of actions. When we say 'He beat his wife because he was angry' we are explaining a person's actions, and only in so far as this is our purpose can this be counted as an explanation in terms of motive. One must, of course, be aware that the term 'motive' is being used in a somewhat extended sense when it is made to cover moods, such as anger. But those who think that Hume considers that we always evaluate motives must be using the term in this extended sense. If I condemn anger as a motive, and say that a person ought not to be motivated by anger, I am not condemning the feeling as such, but only claiming that the person should control himself, should not let anger lead him into beating his wife and other undesirable behaviour. But Hume's main point is that this is not our only reason for condemning or disapproving of an irascible man. We do not only disapprove of him because he is prone to act in a mischievous way, but also simply because it is disagreeable for the man himself to be angry. We disapprove because the emotion or mood is disagreeable as such,

and not just because it is a bad motive.[1] This is because we may sympathize with the feelings of *the man whose character we are judging*, as well as with the feelings of those who are affected by his actions. It may be the case that no virtue is approved of merely because it is agreeable to the possessor; but this is one of the causes of approval, even of such virtues as benevolence, that undoubtedly derives most of its merit from the fact that it leads to behaviour which on the whole increases the pleasure of others.

(2) *Qualities immediately agreeable to others.* It can be argued that these qualities are approved of immediately and do not need sympathy to be perfectly intelligible to us. Among the chief of these virtues are good manners, wit and ingenuity. The witty person pleases us immediately, and the reason is not that he is pleased himself. It is not through sympathy with his pleasure that we come to approve, in so far as this is a virtue immediately pleasing to others; part of our approval is surely derived from the consideration that wit causes pleasure in other people. It is not only the pleasure of the person making the assessment that determines the approval. But there is an ambiguity in the term 'value' here, for even though we may not need sympathy to explain the fact that we value a witty acquaintance, seek his company on account of his wit, and would not want to be deprived of it, we do need sympathy in order to explain that in another sense of 'value' we count as equally valuable the wit of an acquaintance and the wit of a person wholly unknown to us. This is the kind of valuation that justifies the use of the expression 'He is a witty person'. It is obvious that I might be amused by someone, but still not feel justified in calling him witty: I might be aware that my sense of humour is highly eccentric. But as regards the source of value we are considering, we can see again that we do not value persons merely on account of their motives, for neither wit nor politeness would normally be classified as motives even in the more extended use of the term.

(3) *Qualities useful to ourselves.* Hume is again quite explicit that we are not talking specifically about motives but habits and qualities of character:

> It seems evident, that where a quality or habit is subjected to our examination, if it appear in any respect prejudicial to the person possessed of it, or such as incapacitates him for business and action,

---

[1] It must be stressed that I am not myself willing to subscribe to the view that moods are motives.

it is instantly blamed, and ranked among his faults and imper-
fections. (EPM, 233)

Thus even intelligence is esteemed a virtue on this account and no one
would suggest that intelligence is a motive. Hume's teaching on this
point is the same in the *Treatise* as in the *Enquiry*.

(4) *Qualities useful to others.* Hume emphasizes that this quality is
a very common source of merit. Many of those virtues which are useful
to the agent, or immediately pleasing to the agent, may also be useful
to others. The merit of virtues may be drawn from more than one
source. There is, however, one class of virtues that is peculiar in that
these virtues derive all their merit from their usefulness to others. I
am referring to the class of artificial virtues, such as justice and chastity.
A person may form a settled disposition to be just or chaste from more
than one motive, but whatever the motive, such a disposition is approved. The concept of an artificial virtue will be discussed later, but
we may notice here that the source of the value of these virtues is
obviously to be explained by an appeal to the principle of sympathy, for
unless we were affected through this principle by the happiness or unhappiness of others, considerations of utility would in no way affect us.
It is because of our sympathy with the happiness of others that we
approve.

It has been suggested that there is an inconsistency in Hume's appeal
to sympathy in order to furnish a common principle which will explain
valuations based on the various sources of merit already mentioned.
Hedenius claims that ' . . . those virtues which are immediately agreeable to other persons are outside the general scheme of Hume's ethics'
(SHE, 398). His reasons for this are simple, for he claims that

> the definition implies that they are virtues, because they are
> qualities that are approved of, but such a definition must for
> Hume imply pure tautology: they are virtues because they are
> virtues, qualities approved of because they are qualities that are
> approved of. (SHE, 398)

If Hedenius is right, it is obviously superfluous to appeal to sympathy
in order to explain why the presence of these qualities elicits approval,
and this would be the same as to explain why they are virtues. The
assumption upon which this criticism is based is simply that to be
pleased by the wit of a person is to consider the wit a virtue, to 'morally'
approve of it. This is so, because Hume is alleged to teach that a
pleasurable consciousness of something is the approval of it. But a

careful reading of the chapter in the *Enquiry* in which Hume discusses this topic, reveals that he distinguishes between the explanation of why the qualities under consideration are immediately agreeable to others, and the explanation of our approval of those qualities.

In the case of wit, it might be impossible to explain with the help of psychological concepts, why the behaviour or conversation of the witty person gives immediate pleasure to others. But when we come to explain the fact that wit is counted a virtue, and not just liked by those who enjoy the company of the witty person, we must appeal to the principle of sympathy. The final paragraph of the chapter makes this clear:

> We approve of another, because of his wit, politeness, modesty, decency, or any agreeable quality which he possesses; although he be not of our acquaintance, nor has ever given us any entertainment, by means of these accomplishments. The idea, which we form of their effect on his acquaintance, *has an agreeable influence on our imagination* and gives us the sentiment of approbation. This principle enters into *all*[1] the judgments which we form concerning manners and characters. (EPM, 267)[2]

Is it not obvious that the words 'this principle' refer to sympathy, and could Hume be more explicit than he is when he says that this enters into *all* our approvals of the qualities under consideration? Hedenius' confusion is perhaps caused by a failure to see that we may be 'spectators' in two different ways: we may be pleased as spectators of the antics of a clown, or when we see a polite person's behaviour. But when Hume talks of our taking up the position of a spectator, he is thinking of a judgment of a particular quality as a source of pleasure generally; we have not taken up an unbiased view unless we do this. Here sympathy with the pleasure of others inevitably comes into the picture and influences our feelings of approval or disapproval. Thus, although the immediate pleasures derived from the company of the witty and the polite are undoubtedly the *source* of the 'virtuous' character of wit and politeness, we must understand the term 'source' in the sense in which a causal factor is a source of its effect.

When Hume, just before the passage quoted above, mentions the fact that certain people seem to possess an indefinable something which

---

[1] My italics.
[2] Though this quotation is from the *Enquiry*, Hume here expresses a view implicit in the *Treatise*.

'catches our affection' in an inexplicable manner, it should be noticed that he does not say 'commands our approval'. Sympathy cannot explain why these characteristics catch our affection, but this is very different from saying that we may come to *approve* of these characteristics without the assistance of the principle of sympathy.

The recognition by Hume of the influence of *comparison* adds a further complication to his system. Hume thinks that pride, when justified, is a most valuable asset; it helps us to achieve our purposes and is generally found in people we call great men. In spite of this, expressions of pride are thought to indicate bad breeding. In order to explain this, we must refer to the fact that people generally have a tendency to think more highly of themselves than seems to be justified. An expression of pride operates upon others through the principle of comparison, and this, as we have seen, has an effect opposite to that of sympathy. Our knowledge of the high opinions someone else has of himself makes us see ourselves as less significant by contrast. This pains us, and it is for this reason that the general rule is formed that pride, even when justified, is not to be allowed full and unhindered expression:

> . . . we establish the *rules of good breeding*, in order to prevent the opposition of men's pride, and render conversation agreeable and inoffensive. (THN III, 292/597)

There is no doubt that the explanation Hume gives of the fact that we dislike a boastful man has a lot of truth in it. He also makes some rather interesting observations on the difference between occasions when sympathy operates and occasions when we are affected by comparison. Let us imagine our feelings, during a bad storm, when we come to know of a boat in distress. If we are at a relatively safe distance, this may raise in us a feeling of satisfaction with our own lot by comparison. If, on the other hand, we are on the seashore and can actually see the men falling overboard and the panic on their faces, we are likely to be affected by sympathy with their plight, and gripped by pity or compassion. This observation is probably sound, but it raises the question whether it is possible to give any general rule for deciding when our knowledge of the suffering of others would influence us by comparison as opposed to sympathy. When we remember that specifically moral approvals arise when we take up a relatively detached attitude, we should, perhaps, have expected that our knowledge of the suffering of others would make us more satisfied with our lot, rather than pain us through sympathy. But perhaps one ought not to talk here in terms of exclusive alternatives: possibly our satisfaction with our own situation, as contrasted with the lot of unfortunate people affected by the deeds of an evildoer, strengthens still more our disapproval of him. The plight of the sufferers seems greater by contrast with our own relatively happy situation, and this could make the person responsible for the suffering seem even more abominable.

Hume makes it quite clear that certain virtues are virtues only when accompanied by benevolence:

> Courage and ambition, when not regulated by benevolence, are fit only to make a tyrant and public robber. It is the same case with judgment and capacity, and all the qualities of that kind. They are indifferent in themselves to the interests of society, and have a tendency to the good or ill of mankind, according as they are directed by these other passions. (THN III 297/604)

Thus, for Hume, the benevolent and tender passions are of peculiar importance. It is indeed the case that there is nothing which is more lovable than 'any instance of extraordinary delicacy in love or friendship'. This is not merely because of the general utility of these passions; it is rather that the passion communicated by sympathy is love itself, and this love need only change its object, so to speak, and come to be directed to the loving people. Since any mental quality which excites love is a virtue, we need not be surprised that the tendency to this passion should be much admired. Hume does not always distinguish as clearly as he should, between valuing in the sense in which to *love* a man is to value him, and the valuing which would be properly expressed by saying he is a good or a virtuous man. The reason, no doubt, is, that since approval is only a more imperceptible love, it is made more violent, and becomes what we normally call *love* when we are acquainted with the person of whom we approve. In these cases we are also quite often conscious that our love is determined by merit, and not by the fact that we are closely related to the person whose propensity to the tender passions we so much admire. Here, we have an instance of a calm passion that, in this particular case, happens to be violent.

Although Hume rates the 'tender passions' so highly, we must never forget that not all 'angry passions' are vicious. When, however, these passions give rise to cruelty, we have an example of the most abominable of vices.

Hume places his main emphasis on the tender virtues and the artificial virtues, but he is prepared to count as a virtue such a thing as a good judgment or wit. These do not excite approval of quite the same kind: 'Good sense and genius beget esteem; wit and humour excite love' (THN III, 301/608).

Apart from the strangeness of calling these qualities virtues, it is important to note that Hume realizes that we *feel differently* about the various characteristics we value under the name virtue; different qualities affect our emotions differently. The following footnote shows what is common and what is different in the evaluations implied in loving and esteeming:

> Love and esteem are at the bottom the same passions, and arise from like causes. The qualities that produce both are agreeable, and give pleasure. But where this pleasure is severe and serious; or where its object is great, and makes a strong impression; or where it produces any degree of humility or awe; in all these cases, the passion which arises from the pleasure is more properly denominated esteem than love. Benevolence attends both; but is connected with love in a more eminent degree.
>
> (THN III, 301/608, footnote)

Since there can be only four basic indirect passions, according to Hume's psychological theory, it should be obvious to us why love and esteem must be thought basically the same. What is interesting here is the relation between awe or humility and esteem or respect. In a case where by contrast we tend to feel small and insignificant in relation to the object, it would be proper to say we esteem or respect the object. Love does not seem to have in it this element of 'looking up to', although, as Hume points out, it tends to be more closely connected with benevolence. We are more solicitous for the welfare of persons we love than for the welfare of those we esteem or respect. We also tend to call great what commands our esteem, and good what commands our love.

But is Hume not guilty of a gross confusion between the moral and non-moral qualities a man may have? He is well aware of the fact that he is extending the scope of the term 'virtue', but he thinks he can show that there are good grounds for emphasizing the similarities between virtues and talents, moral and non-moral qualities in general. Hume points out that people seem to value their intellectual capacities as much as what we normally call their moral virtues. They might become more angry if called fools than if called knaves. It is, furthermore, undeniable that natural abilities 'give a new lustre to the other virtues;

and that a man possessed of them is much more entitled to our good will and services than one entirely void of them' (THN III, 300/607). It is certain that we do not estimate a man's virtue *simply* by his intention. A man who forms his intentions, however benevolent, on the basis of unrealistic assessment of his abilities, would perhaps be described as kind but foolish. The 'but' indicates reservation in our praise.

We have already seen that different virtues inspire different kinds of feeling. It would thus be quite possible for what we call natural abilities to inspire different kinds of emotions from other virtues – we might feel differently about them; but this is not sufficient to justify thinking of them as being of an entirely different kind, since the same holds good for different qualities admitted to be virtues, for example the awe-inspiring and the lovable.

Since it is the pleasures and pains arising from the contemplation of personal characteristics that determine approval and disapproval, we can easily see that they may result from non-voluntary characteristics. This would not furnish an adequate criterion for distinguishing virtues from talents. As regards the criterion that virtues are the result of free activities, whereas talents are not, Hume points to his discussion of freedom, according to which the 'voluntary' is not necessarily 'free'.

Hume does, all the same, recognize that the distinction between the voluntary and the involuntary can explain to us why moralists have invented the notion of *moral virtue*:

Men have observed, that, though natural abilities and moral qualities be in the main on the same footing, there is, however, this difference betwixt them, that the former are almost invariable by any art or industry; while the latter, or at least the actions that proceed from them, may be changed by the motives of rewards and punishment, praise and blame. Hence legislators and divines and moralists have principally applied themselves to the regulating these voluntary actions, and have endeavoured to produce additional motives for being virtuous in that particular. They knew, that to punish a man for folly, or exhort him to be prudent and sagacious, would have but little effect; though the same punishments and exhortations, with regard to justice and injustice, might have a considerable influence. (THN III, 302/609)

P. H. Nowell-Smith tries to distinguish moral from non-moral qualities or characteristics in terms of amenability to praise and blame:

Both he [the weak-willed] and the wicked man differ from the
addict or compulsive in that the latter will respond neither to
threats nor to encouragement. (*Ethics*, 306)

The trouble with this is that the really hardened criminal, the person
who is beyond redemption, does no more respond to threats or encour-
agements than the addict; and although we distinguish between them
there are no grounds for doing so, if Nowell-Smith's account is accepted.

Hume is entirely clear about the difference between the sense in
which you can *decide* to approve or disapprove, with a view to altering
people's behaviour, and the other more fundamental sense in which
you *find* yourself approving or disapproving, as you find yourself loving
or hating someone. This latter sense is, for him, the primary sense of
moral evaluation, and is to be distinguished from the use moral language can be put to in encouraging or discouraging behaviour. The
following quotation from Nowell-Smith can be defended only if by
'appraising', 'praising' and 'blaming' we mean doing something overtly:

Appraising, praising, and blaming are things that men *do* and can
only be understood on the assumption that they do them for a
purpose and use means adapted to their purpose. (*Ethics*, 301)

According to Hume, and in this I think he is right, we cannot choose
to evaluate in one way rather than another, although we may choose
to use evaluative language for the purpose of encouraging certain behaviour and discouraging other behaviour. It is for this reason that I
think Nowell-Smith is misleading in his account of this matter:

Moral approval and disapproval play the same role as [rewards
and punishments]. It is not just an accident that they please and
hurt and that they are used only in cases in which something is
to be gained by pleasing or hurting. (*Ethics*, 304)

In the basic sense of 'approve' or 'disapprove', we cannot use our
approvals or disapprovals in the sense in which we may use bad language. If we want to express in language our approval or disapproval,
we need have no reason for doing so other than the fact that we
approve or disapprove. This is not to deny the fact that we may also
express our approval or disapproval in order to modify people's conduct.

Hume widens the concept of virtue, but not in such a way as to want
to justify punishments for lack in certain abilities or talents. He is
primarily interested in the ways in which we evaluate human character
and he is perhaps right in thinking that no clear-cut criterion to distinguish the specifically moral is in use by ordinary people. We do not, for

example, enquire whether a man's courage is native to him before we call it a virtue. This is not at all to deny that it is only reasonable to use moral language for exhortations, where we think they may modify conduct.

8

THE ARTIFICIALITY OF JUSTICE

The word 'artificial' is often used in opposition to 'real', although 'real' has, of course, many other opposites. Thus we talk about the real and the imaginary, and the distinction between the real and the apparent is perhaps the best known distinction to be found in the history of philosophy. But when Hume calls justice an artificial virtue, he is not distinguishing it from real virtue. He is certainly not saying that it appears to be a virtue but really is no virtue at all, nor is he implying that it is an inferior kind of virtue. It is important to remember this, for sometimes the word 'artificial' is used in such a way as to throw doubt upon the value of an object. It is used as the opposite to 'genuine'. To describe jewellery as artificial is not to praise it.

As used by Hume, 'artificial' has neither 'real' nor 'genuine' as its opposite. It is not a value term at all, but has a purely descriptive force. An 'artificial' virtue is contrasted with a 'natural' virtue, and both these terms are to be taken in a strictly descriptive sense. Thus we must not confuse this contrast with that between natural and unnatural; for to describe a passion as unnatural would involve condemnation or disapproval of it. Hume's use of 'artificial', in the context we are considering is not unlike the use of this term in 'artificial silk', where the word is used to indicate that the silk is not a natural product, but is produced by human inventiveness. The analogy is not as close as it may seem, for 'artificial silk' is sometimes distinguished from 'real silk' and here the use of 'real' indicates that this kind of silk is somehow better, or at least more truly entitled to be called silk, than the artificial variety, which is not really silk though it masquerades as such. In some cases, of course, people may come to prefer the artificial product to the real thing. There will then be a tendency for the term 'artificial' to cease to be disparaging. The artificial variety is no longer looked upon as a poor substitute. But we must, at the outset, rid ourselves of the inclination to think that Hume, by calling some virtues artificial, wanted to indicate that they were either less valuable, or less entitled to the name 'virtue', than the natural variety.

Hume entitles the second part of Book III of the *Treatise* 'Of Justice and Injustice'. This is slightly misleading, for he treats, under this general heading, other virtues, such as allegiance and chastity and modesty. In general, one might say that this part of the *Treatise* is concerned with artificial virtues as distinct from natural virtues, but, of these, justice is considered by Hume to be the most important. It must also be remembered that the second part of the book is the longest, and that the third part, entitled 'Of the Other Virtues and Vices', contains only a relatively short chapter on the origin of the natural virtues. This may serve to indicate that Hume considered his discussion of justice and injustice of great importance.

As far as Hume's arguments for the artificiality of *justice* are concerned, this chapter will contain only some general observations; nor do I intend to discuss the bearing of these arguments upon his political theory. My main concern is to explain the concept of an artificial virtue in its relation to Hume's views about human psychology, and to the evaluation of actions and of people.

Hume rejects, without reservation, the view that we can explain why any particular conduct is a sign of virtue by simply appealing to a moral sense. This would hardly be an explanation: it is rather an expression of our inability to explain. A simple appeal to an original instinct

> is not conformable to the usual maxims by which nature is conducted, where a few principles produce all that variety we observe in the universe, and everything is carried on in the easiest and most simple manner. (THN III, 181/473)

We explain by showing how apparently diverse occurrences were to be expected because of the presence of one property common to each. The model is that of scientific explanation, or a special kind of scientific explanation. Hume would have endorsed completely the following remarks made by Jeremy Bentham:

One man says, he has a thing made on purpose to tell him what
is right and what is wrong; and that it is called a *moral sense*: and
then he goes to work at his ease, and says, such a thing is right,
and such a thing is wrong – why? 'because my moral sense tells
me it is'. (PML, 17, footnote)

Such an explanation would, indeed, be like saying that a drug puts you
to sleep because it possesses a 'virtus dormitiva'.

Where are we to look for the common principle that would explain
the occurrence of approval and disapproval? Are these principles found
in nature? Hume's answer to this question is instructive: he distinguishes various senses of 'natural' and considers the answer in terms
of each. In so far as we oppose the natural to the miraculous, we can
anticipate his answer, for everything that happens is natural, Hume
contends, although he adds, with his tongue in his cheek, *'excepting
those miracles on which our religion is founded'* (THN III, 181/474). In
the sense in which we contrast the natural and the unusual, we find
that the boundary between these concepts is not very sharply defined.
We may, all the same, affirm that the 'sentiments of morality' are in
this sense natural, for

> there never was any nation of the world, nor any single person
> in any nation, who was utterly deprived of them, and who never,
> in any instance, showed the least approbation or dislike of
> manners. (THN III, 182/474)

Here, the mere fact that people approve and disapprove of actions is
taken as evidence that they have moral sentiments. It seems we can
know that a man is capable of moral sentiments, without knowing of
what he approves and disapproves. It is a contingent fact about human
nature that the passions we call approval and disapproval have the
'causes' Hume ascribes to them.

From one point of view, things that arise from 'artifice' are entirely
natural:

> We readily forget that the designs, and projects, and views of man
> are principles as necessary in their operation as heat and cold,
> moist and dry; but, taking them to be free and entirely our own,
> it is usual for us to set them in opposition to the other principles
> of nature. (THN III, 182/474)

There is thus a sense in which artifice is to be expected from man:

> Mankind is an inventive species; and where an invention is ob-
> vious and absolutely necessary, it may as properly be said to be

natural as anything that proceeds immediately from original principles, without the intervention of thought or reflection. (THN III, 190/484)

Hume even thinks there are good grounds for calling the rules of justice *Laws of Nature*, for he thinks *some* such rules 'inseparable from the species'.

One certainly can not distinguish vice from virtue by saying that virtue is natural and vice is unnatural. Hume is decidedly not concerned to advocate that we should follow nature, on the ground that vice is contrary to nature. Vice is as natural as virtue, and we are, as moral philosophers, concerned with the problem of explaining *'why any action or sentiment, upon the general view or survey, gives a certain satisfaction or uneasiness'* (THN III, 183/475).

Hume stresses the view that we always approve of the 'motives that produce [actions]' (THN III, 184/477). The external action has no value or merit, unless it is taken as a sign of a motive at work in the agent. His doctrine appears to be that actions derive their moral character from the motives that give rise to them. This contention he supports by the argument that in a situation where we consider a man is actuated by a certain motive of which we approve, we do not think any the less of him if external circumstances hinder him from performing the action:

> If we find, upon inquiry, that the virtuous motive was still powerful over his breast, though checked in its operation by some circumstances unknown to us, we retract our blame, and have the same esteem for him, as if he had actually performed the action which we require of him. (THN III, 184/477-8)

It is by no means obvious that the statement quoted supports Hume's contention that the motive determines the moral character of an action. It seems to depend upon the meaning we ascribe to the term 'motive'. Thus Bentham insisted that any motive could lead to both right and wrong conduct, although certain motives were more likely to lead to right conduct than others. Certain motives are more or less universal throughout the species. Sexual desire would be an example: we do not praise or blame a man for his sexual desires. But a man may have developed a tendency to attempt to gratify these in ways, and upon occasions, that are considered socially injurious. In the case of such a man, we should be inclined to call his motive 'lust', a word which indicates our disapproval. A man who has, on the other hand, developed a disposition to attempt to satisfy his desire in lawful ways, for example in marriage only, is not disapproved of. In his case, we might even call his motive 'love', to indicate our approval.

Hume's position seems to have certain implications that are not explicitly stated. Thus he can claim that his argument is plausible only if 'motive' is used in such a way as to indicate an inclination or a tendency to perform a kind of action which can be known to be good or bad if the motive is known. The motive cannot be neutral with regard to value in the way in which Bentham thought sexual desire neutral. By 'motive' must be meant something either virtuous or vicious. This must be so if we think the same approval due to the person 'as if he had actually performed the action which we require of him'. We must think of the motive as involving an inclination or a tendency to perform a special *kind* of action, for the value of the motive depends largely upon the pleasurable consequences the type of action has upon those who are affected by it.

But motives cannot, on Hume's account, be *identified* with a tendency to act in a particular way. The importance he attaches to the concept of calm passions clearly shows this. Hume here talks about the constant *union* between certain motives and actions. It is clear that he is not merely wanting to emphasize the obvious, that a disposition to act in a certain way, and *acting* in this way, tend to go together; there is more to a motive than this. Hume considers that there is an occurrent impression of some sort whenever one is *influenced* by a certain motive, however faint that impression may be. Some virtues consist in the tendency to be influenced by certain motives. If different motives tend to lead to specifically different types of behaviour, the doctrine as to the nature of virtue is similar to the view expressed by Nowell-Smith when he says 'Virtues and vices are dispositions to behave in certain ways' (*Ethics*, 248). It must be remembered, however, that this would fit only some 'virtues', according to Hume. If wit is a virtue, it could not be characterized in this way. 'Wit' and 'intelligence' refer to capacities rather than to dispositions, although a person could hardly be called witty unless he is sometimes disposed to say or do witty things, and it may be felt that intelligence similarly involves a disposition to intelligent talk or behaviour.

Since utility enters into the explanation of the value of every social virtue, it is odd to find Hume saying 'Were not natural affection a duty, the care of children could not be a duty' (THN III, 185/478). He seems to be indicating that we approve of the care of children only because the motive which leads to this conduct is already approved of for independent reasons – a most un-utilitarian argument. This may incline people to think that approval is indeed, for Hume, to be equated with an immediate sympathy with the motive of an action, and that this determines the value of the action. This would clearly be inconsistent with the account given in this book of the relation between sympathy and moral approval and disapproval.

Perhaps this problem can be solved in the following manner: Hume thinks that the object of *moral* approval is always a quality of mind or character. When, therefore, we consider an action to be done in spite of a man's character, and thus do not consider it a just or legitimate sign of a disposition in him, we should not approve of the action 'morally', however much pleasure results from it for others. It would not be closely enough related to the agent to arouse love towards him.

If I have been right in the emphasis I have placed upon the analogy between approval and disapproval on the one hand, and the indirect passions on the other, one can understand why Hume should demand a close connection between the agent and a quality that *makes* us approve of him. The point is still more easily understood if one remembers that agents, rather than actions, are the natural objects of approval and disapproval, in so far as these passions are analogous to the indirect passions (see p. 23).

Whatever we may think of Hume's view, it has at least the merit of avoiding the charge that an action could be called *morally right* just because it has fortunate results. Later Utilitarians were somewhat embarrassed by this criticism, for it seemed they had to say an action was right if it contributed more to happiness than other alternatives open to the agent. Since, however, we should not morally approve of these actions where the beneficial consequences were purely accidental, it was claimed that the rightness of an action depended upon the intention rather than the actual consequences. The doctrine that pleasure and the absence of pain are the sole intrinsic goods seems to imply that the rightness of an action is derivative, and nineteenth-century utilitarian doctrines seem to be teleological in such a way as to make the rightness of actions dependent upon the goodness of their consequences. They were, therefore, saddled with two senses of 'right' in their attempts to account for morality. In Hume's philosophy, on the other hand, actions are never to be judged *solely* by reference to an end. In so far as they are morally evaluated, they are always thought of as indicating a quality of mind or character. The object of the evaluation is always a person.

It therefore follows from Hume's doctrine that when we approve of a man's care for his children, we are justified in doing so only because we consider his action a sign of a disposition or inclination in him. In this case, we are dealing with a disposition or inclination which we do not think dependent upon the agent's concern for the rightness or wrongness, goodness or badness of what he is doing. If we thought that a man's care for his children was dependent upon his feeling in some way constrained to do it, we should consider this a sign of weakness in him, a sign that he was somewhat lacking in parental affection, and thus was not as virtuous as he might be. We cannot, therefore, say that the motive to these actions is the sense of their morality. A natural motive is presupposed, for it is only because he possesses a motive involving a certain disposition that we may attribute the virtue to the man.

But it can hardly be denied that Hume seems to be putting the cart before the horse when he says:

> We blame a father for neglecting his child. Why? because it shows a want of natural affection, *which is the duty of every parent.*[1] Were not natural affection a duty, the care of children could not be a duty; and it were impossible we could have the duty in our eye in the attention we give to our offspring. In this case, therefore, all men suppose a motive to the action distinct from a sense of duty. (THN III, 185/478)

Hume appears to be maintaining that (1) it is our duty to be moved by certain motives and (2) that the action to which a motive naturally leads would not be a duty unless the motive for that kind of action were also considered a duty. This view is in sharp contrast with the doctrine put forward by Sir David Ross, who maintains that it is always our duty (1) to *do* something (*The Right and The Good*) or (2) to *set* ourselves to do something (*The Foundations of Ethics*). His view depends mainly upon the contention that whatever is our duty must be subject to our voluntary control. This, indeed, explains his change of doctrine in *The Foundations of Ethics*, for he came to believe that, whereas sometimes our actions are hindered by circumstances beyond our control, we *can* always, if we so choose, *set* ourselves to do an action. It is for this reason, as well, that Ross considers we can never be under an

---

[1] My italics.

obligation to act from some particular motive; our motives are not under voluntary control. The motive has nothing to do with the rightness of an action, nor with a question of duty. It is relevant only in deciding the action's goodness. If it is right to give to charity, it is right to do so even from a self-interested motive. The action would, however, be better if the motive was concern for other people's welfare.

It is possible to attack Ross' views on the relation between motives and duty in two ways: (1) we can deny that our motives are beyond our voluntary control, and (2) we can deny that only those things that do lie under our control are duties. The first of these alternatives may seem initially the more promising: we think it makes sense for a mother to try to love an unwanted child. Hume takes the latter alternative: he refuses to talk of the rightness of actions in abstraction from the motive which would make it legitimate to take the action as a sign of a quality of mind or character. He is primarily interested in the value of human character, and in this he is rather like Kant. In Hume's case the emphasis upon the value of people is less surprising when we remind ourselves that the indirect passions, in which he finds the basis for moral evaluation, have persons as their natural objects. But we must remember two things in interpreting this chapter: (1) Hume thinks we approve as much of a man who is, by external circumstances, prevented from doing benevolent deeds, as we do of the person who has the opportunity to exercise his benevolence. So long as we think the motive prevails the actual *consequences* do not make a difference to our approval; (2) there is this important difference between virtue and duty: when the presence of a quality pleases us in a certain way, we say it is virtuous; when the thought of its absence pains us, we say that possession of it is a duty. Consider the contention that love of children is a duty: it would pain us to know that someone was lacking in parental affection. Unless this were so, our disapproval of a man who neglects his children would not be moral. I might be an emotional person who gets enraged because I see a father beat up his child. But my anger is not righteous indignation, unless I feel the emotion because of my knowledge that the man had a disposition to beat the child. If physical restraint of the man entirely removes my emotion and leaves me unaffected, I cannot have been disapproving, although I may have been pained by seeing the child beaten. My emotion in this situation might have been pity or compassion. It could not have been moral disapproval.

Hume would not have been impressed by the contention that only those things under our direct control can be duties. The feelings of a spectator determine what is and what is not a duty. Lack in parental affection pains us: that settles the matter. We must, in any case, remember Hume's brand of determinism: we are certainly not *compelled* to have the feelings we have; they are thus undoubtedly free, in the sense in which freedom is opposed to compulsion.

Hume's insistence that we can talk about the *virtuous* character of an action only if we consider it as determined by a certain motive which ties it to human character, makes it absurd to say that regard to the morality of an action can be the *first* motive for its performance. There must be a natural motive of which the action is a sign, and which makes the action a virtuous one. He therefore takes it as

an undoubted maxim, *that no action can be virtuous, or morally good, unless there is in human nature some motive to produce it distinct from the sense of its morality.* (THN III, 185/479)

Hume is not denying that conscientiousness or the sense of duty may be the motive of an action. Indeed, he insists that a person who finds himself lacking in the inclination (motives) to virtuous behaviour, may still perform actions which the truly virtuous man would have a natural motive to perform. He may do this, either in order to acquire the virtuous motives through habit, or in order to disguise from himself his own lack of true virtue.

We may even praise such conduct – and quite rightly; for a large measure of the value of actions is derived from their consequences, their effect upon the happiness of others. In these cases we attribute some virtue to conscientious behaviour, because our attention is fixed upon the signs, and we approve those actions which, on most occasions, are signs of virtuous motives. There is in fact nothing strange in this doctrine, for although conscientiousness may be a substitute for natural goodness as a motive, we still do not think the substitute superior to the original.

If a person were asked why he should return a sum of money he has borrowed, the obvious answer would be 'because it is just to do so'. This answer will satisfy only a person who uses the term 'just' as a term of praise; it presupposes that justice is already admitted to be a virtue. But the problem we are interested in is precisely *why* it is a virtue – so the answer begs the question.

Given the accepted senses of 'borrow' and 'lend', there is an air of paradox about suggesting that one ought not to repay what one has borrowed, unless special reasons are given. But if we do not presuppose a system of rules for just dealings between people, there is no paradox involved. What now needs a reason is why it would be virtuous to repay the money. Hume makes this philosophical point by the use of a hypothetical case, where this rule has not been accepted as a moral rule:

> But in his rude and more *natural* condition, if you are pleased to call such a condition natural, this answer would be rejected as perfectly unintelligible and sophistical. For one in that situation would immediately ask you, *wherein consists this honesty and justice, which you find in restoring a loan, and abstaining from the property of others?* (THN III, 186/479-80)

Hume's problem is to explain what 'reasons or motives' could have led to the acceptance of the rules of justice in the first place. There would be a natural reason why we act justly, (1) if we behave in this way by instinct, or (2) if this is in our interest, or (3) if it benefits those connected with us. These reasons are, of course, not mutually exclusive. It is extremely implausible to suggest that justice is the result of instinct. Where we accept such an explanation, there is a general uniformity in the phenomena thus explained. The rules of justice are, in contrast to this, extremely varied. They resemble more the effects of reason than the effects of instinct. The following quotation from the *Enquiry Concerning the Principles of Morals* clearly marks the difference between the effects of these two principles:

> All birds of the same species in every age and country, build their nests alike: In this we see the force of instinct. Men, in different times and places, frame their houses differently: Here we perceive the influence of reason and custom. A like inference may be drawn from comparing the instinct of generation and the institution of property. (EPM, 202)

In the case of (2) and (3) above, there would not just *be* a reason why people act justly: people would *have* a reason for so acting.

Undoubtedly we approve of just conduct, but on considering any particular instance of 'just conduct', abstracted from the system of justice, there may not seem to be any reason at all why we should engage in it; for just actions sometimes seem to be contrary to our own interest, and even contrary to the public interest, when taken in isolation. Even in these cases we feel under an obligation to act justly, although, as we have already seen, we cannot appeal to this feeling in order to account for the obligatory nature of justice, without circularity. It is absurd to suggest that a conscientious motive is the source of our allegiance to justice, since it presupposes that just behaviour is antecedently believed to be virtuous.

We may now consider some possible answers to Hume's problem. It is tempting to say that the source of justice is self-love. But this is somewhat paradoxical, for we consider self-love a great source of all manner of injustice.

Could it then be that '*regard to public interest*' is the reason for just conduct? This answer is also rejected by Hume, on the grounds that the public interest is not necessarily served by attachment to behaviour in conformity to the rules of justice; it is only attached to such behaviour if we presuppose a convention. The point really is that unless there is a general adherence to 'just' conduct, such conduct on the part of an individual need not be to the advantage of the public at all. A person could act justly when concern for the public interest would not dictate such behaviour.

In cases where a transaction between people is secret, and its fulfilment has effects only upon the people concerned in the transaction, the public has no interest in the matter, and the obligation ought, according to the hypothesis, to be removed. This we find not to be the case. It is furthermore to be observed that people, on the whole, can hardly be said to keep the public interest in mind whenever they repay a loan or keep their promises. This last point does not, of course, show that the public interest may not ultimately be the source of the obligation to be just.

The problem we are concerned with here is this: Why do people adhere to rules of justice? It is assumed that the answer must demonstrate that this naturally follows from a certain motive. The suggested motives are rejected as inadequate explanations, because they would quite often lead to conduct contrary to justice. But could we not say the same of a natural motive such as benevolence? It certainly is true that a benevolent action does not always lead to consequences that increase the welfare of the person intended to benefit from it. It follows, all the same, that if this were known to the benefactor before the act, he would refrain from performing it if his motive truly were benevolence. On the other hand, he might know that a just action does not as such benefit anyone, and thus the motive of benevolence would not prompt him to do it. The fact remains that he still thinks it ought to be done, although he may not see any possible benefit accruing even to himself. Thus benevolence cannot be the motive for justice.

The upshot of Hume's argument, then, is that, given an established code of justice, none of our natural motives can explain the obligation we find constraining us to act justly and refrain from injustice. The only explanation we seem to be able to give of a just man's adherence to justice, in spite of contrary inclinations of benevolence or self-love, is conscientiousness or 'a sense of duty'. But this motive cannot be appealed to unless we presuppose that justice is known to be virtuous, and unless we presuppose a system of justice which we accept as imposing obligations upon us.

Hume's problem is: can we give an intelligible account of the origination of these rules of conduct in the first place, without circularity, by appealing only to natural motives in our explanation? This problem is a real one, for even though justice is useful and benefits human beings generally, Hume cannot maintain that *extensive benevolence* is the original motive to justice; he cannot appeal to such benevolence as a natural principle, simply because he has denied its existence. Human passions are naturally biased in favour of the self and those closely related to us. In the same way, love is influenced by merit in such a way as to clash, on occasions, with the attitude dictated by strict equity. It is important to bear this point in mind, one which Hume stresses in the following passage:

> In general, it may be affirmed, that there is no such passion in human minds as the love of mankind, merely as such, independent of personal qualities, services, or of relation to ourself. It is true, there is no human, and indeed no sensible creature, whose happiness or misery does not, in some measure, affect us, when brought near us, and represented in lively colours: but this proceeds merely from sympathy, and is no proof of such an universal affection to mankind, since this concern extends itself beyond our own species. (THN III, 187-8/481)

The only benevolence which is natural to human beings is 'biased', because it is accounted for by an appeal to the principle of sympathy, which varies with the nature and closeness of relations. This principle, furthermore, influences our conduct towards animals as well as men. It cannot, therefore, be the sole foundation of justice, which relates only to our dealings with human beings. We can be unkind to animals but not unjust, Hume seems to be implying. The reason for this is that animals cannot enter into the kind of convention that leads to justice. It certainly cannot be put down to their lack of sympathy, for

> It is evident that *sympathy*, or the communication of passions, takes place among animals, no less than among men.
>
> (THN II, 112/398)

It is, similarly, their incapacity for objective judgment which explains why animals are capable of the indirect passions, and yet cannot morally approve and disapprove.

Private benevolence, or 'regard to the interests' of the party concerned, would quite often prompt behaviour contrary to justice:

> For what if he be my enemy, and has given me just cause to hate him? What if he be a vicious man, and deserves the hatred of all mankind? What if he be a miser, and can make no use of what I would deprive him of? What if he be a profligate debauchee, and would rather receive harm than benefit from large possessions? What if I be in necessity, and have urgent motives to acquire something to my family? In all these cases, the original motive to justice would fail; and consequently the justice itself, and along with it all property, right and obligation.
>
> (THN III, 188-9/482)

Thus we can neither explain why people have come to behave justly, nor account for the emergence of the obligations to just acts, by treating these as natural results of a motive of which we already approve. We must, therefore, conclude that the only motive for justice is conscientiousness or the sense of duty. Since this motive can be effective only if we presuppose that justice has been accepted as virtuous, we are committed to accepting the circular argument already referred to:

> From all this it follows, that we have no real or universal motive for observing the laws of equity, but the very equity and merit of that observance; and as no action can be equitable or meritorious, where it cannot arise from some separate motive, there is here an evident sophistry and reasoning in a circle.[1]
>
> (THN III, 189/483)

The only solution to the problem seems to be that the sense of justice arises 'artificially, though necessarily, from education and human conventions' (THN III, 189/483).

Hume has to explain how people's natural motives come to establish

---

[1] I shall later refer to this simply as *the circular argument*.

the convention that gives rise to justice. He thinks he must use different arguments to show why justice comes to be regarded as a virtue, why the term becomes a term of praise, and its contrary, 'injustice', a term of condemnation. Let us discuss the two problems in the order in which Hume himself tackles them.

In explaining the pattern of human actions it is not enough to point to men's motives alone. We must take into account the situation in which men find themselves, and their ability to satisfy their interests in that situation.

Hume points out that the physical endowments of human beings seem strikingly inadequate to satisfy their many needs. It is not surprising that men should come to co-operate in societies, for this seems the most efficient method for securing the satisfaction of men's needs, in spite of the deficiencies of each individual taken separately:

> By the conjunction of forces, our power is augmented; by the
> partition of employments, our ability increases; and by mutual
> succour, we are less exposed to fortune and accidents. It is by this
> additional *force*, *ability*, and *security*, that society becomes advantageous. (THN III, 191-2/485)

Hume, however, is careful to remember that utility alone will not explain the origin of society. People might never have *discovered* the utility. He therefore emphasizes that there is a primitive instinct drawing people together – the sexual instinct. He sees in the family the seed of larger society. The human child must be cared for through a long period of development if it is to survive at all. Hume believes parents have a natural inclination to protect their offspring and prepare it for independence.

But, granting these social inclinations that are, in any case, limited in extent, Hume is well aware that there are features in human nature which would seem, at first sight, to stand in the way of effective co-operation. The chief of these is the selfishness of man.

I have already argued that Hume is not a psychological egoist, but he always stresses the 'biased' nature of even our *benevolent* natural inclinations. This would be as great a hindrance to effective co-operation in society as narrow selfishness, though the anti-social tendency of these motives would become much more obvious as the society grows larger:

> For while each person loves himself better than any other single
> person, and in his love to others bears the greatest affection to his

relations and acquaintances, this must necessarily produce an opposition of passions, and a consequent opposition of actions, which cannot but be dangerous to the new-established union. (THN III, 193/487)

The motives just mentioned become most anti-social in the case of goods that are transferable in such a way that those from whom the transfer is made are necessarily left with less. In the sense in which I can transfer enjoyment to another my own enjoyment is in no way decreased. My physical advantages cannot be transferred from me to another. Only external goods can be transferred in the way mentioned, and it is consequently with regard to these that friction is most likely to arise.

Hume does not mention here the obvious fact that we may be tempted to impair another's physical endowments, in order to make him incapable of acquiring or defending goods we desire. Thus it would seem the rules of justice could be looked upon as relating to physical violence, as well as the violation of property rights in the narrower sense. Hume could not accept the notion that we have a *natural* property in our body, nor could he accept the labour theory of property rights that John Locke based upon this notion (Locke, *Second Treatise of Civil Government*). But it is entirely consistent with Hume's view that there should be a convention established to restrain us from impairing our fellow-men's physical capacities. There is no reason at all why this should not count as part of justice.

At this point we might remind ourselves that the natural passions, essentially biased, are not corrected by our evaluation of them. Our approval of them, on the contrary, depends upon their being biased in this way. Thus we think greater concern is due to friends and family than to strangers. We blame a man for neglecting the former completely in favour of a total stranger, although we should also blame a man who 'centres all his affections in his family'. Here we are reminded of the notion of a due mean in our affections, so much insisted upon by Adam Smith. It is clear that an unbiased evaluation need not necessarily condemn men's natural bias in favour of close relations.

The important point to remember here is that we cannot merely appeal to 'natural morality' as the agency which corrects the bias which justice must overcome:

The remedy, then, is not derived from nature, but from *artifice*; or, more properly speaking, nature provides a remedy, in the judgments and understanding, for what is irregular and incommodious in the affections. (THN III, 194/489)

It is obvious from the way in which Hume goes on to explain his meaning that the judgment or understanding do not give rise to any new motive which opposes, and can be contrasted with, the passions. The understanding changes only the *direction* of the passions. By a change in direction is meant simply that the same passions or motives give rise to different actions; but the passions themselves are the same and point towards the same *end*. It is only that we realize that there are more efficient means of satisfying them. Thus, reason still furnishes no motive to the will, and Hume is in no way constrained to change his view that all the ends of human actions are determined by the desires and passions. Reason is still the 'slave' of the passions.

Our selfishness and limited benevolence seem to be the greatest obstacles to the establishment of society and justice. Yet it is these very same motives that give rise to the convention through which justice is established. This comes about when people see that they can best serve their own interests, and those of their friends, by having some rules regarding the possession of property. This is seen to be essential, because of the unstable nature of material goods already referred to, and the relative scarcity of some of them. People soon realize

> that the principal disturbance in society arises from those goods, which we call external, and from their looseness and easy transition from one person to another. . . . (THN III, 195/489)

They therefore

> seek for a remedy by putting these goods, as far as possible, on the same footing with the fixed and constant advantages of the mind and body. (ibid.)

Because the inherent sexual instinct in man gave rise to some sort of family group Hume considered it fanciful to assume that a state of nature preceded society, a state of nature where justice would be unknown. It would be reasonable to presume that such a state of nature existed only if we have grounds for believing that at some stage in the past history of man basic commodities were so plentiful that division of them was unnecessary. Perhaps, in extreme necessity, each man would be exclusively ruled by the motive of self-preservation, assuming the principle that each individual loves himself more than he loves anyone else. Even then, one might think that factions would tend to arise because of man's limited generosity. There is thus little likelihood that there was ever a state of affairs that could legitimately be described as the war of *all against all*.

There might have been a state of nature preceding justice, if human nature has radically changed, if, for example, we could assume that at some distant time in the past, our ancestors possessed complete and universal benevolence. But we should be justified in believing this only if we had some empirical evidence in support of that belief. Hume does not seem to think there is any such evidence. He takes human nature as he thinks it is and asks whether we can, on the basis of our knowledge of human motives, explain why people have come to invent rules of justice.

It is not altogether clear that justice would not be established if man were wholly egoistic. At first sight egoism would seem to necessitate a war of all against all. As long as we consider intelligence to be part of our nature, and presume a certain amount of foresight in man, we can see how justice may arise from prudence; but it is not at all obvious that it would arise necessarily in the family. The male, being the stronger, might restrain the wife by force, and might even welcome some friction among the children, in order to make a combined attack upon himself less likely. He might find that prudence would dictate for him the well known policy 'divide et impera'.

One might say that Hume does not give enough weight to the possibility of the love of power standing in the way of the establishment of justice. In defence, he would say that a tyrant must have rules regulating what those under his authority can do with impunity, and that therefore justice inevitably comes into the picture. But in such an autocracy these rules would certainly not be established by a mutual compact of the nature Hume proceeds to describe, for the simple reason that *mutual restraint* of the passions would not be involved. We must remember, in any case, that Hume is not telling us how justice arose, but demonstrating how it could have arisen from natural motives; he is making the origin of justice intelligible.

In his account of the nature of the contract that gives rise to justice, Hume is most insistent that we are not to understand that people consider themselves bound by the contract because it is in the nature of a promise. We cannot understand the contract in this way, for the simple reason that promise-keeping is itself an artificial virtue. To fail to keep a promise is vicious because it is a violation of a rule established by an artificial convention. The contract is rather to be understood to involve a tacit understanding between people to behave towards each other in a certain way, not from the motive of duty, but simply in order to satisfy limited benevolence and self-interest. There is, we might say, a natural obligation but not a moral obligation to justice, and this state of affairs might conceivably persist, even after a system of rules of justice has been firmly established. These natural motives come gradually come to bind us to just conduct 'by a slow progression, and by our repeated experience of the inconveniences of transgressing it' (THN III, 196/490).

Hume compares the establishment of justice with the way in which human conventions gradually give rise to language. There is no reason to believe that we come to use a common system of signs in communicating with each other by any explicit mutual promise. Again, there is no reason to assume that the motive leading to the establishment of language has been anything but an awareness of the convenience of this method of communication for satisfying our needs and interests. Above all, we may not assume that, because of the immense general utility of language, the motive leading to the emergence of languages must have been general benevolence.

Let us assume that there is an established system of rules concerning the stability and transference of property. We can then give sense to the concept of right which is to be defined in terms of the rules; this right would be, admittedly, more akin to a legal than a moral right. We can then give sense to the concept of property which involves in its definition the concept of right. We can also give sense to the concept of obligation, for this, too, would be defined in terms of the rules established by the convention.

The sense of 'obligation', in this context, seems to be different from the sense of duty referred to earlier in this chapter. Obligation is here specifically tied to the artificial virtues. Since Hume maintains that it is possible to do from a sense of duty the actions a benevolent man would naturally do, we can see that the motive of duty is not tied to the performance of actions in conformity with the artificial virtues.

Hume insists that it is a mistake to define justice in terms of property. There are good reasons for this; for we can make no sense of the notion of property, unless we already have the notions of justice and right, in terms of which we must define it. The relation a man has to his property is not a natural but a 'moral' relation. His property is what he has a 'right' to, and what others are obliged to allow him to dispose of according to *his* will. The rules established by the convention give rise to property and justice together. Another reason why one cannot define justice in terms of property is that there are conventions leading to the emergence of justice other than the convention regarding property, for example the convention which leads to promises.

But it does not seem at all obvious that the convention gives rise to the concepts of 'right' and 'obligation' in a *moral* sense; we still do not know why 'respecting' property rights is a *virtue*. I have so far shown only how known human motives may have led to the formation of a convention which gives rise to property rights and justice. Hume, himself, has indicated that a separate explanation must be given of our reasons for calling justice a virtue. We should also have to explain why obligation, considered as a motive, should be attached to justice by the mere existence of a convention. Can Hume be referring to the natural obligation to justice, that is self-interest and limited benevolence? This is possible, but hardly plausible, because there seems no reason to believe that obligation, in this sense, is *unintelligible* without presupposing the convention. It seems more plausible to assume that the terms 'right' and 'obligation' are considered here as legal terms. They are both defined in terms of the laws of society, written or unwritten, established by the convention.

If the preceding account is correct, we still have to account for the way in which we come to consider ourselves under a *moral* obligation to be just and we still have not explained how there arises in man a separate *motive* for adhering to justice, which is capable of overriding the strongest natural inclinations of self-love and limited benevolence. This would be the specific motive to justice.

Hume at this stage argues that avarice, the strongest enemy of justice, can be restrained only by itself. Here we might understand by 'avarice' desire for things for ourselves and those closely related to us. There is no other 'natural' motive strong enough to keep us steadfast in the path of justice. Since we are dealing with a natural motive that can lead to either desirable or undesirable conduct, according to the adequacy of the factual judgments which direct the course of the actions it leads to, it would obviously serve no useful purpose to call it either wicked or good as such. We nowhere get a clearer indication of Hume's view that self-interest is not necessarily a vicious motive. He most emphatically rejects the view, apparently held by Hutcheson, that benevolence is the only good motive. Nor, would it seem, can one defend commentators who think that Hume deems virtuous only those actions that issue from a limited class of motives which might be called social.

I have emphasized that the natural motives for justice are self-interest and limited benevolence, but Hume insists that the connection of the rules of justice with self-interest is 'somewhat singular, and is different from what may be observed on other occasions'. Even when people have come to identify their own interest with the public interest, through enlightened 'self-love', a single individual act of justice may neither serve the public interest nor benefit the agent himself:

> When a man of merit, of a beneficent disposition, restores a great
> fortune to a miser, or a seditious bigot, he has acted justly and
> laudably; but the public is a real sufferer. (THN III, 201-2/497)

Hume, however, seems to think that were our self-interest enlightened enough, we should see good prudential reasons for adhering scrupulously to justice, even in these cases. If we were only to become sufficiently aware of the fact that without rules of justice strictly adhered to there could be no effective co-operation in society, we should see that the alternative is less attractive:

> And even every individual person must find himself a gainer on
> balancing the account; since, *without justice, society must immedi-*
> *ately dissolve,*[1] and everyone must fall into that savage and soli-
> tary condition, which is infinitely worse than the worst situation
> that can possibly be supposed in society. (THN III, 202/497)

Hume's argument here is not altogether convincing, for there is little reason to believe that the alternatives are as clear cut as he seems to think. When one sacrifices justice for the welfare of the public, in an individual case, one has not thereby chosen the dissolution of justice altogether. We need only remind ourselves that unjust actions are frequent, and yet we have not sunk into that 'savage and solitary condition' which Hume speaks of. If, in fact, widespread unjust actions had *only* the natural consequence of making co-operation more difficult, our temptation to act unjustly would be much greater than it actually is. Many people are kept on the straight and narrow path of justice, not by these 'natural' considerations, but rather because of the sanctions attached to injustice by the law.

The reason why Hume does not mention this incentive to just behaviour is obvious: he is explaining the origin of justice through the

[1] My italics.

workings of 'natural' motives, and the 'natural' condition in which man finds himself. In showing the possibility of the contract being formed, he cannot therefore assume, as an incentive, any consequences which follow injustice only in an established society with an orderly system of laws and punishment. If he did this, he would be begging the question, since 'punishment' for injustice presupposes that justice has already been established.

Must we then say that the 'natural' motives that Hume appeals to are insufficient to account for the convention being formed? The first thing to notice is that Hume need not commit himself to the view that these natural motives will ensure that the parties to the convention will universally and always act justly. It is enough if he has made intelligible how individuals have come to appreciate the general advantage of fixed rules about property. One can then see how following the rules of just conduct may come to be associated in a man's mind with his own interests, and how this furnishes a countermotive to the immediate satisfaction of a short-term interest.

We have already observed that Hume considers that society has grown from its origin in a small group, and that the first trace of social life can be seen in a family unit. In a small group of men, it is much easier to see how co-operation is essential in order to derive the benefits of the group membership, and how an individual can come to look upon his own interests as dependent upon successful co-operation. The alternative is to be left alone, to be banished from the group. This is perhaps why Hume thinks one must abide by the convention or alternatively 'fall into a savage and solitary condition'; he probably had a small group in mind when he wrote this. In addition the influence of the 'confined benevolence', which Hume takes to belong to our nature, would be much greater in a small group, and would make us more sensitive to the interests of other members of the group; there would be no 'total strangers'. We should be more affected by the pleasures and pains of others through sympathy.

We must imagine that we are dealing with a society of this kind, a small group, when considering how justice comes to be regarded as a virtue. The moral approval of the just man's behaviour is supposed to depend upon the utility of justice. This utility is much more easily seen in a small society, although the natural motives may be less obviously in need of the additional moral incentives in order that the system may be upheld.

If we have in mind a tacit agreement between people to behave in a certain way, we see that a failure to do so will cause disappointment in the other parties to the agreement who have come to count upon our behaviour. Thus injustice comes to have an injurious consequence in virtue of the convention having been formed. Combine with this an awareness that the rules of justice generally make social life safer and more 'commodious'. Although this may be more easily overlooked in a large society, we cannot avoid noticing the ill effects of suffering injustice when we ourselves, or those close to us, are the sufferers. We thus come to think of unjust actions as the causes of unpleasantness and pain. We sympathize with those who are adversely affected by them and come to dislike the causes of them, ultimately the agent. This dislike becomes moral disapproval when we look upon injustice as impartial spectators. It may be noticed that this account makes it much more obvious why we should disapprove of injustice than approve of justice, since the utility of the latter is not so easily seen as the ill effects of the former. This may not be thought a grave fault in the theory, for we find, in fact, that justice needs to be exceptional for it to be warmly approved of, whereas we disapprove of all manner of injustice. The reason for this may well be that a minimum standard of justice is required of us. It is only when the minimum requirement is surpassed that justice is considered a virtue in a man.

We have seen that our approval of justice and disapproval of injustice arise out of our contemplation of the actions of others. We extend it, however, to cover our own case, and approve of justice in ourselves, and disapprove of our injustice:

> The *general rule* reaches beyond those instances from which it
> arose; while, at the same time, we naturally *sympathize* with others
> in the sentiments they entertain of us. (THN III, 204/499)

Hume insists in this chapter that a full account of the reasons why we approve of justice, and disapprove of injustice, cannot be given before the natural virtues have been examined. This is because he has not yet given an account of objectivity in evaluations – the way in which we come to evaluate actions and characters from an impartial point of view. His order of exposition is unfortunate, and has given more plausibility to a wrong interpretation of this particular statement.

Hume explains how our sympathy with the judgments others form of us helps to make us approve and disapprove of ourselves, and it seems that this approval or disapproval stems from a desire to be thought *well of*. This is the outlook of someone who wants to be respectable. Thus the feeling lingers that this would nòt be genuine moral disapproval. This, however, is too one-sided an interpretation, for Hume's statements must be understood in the light of his doctrines as expressed in Book III, Part III, Section 1. There is reason to believe that sympathy with the unfortunates who suffer from our own injustice has something to do with our disapproval of injustice in ourselves: when we look upon ourselves with approval or disapproval, we view ourselves *as if we were* any other person.

It might further be pointed out that when Hume uses the phrase 'sympathize with others in the sentiments they entertain of us', he may simply mean 'agree with others in their condemnation or praise of our actions'. If theirs is a genuine approval or disapproval, based upon the same factual judgments of the case as we ourselves make, we would naturally sympathize with their judgments of us.

Hume is concerned to show how our motives for justice come to be strengthened so that we often act justly against our own, and even against the public interest. He emphasizes, and rightly, that once justice comes to be considered a virtue, politicians and educators may strengthen people's allegiance to just conduct, by utilizing the evaluative force of the term. He can also quite legitimately point out that people's desire for respectability may be used for this purpose. Parents may see that a just man gets on better in the world than an unjust one, and consequently indoctrinate their children in such a way as to make them see that it is prudent to be just. It would be rash to deny that these motives are powerful in counteracting the force of temptations to behave in unjust ways.

Here, we meet with a real difficulty in Hume's argument. Sympathy with the general utility of justice may be enough to account for our approval of the just man; but Hume cannot, consistently with his view of the biased nature of benevolence, maintain that public benevolence is the *motive* which keeps people to the path of justice, even in a case where this motive opposes strong self-interest or limited benevolence. This is why he has to search for additional influences which may help to explain the just man's steadfast adherence to the rules of justice. We must, in any case, remember that in society most people would probably not be fully aware of the public utility of justice, and would thus not be able to value it for the right reasons.

But when justice is classified with the natural virtues people generally come to have the same outlook towards it, strengthened by the propaganda of politicians in their quest for an orderly society, and the influence of parents who desire the welfare of their children. But this propaganda presupposes, is parasitic upon, our natural moral sentiments:

> Any artifice of politicians may assist nature in the producing of those sentiments, which she suggests to us, and may even, on some occasions, produce alone an approbation or esteem for any particular action; but it is impossible it should be the sole cause of the distinction we make betwixt vice and virtue. For if nature did not aid us in this particular, it would be in vain for politicians to talk of *honourable* or *dishonourable*, *praiseworthy* or *blameable*. These words would be perfectly unintelligible, and would no more have any idea annexed to them, than if they were of a tongue perfectly unknown to us. The utmost politicians can perform, is to extend the natural sentiments beyond their original bounds; but still nature must furnish the materials, and give us some notion of moral distinctions. (THN III, 204/500)

This is in harmony with Hume's general associationist scheme. The word calls up a certain idea which may be enlivened into a real impression – a passion. But this association could not be formed without a previous impression, of which the idea is a copy. This explains the inability of politicians to give meaning to words of praise in the first place. The association presupposes real approval and disapproval, these being passions of a special sort with which the terms come to be associated. A word is not a natural cause, but acquires its causal efficacy by convention, through its association with some experience, some perception.

The concepts of duty and obligation do not play a prominent part in Hume's philosophy, although the circular argument, mentioned earlier seems to entail that the only adequate motive for justice is the sense of its morality. Hume cannot, of course, admit that actions possess a characteristic which may be called their 'obligatoriness'; yet we here seem to be faced with the difficulty that regard for the morality of an action may be a motive for performing it. Furthermore, it is the specific motive of the *just man*. If then the moral characteristic of an action derives from the nature of the motive, it seems that some actions derive their morality from regard *for* their morality. This reasoning appears to be circular and is taken by Hume to be so. In fact, this is the dilemma he states in posing his problem about the artificial virtues.

From this, it might be concluded that public utility is the ultimate reason why justice is approved as a virtue. But has Hume not denied that there is any such principle as public benevolence? How then can the consciousness of the public utility of justice come to furnish a motive for just conduct?

It must be firmly kept in mind that Hume nowhere maintains that a just act, in one sense, is always performed from the same motive; it would indeed be absurd if he did maintain this. Let us imagine a man repaying a loan: this is undoubtedly an action in conformity with established rules of justice; it would be thought unjust not to pay. Yet it is obvious that the motive might not be a sense of duty at all. The action may arise from the thought that the creditor needed the money, and a consequent desire for *his* happiness. The point is, of course, that benevolence may often lead to behaviour we should describe as just. On other occasions, self-love might be the motive: we might want to enhance our reputation, or our intention might be to secure the possibility of another loan from the same source later on. There is thus an obvious sense in which it is untrue to say that the *only* motive to conduct called just is a sense of duty.

But we must remember that, in the cases listed above, we should not describe *the agent* as just if we inferred his motive to be self-love or benevolence. We should call him prudent or benevolent, as the case might be. In what circumstances would the man be described as just, if we distinguish one virtue from another by a difference in motive and if Hume has denied that there is a special natural motive to just conduct?

It is here that the problem of the motive of duty intrudes itself, and it is assumed that justice is distinguished from the other virtues in that the just man is motivated by a 'sense of duty', as distinct from benevolence or self-interest. The just man is the man who adheres steadfastly to the rules of justice, even when benevolence and self-interest may seem to prompt different behaviour. He is able to do this because the motive of duty has come to be so highly developed. We have seen that if this motive were supposed to result from the realization of the utility of justice, its strength could not be accounted for. Propaganda and education help to create a situation where the non-performance of just actions comes to be firmly associated with pain in our minds. This helps to strengthen the behavioural pattern we call just behaviour. So long as we think of the 'sense of the morality' of an action as benevolence resulting from moral approval, Hume cannot be made consistent. By 'sense of duty' we must understand 'being pained at the thought of the absence of an action or character'.

But Hume has put forward two apparently incompatible views: (1) that no virtue has the sense of duty as its motive; and (2) that this is the characteristic motive of the just man. Perhaps it is due to awareness of this that he sometimes insists that *properly enlightened* self-interest would suffice to keep a man to the path of justice. This would, however, reduce justice to prudence. When the just man acted from a sense of duty this would be an indication of a lack of this virtue of prudence; he would be doing what the prudent man would do.

I cannot see that the difficulty mentioned in the previous paragraph is ever fully resolved by Hume. There is a sense in which a virtue whose characteristic motive is the sense of duty is impossible according to his theory.[1] This would entail that justice is impossible as a separate virtue. Yet we must remember that even though our sense of duty may be impressed upon us partly through an appeal to self-interest and our limited benevolence, this need not entail that when we come to achieve objectivity in our attitude our feelings of duty are entirely non-moral. Do we not in fact recommend the virtuous life to our children very largely through an appeal to one or other of these motives?

Hume denies that justice 'admits of degrees' in the way in which natural virtues do. These run insensibly into vice: we become less and less benevolent until our lack of benevolence has become a vice. We must not understand this to mean that a man cannot be more or less just, as he can be more or less benevolent: the man who is more just follows the rules of justice more consistently. But an individual act, and this is Hume's point, must be either just or unjust; a man's action may be more or less benevolent, but there is no such sliding scale in the case of justice. The main reason for this is to be found in the fact that property admits of no degrees: either we own something or we do not. Once we remember how closely Hume ties justice to property his view becomes more easily understood. Even so, he admits that claims to property may, by an arbitrator, be deemed so equal that a division in property is called for. It remains true that Hume thinks in terms of inflexible rules which the just man is obliged to follow:

Were men, therefore, to take the liberty of acting with regard to

[1] My treatment of this problem has been much assisted by Hedenius' *Studies in Hume's Ethics*.

the laws of society, as they do in every other affair, they would conduct themselves, on most occasions, by particular judgments, and would take into consideration the characters and circumstances of the persons, as well as the general nature of the question. But it is easy to observe, that this would produce an infinite confusion in human society, and that the avidity and partiality of men would quickly bring disorder into the world, if not restrained by some general and inflexible principles. (THN III, 233-4/532)

I agree with MacNabb that Hume's view is open to the interpretation that not only are the *rules* inflexible but our *observance* of them should be inflexible. According to MacNabb, a principle may have many qualifying clauses indicating conditions where it would not apply and yet still be inflexible. Given these exceptions, there is no further latitude. He takes the example of a friend who falls ill in his (MacNabb's) house. The telephone wires are broken and the roads blocked. A previous visitor has left a bottle of medicine in the house which would save his friend's life. MacNabb now asks:

> Is it theft to use the medicine, however valuable? Surely not; the principles of private property tacitly provide for such exceptions. And if the owner of the medicine subsequently sued me at law, it would be open to the courts to mark a technical offence, but dismiss the charge as trifling under the probation of offenders act.
> (DHTK and M, 184)

I think Hume would be bound to say that, in the legal sense, it was indeed theft to take the medicine. Hume seems primarily to have in mind the legal sense of 'justice' in writing the passage quoted above. It is, as MacNabb says, a 'technical offence'.

Let us remember that if the person in MacNabb's story refrains from taking the medicine, on the ground that it is not his property, he could not be charged with *injustice*. We might, however, condemn this behaviour as *inhuman*. This might be one occasion where we should not approve of behaviour in accordance with the rules of justice. It is the benevolent man of whom we should approve in this situation.

We now see, perhaps, one further reason why Hume should be inclined to talk as if the man must follow the rules of justice inflexibly. Justice must involve a disposition to behave in a particular way. Where humanity (benevolence) or self-interest bids us act contrary to these rules, there may be individual occasions where we should approve of these exceptions. We still cannot say that it is in virtue of a man's justice, rather than his possession of the natural virtues, prudence or benevolence, that he makes the exception.

Hume maintains that justice arises from prudence and limited benevolence. Yet it is a separate virtue that can neither be reduced to benevolence nor prudence nor a combination of the two. This chapter has been concerned with Hume's attempt to explain how the admission of a *separate* virtue of justice can be made consistent with his general view about the nature of virtue. Since a virtuous action is derived from the virtue of the motive which ties the action to a person's character, one should not be surprised that Hume emphasizes the search for the specific motive for justice.

9

EVALUATIONS AND THEIR LINGUISTIC EXPRESSION

In the *Treatise*, Hume explains the nature and origin of evaluations; but he is not concerned with evaluative language. This is why I have so far said nothing about the question to which commentators have given different answers: how does Hume think evaluative linguistic expressions ought to be analysed? I shall examine three answers to this question, and attempt to trace the sources of certain mistaken interpretations of Hume's words.

Hume is sometimes accused of reducing Ethics to Psychology. This is in a sense true, although it would be fairer to say that once the nature of evaluation has been established, there is no room for a *normative* science of Ethics, as distinct from an empirical enquiry into the principles in accordance with which people evaluate. Thus we might say, with some justification, that, for Hume, a science of Ethics is possible only as a branch of Psychology, depending for its data upon history and knowledge of man's social behaviour. The statements of this empirical science would be about evaluations; they would not be evaluative expressions. It must, of course, also be borne in mind that some of Hume's 'psychology' is of interest when understood as conceptual analysis. I have, indeed, emphasized this in Chapter 2 of this book.

It is of the utmost importance to understand precisely in what sense Hume reduced Ethics to Psychology, for it is not uncommon to attribute to him the doctrine that evaluative expressions are descriptions of psychological facts. I shall attempt to show that the general trend of Hume's arguments is at variance with such an interpretation, and that some accepted interpretations make nonsense of his views.

It is true that Professor C. D. Broad bases his interpretation of Hume upon the *Enquiry*. His interpretation could hardly have been arrived at by an unbiased reading of the *Treatise*. My justification for mentioning Broad's view here is that he writes as if he were representing all Hume's thought on the subject: 'The best account of Hume's theory of ethics is to be found in his *Enquiry Concerning the Principles of Morals*' (FTET, 84). This certainly does not suggest that Hume may have put forward a different and, perhaps, a more adequate theory in his *Treatise*.

Discussing Hume's view on 'the meaning and analysis of ethical predicates and propositions', Broad gives the following interpretation:

> There is a certain specific kind of emotion which nearly all human beings feel from time to time. This is the emotion of *Approval* or *Disapproval*. It is called forth by the contemplation of certain objects, and it is directed towards those objects. Now for Hume the statement '*x* is good' *means* the same as the statement '*x* is such that the contemplation of it would call forth an emotion of approval towards it in all or most men'. (FTET, 84-85)

The definition of '*x* is bad' would be the same, with 'disapproval' substituted for 'approval'. The interpretation is plain enough, although it is vague on one point. The statement '*x* is such that it would call forth an emotion of approval towards it in all or most men' is, one presumes, to be amplified by 'when people think of *x*, or meet with *x* in life'. The value-judgment is then taken to state what the feelings of people would be when confronted with *x* in thought or experience. It would thus claim to be a statement of fact, and would be verified or falsified by examining what people really felt when confronted with *x*.

Hume's doctrine would, on this interpretation, be a perfect example of the naturalism which G. E. Moore attacks in his *Principia Ethica*. One would not have been surprised if Broad had asked whether it was a tautology to say that what all or most people approve of is good. The statement, as it stands, would clearly not be tautological. We consider it at least logically possible that the minority is correct about the evaluation of certain things. This entails the possibility that what most people approve of is bad; but if the above definition of '*x* is good' is accepted it would be self-contradictory to entertain such a possibility. It would, indeed, be like claiming that what is approved of by most people might not be approved of by most people.

Broad almost certainly means by 'all or most men' what could be equally well expressed by 'at least most men'. He could hardly wish to indicate that by '*x* is good' we sometimes mean 'most men approve of *x*', and at other times 'all men approve of *x*'. But there is one obvious reason why it is not very plausible to suggest that '*x* is virtuous' means 'at least most people approve of *x*'. The latter statement seems to be a general statement *about* people's evaluations rather than a value statement itself. '*x* is good' is a value statement; it expresses an evaluation. It seems obvious that when people approve of *x* they can express this approval by the statement '*x* is good'. But, if Broad's interpretation is correct, it would be possible for a person to approve of *x*, and at the same time believe that *x* is not good, because in believing that *x* is good, one would be believing the truth of a proposition about other people's approvals as well as one's own. The proposed analysis would make it impossible to think that *x* is good because one approves of *x*, knowing, or believing, that one is not concurring with most people's evaluations, since to think that *x* is good is to believe a proposition about most people's emotions. But surely one could think that one was both in the minority and in the right in one's evaluation: one might think that other people were morally immature, or perverse in their moral judgments.

A further difficulty arises about the extension of the class of people. It may include only those who have lived up to the present, or it may include all future generations. According to the first interpretation, the expression '*x* is good' would be a historical statement, and its truth would be entirely determined by what is the case or has been the case, as opposed to what will be the case. This would make the status of the moral teacher, the innovator, a peculiar one. He would be a man who discovers something about the past and present, rather than a man who lays down the law for the future. He would, indeed, be in the same position as any other historian making a discovery about the past and present.

If we include future generations in the class of people, it would follow that we could *never* be quite certain that the statement '*x* is good' is true. The explanation for this would not be that people have *different ideas* of what constitutes goodness; this would be easily understandable and is most likely true. The reason is that we could never be certain that we have in fact examined all people, or even most people. We may have a hundred per cent agreement now: all the cases in the future might turn out to be unfavourable. This entirely misrepresents our uncertainty when we are in doubt about whether someone is a good man or not. It would be misleading to suggest that what we doubt is whether all other people would feel the same way as we do about the person in question. This is not to deny that it may be relevant to consider other people's opinion about a person, when we are assessing the value of his character.

It may, of course, be said that there are uses of '*x* is good' and '*x* is virtuous' that fit the analysis Broad attributes to Hume. Thus there may be occasions when to say '*x* is good' is treated as equivalent to giving the information that people in a certain society generally approve of *x*. I might be studying a certain culture and be interested in finding out what the inhabitants thought good. I might try to get the information by asking questions of the form 'Is *x* good?' If Mr Obu, to whom I am talking, understands what I am after, he may answer 'Yes', even in a case when he himself disagrees with the majority. It must be agreed, however, that the sense in which '*x* is good' means 'most people approve of *x*' cannot be considered the primary evaluative sense of the expression. We might even want to say that Mr Obu ought to have said 'Most people here *think* *x* is good but I don't agree'.

The main point to be emphasized is, of course, that Hume never accepts 'all or most people approve of *x*' as justifying, by equivalence of meaning, the statement '*x* is virtuous'. Knowledge of what people approve of is, all the same, very relevant to our own approvals and disapprovals, not as evidence, but as a causal factor which may operate through sympathy.

It is not uncommon for the interpretation of the doctrines of major philosophers to harden into dogmas. In the end it becomes difficult to achieve an unbiased reading of the original text, because of the almost irresistible tendency to find what one's teachers and commentators have led one to expect. In the particular case I am now going to discuss, there are in fact two dogmas, two incompatible interpretations, each of which claims to represent Hume's real view. What follows explains why I think that both sides in this combat are wrong; this is a battle no one deserves to win.

I shall confine my attention to evaluation in terms of the virtue or vice of actions or people. The question is whether Hume is a Subjectivist or an Emotivist. One may conceive of the issue between these theories in one or other of two ways: (1) as concerned with the correct interpretation of evaluative language; and (2) as having to do with the nature of evaluations themselves.[1] I shall use the names 'Subjectivism' and 'Emotivism' exclusively for doctrines about the function of evaluative language. I have, for the sake of clarity, given the names Emotionism and Reflectivism to two theories about the nature of evaluations themselves that might be confused with Emotivism and Subjectivism.

The Subjectivist maintains that '*x* is virtuous', and similar expressions, are to be understood to make statements about the feelings of the speaker.[2] They are true or false according to whether or not the contemplation of an action, or a person's character, arouses a certain feeling in the person using the expression.[3] The Emotivist, on the other hand, considers that the evaluative expressions we are discussing do not make true or false statements. They are used rather to express the feelings one has in contemplating some person or an action. Evaluative expressions are not to be thought of as true or false.

I am fully aware that some may want to quarrel with my use of 'Subjectivism' and 'Emotivism' on the ground that both terms have been used differently in the past. Thus it may be pointed out that Emotivism has taken various different forms, some of them more refined than the doctrine I here state under that title. But my intention is not to give a historically accurate account of the way these terms have been used, and the blunt way in which I have drawn the distinction does, I hope, serve to bring out the main points I want to make.

Let us now turn our attention to Emotionism and Reflectivism. The Emotionist contends that evaluations *are* emotions, whereas the Reflectivist maintains that they are *judgments* that one has certain emotions. On the first interpretation, the evaluation, it seems, could not be thought of as true or false, since feelings are not assessed in these terms. (I am not forgetting that one may talk of, for example, love as

---

[1] Broad does not draw this distinction. Although he puts his view forward as an account of Hume's doctrine about linguistic evaluative expressions he probably thought that he was also, by implication, analysing Hume's account of the nature of evaluations themselves.

[2] In what follows I want what I say about '*x* is virtuous' to be understood to apply also to '*x* is vicious' with relevant but obvious modifications.

[3] I use the noun 'expression' in its ordinary sense so as not to beg any questions about what is expressed. It could be an emotion or a proposition.

being true; but this sense of 'true' is different from that in which propositions, statements and judgments may be true.)

I began this chapter by emphasizing that Hume, in his *Treatise*, is not mainly concerned with the elucidation of the function of evaluative language. His chief objective is to explain the origin and nature of evaluations themselves.[1] It is perfectly possible, although perhaps not plausible, to maintain that evaluations are emotions, and yet to think that the verbal form '*x* is virtuous' is used to make a true or false claim that one is having the emotion in which our evaluation *consists*. One can with logical consistency adhere to both the Emotionist and the Subjectivist position. But in that case it follows that the words '*x* is virtuous' make a statement *about* an evaluation and are not an evaluative expression in themselves. If, on the other hand, evaluations are *judgments* that one is having an emotion, then the natural linguistic expression for this judgment would make a statement about the feelings of the speaker. The linguistic expression of this would then be a genuinely evaluative expression and would not make a statement *about* an evaluation, although this is what it appears to do. It seems natural for a Reflectivist to maintain the Subjectivist position; for, if evaluations are judgments about the feelings of the person judging, one would expect evaluative expressions to make statements *about* the feelings of the person making the statement. A statement *about* an evaluation would, in this case, be a statement to the effect that one judges that one has a certain emotion. It would be a statement about the judgment that constitutes the evaluation – it would, to put it another way, express a second-order judgment.

By the term 'judgment' I mean only a true or false thought that a person has at a particular time. It is obvious that one often has true or false thoughts. These can not be equated with *saying* things to oneself. I now think (I hope truly) that my wife is making lunch. I could have thought this without saying anything to myself. I do not think the word 'judgment' ought to engender any confusion, although it is sometimes used in a wider sense: people talk about 'moral judgment' in such a way that it is not a contradiction to talk about the Emotivist analysis of moral judgments. In my terminology, to say that *x* is a judgment entails that *x* can be assessed in terms of truth or falsity.

[1] On this point, and some others, there is close similarity between Professor Antony Flew's and my own reading of Hume. See 'The Interpretation of Hume', *Philosophy*, April 1963.

Underlying this is the assumption that evaluations in words are possible, that when we say 'x is virtuous' we are simply evaluating publicly, rather than keeping our evaluation to ourselves. There may, of course, be certain reasons why we should decide not to keep our evaluation to ourselves. We may, for example, want to affect the attitudes of other people. What we say will, of course, also give information about ourselves; but this is not the point of an expressed evaluation, although it may be the point of expressing it. There is a logical absurdity about the question 'What is the point of approving of x?' or 'What is the point of thinking x virtuous?', but there is no such oddity about 'What is the point of saying you approve of x?' or 'What is the point of saying that x is virtuous?' The fact that asking someone for his purpose in saying that x is virtuous would normally be taken to imply that the speaker is insincere, or has an ulterior motive for saying this, does not in any way affect my main point. One can decide to say things or to keep them to oneself, but one cannot decide to evaluate in one way rather than another. Whether one thinks a person virtuous or vicious is not a matter of decision at all, though one may decide to keep this to oneself or to evaluate openly by saying 'x is vicious', or 'x is virtuous', as the case might be. I do not want to deny that we do often say that we decide what to think of things, or how to value them: 'I decided he was no good' is a perfectly natural, if ungrammatical, way of talking. But decision, in this sense, is determined by the evidence, if it is a genuine decision at all; in a sense, the decision is not free. Having decided that someone is a scoundrel, one may decide to tell him this or to remain silent; this decision is free, in that it is not determined by the reasons for or against. It is always possible to decide to do what there are good reasons for not doing; but it makes no sense to suggest that a person may, in this sense of 'decide', *decide* to alter his evaluation of someone or something. Our freedom to decide what to think is strictly limited, in a way in which our freedom to act is not. Thus we can decide to say, from ulterior motives, that a person is a villain. To suggest that we can decide to think, from ulterior motives, that someone is a villain is plainly absurd.

To use language for openly evaluating is specifically different from talking about one's evaluations. The point of the first is to pass judgment on the object evaluated, although what is said also allows people to make an inference about the person talking – that he evaluates in a certain way. If what one says concerns the way one feels about things, or how one values something, one is talking *about* one's evaluations rather than openly *evaluating*. A typical instance of this would be the pronouncements of a person on the psychiatrist's couch about his own feelings and values. If we want to preserve the distinction between openly evaluating and talking about evaluations, and consider that both must be allowed to be possible, it seems that Emotivism as a doctrine about language most plausibly fits Emotionism as a doctrine about evaluations, and that the same holds for Subjectivism and Reflectivism. If to think that x is virtuous is to think that one has an emotion, then the natural way to express this evaluation would be to say that one has the emotion. But, if this is an evaluating expression the difficulty is to see how one can, in contrast with this, make a statement about one's evaluation; the two would be the same. If, on the other hand, to think that x is virtuous is equivalent to having the emotion of approval, then the natural way to construe 'I have an emotion of approval' is to think of this as a statement about one's evaluation, rather than an expression of it, or an evaluation in words. The emotive way of interpreting evaluative expressions would get one out of the difficulty, and enable one consistently both to evaluate openly and to talk about one's evaluations.

When one turns to the text of the *Treatise*, one is struck by the fact that Hume's pronouncements about the nature of evaluations appear ambiguous, although he does say: 'To have the sense of virtue, is nothing but to *feel* a satisfaction of a particular kind from the contemplation of a character. The very *feeling* constitutes our praise or admiration' (THN III, 179/471); this seems to imply an Emotionist interpretation. But a little later, in the same paragraph, he writes ' . . . but in feeling that it pleases after such a particular manner, we in effect feel that it is virtuous. The case is the same as in our judgments concerning all kinds of beauty, and tastes, and sensations. Our approbation is implied in the immediate pleasure they convey to us' (THN III, 179/471). One might think that this passage implies that evaluations are judgments and that 'feeling that' is, as it often is today, an alternative for 'believing that'. In another place,[1] Hume talks of matters of fact as objects of feeling. Thus one may think Hume wants us to construe an evaluation as feeling that something is the case, and, therefore, as true or false, according to whether this turns out to *be* the case. It may be felt that it is not Emotionism but Reflectivism that Hume is advocating.

[1] THN III, 177/469.

Which is Hume's real view? In what follows, I hope to go some way towards explaining why this has proved so difficult to decide. Although one may conclude that Hume is an Emotionist, and not so obviously, an Emotivist, there are certain special peculiarities about his position. I shall be concerned mostly with those who attribute Subjectivism to Hume, although I shall also give some reasons for considering it misleading to call him an Emotivist. As an example of an attribution of Subjectivism to Hume, we may look at an article by Geoffrey Hunter.

In the April issue of *Philosophy*, 1962, Hunter makes the following statement about Hume's analysis of moral judgments:

Hume's analysis of moral judgments is mistaken. For, among other things, it has the consequence that if one person says of an action that it is wholly virtuous and another person says of the same action that it is wholly vicious, these two people would not be contradicting each other, since one is saying the logical equivalent of 'I (Smith) feel a peculiar sort of pleasure, and I do not feel a peculiar sort of pain, on contemplating this action', while the other is saying the equivalent of 'I (Jones) feel a peculiar sort of pain, and I do not feel a peculiar sort of pleasure, on contemplating this action', and both these statements could be true. If they were both true, and Hume's analysis were correct, then one and the same action would *be* both wholly virtuous and wholly vicious, which, in the ordinary senses of the words used, is absurd. (op. cit., 151-2)

In 'A reply to Professor Flew', in the April issue of *Philosophy*, 1963, Hunter withdraws some part of the view expressed in the passage quoted above. He no longer thinks that it follows from Hume's analysis of 'moral judgments'[1] that the same action could be 'both wholly virtuous and wholly vicious'. He thus abandons what he had put forward as his reasons for considering Hume's analysis absurd. But he gives no hint that he has changed his view about the interpretation to be given of Hume's analysis of moral judgments, nor does he give us any reason to believe that he now considers Hume's analysis tenable. All we are told is that one absurd consequence does not follow from Hume's view. If Hume's alleged analysis is meant to capture the ordinary sense of

[1] The way Mr Hunter expresses himself tends to mask the distinction that I have drawn between Subjectivism and Reflectivism. I expect, however, that he wants to attribute both these doctrines to Hume. He makes it unambiguously clear that he thinks Hume is a Subjectivist.

'x is virtuous', then all that is needed for this to be asserted truly, is that the person using the expression should, in fact, approve of x. When, therefore, another person asserts that 'x is vicious', he is making a claim about a different speaker, namely himself. When these expressions are used by different speakers, there is therefore no contradiction between the two assertions. But it is implausible to suggest that, according to the ordinary meaning of 'x is virtuous' and 'x is vicious', these are statements about the speaker, and thus systematically change in meaning with the identity of the speaker. It is paradoxical to maintain that two men who equally condemn an action by calling it vicious, and do so for the same reasons, are not saying the same thing about it, but are making statements about their respective feelings. When two people say about x 'x is virtuous', one of them might be saying something true, and the other might be uttering a falsehood; this is surely an unacceptable paradox. And yet, in establishing the truth or falsity of either assertion, a third party ought, given the analysis, to find out who the speakers were, and try to assess whether, indeed, they do have the feelings they claim to have. This is manifestly not the way we establish whether an action, or a person, is virtuous. Yet, on this analysis, it would be the way to establish the truth of 'x is virtuous', when stated by other people. The decision procedure would be different if we attempt to decide whether our *own* assertion, 'x is virtuous', is true. This we can only assert truly on the basis of the feelings we have ourselves on contemplating the object.

It can hardly be denied that, assuming it to express a proposition, the statement 'x is virtuous' can be understood, and its truth or falsity established, without knowing who the speaker is. If it is true, it would be true whoever said it. Hunter's thesis is, as I understand it, that Hume thinks that 'x is virtuous' is a statement about the speaker's feelings, and that from this it follows that what is stated varies systematically with the speaker.

The interpretation Hunter advances for Hume's analysis of 'x is virtuous', where 'x' stands for an action, is, I believe, widely accepted. The same sort of account would presumably be given of Hume's analysis of the meaning of 'x is virtuous' where 'x' is a person.

It has always seemed to me strange that Hume, surely a most perceptive thinker, should not have noticed the implausibility of this view. Commentators have found little difficulty in finding fault with this doctrine. If Hume held it, what precisely led him to put forward a view that has so little to recommend it? I have nowhere seen a serious attempt made to explain this. Surely if you want to attribute to a major thinker a theory that is obviously untenable it is important to give a satisfactory account of the reasons why he holds it. I shall, later on, attempt to show that there are reasons for believing that he did not hold this view. I shall also attempt to explain why he should write in a way which has led people to believe that he was advocating the subjectivist doctrine.

One point is not clear in the analysis attributed to Hume. Does the truth of the so-called 'moral judgment' depend upon the existence in the speaker of a certain feeling *at the moment of speaking*? Does 'This action is virtuous' mean 'I *now* have a certain feeling of pleasure in contemplating this action'? The alternative is that 'x is virtuous' means 'whenever I contemplate x I have a certain feeling of pleasure'. It is obviously of some importance to decide which of these analyses is taken to represent Hume's view. By 'Subjectivism' I mean the first of these views. I shall not consider the other interpretation; it is essentially obscure and it would take too long to elucidate its precise meaning. Are we to say, for example, that the statement 'x is virtuous' is falsified if at some time in the past I contemplated x without having a feeling of approval?

In the same chapter in which Hume appears to maintain that moral judgments are statements of psychological fact, he writes that a certain feeling we have in contemplating a character 'constitutes' what we call praise or admiration. He implies that what we normally, in ordinary language, call 'thinking that x is virtuous' is, in effect, simply having a certain feeling. The Subjectivist analysis of moral language does not fit in well with Emotionism; for, if 'x is virtuous' makes a statement about the speaker's feelings, there is no linguistic means of expressing the emotion which constitutes the evaluation. What we are expressing when we make a so-called 'moral judgment' is that we have the feeling which constitutes our feeling that something is virtuous. On this account the feeling which 'constitutes our praise or admiration' corresponds to what we normally call 'moral judgment'. It certainly has to be differentiated from the judgment expressed by the words 'I (Paul) feel a peculiar sort of pleasure, and I do not feel a peculiar sort of pain on (now) contemplating this action'. This statement would normally be considered to give information about the way in which I feel about, and, indeed, the way I do not feel about the action. Since this is so, it is not contradicted by a statement to the effect that someone else (Smith) feels differently about it. But when we understand an utterance in this way we are not taking it to *express an evaluation*; we take it to be a statement of psychological fact. It is to be challenged by attacking the speaker's truthfulness about his inner state, or his capacity for correctly describing the nature of his feelings.

The important difference between statements about emotions and expressions of evaluations can perhaps be brought out by the following consideration. When John, in talking to his psychiatrist, describes to him what his feelings are, his statement 'I have feelings A, B and C' has precisely the same truth conditions as the psychiatrist's statement to John 'You have feelings A, B, C' and his later report 'He (John) had feelings A, B, C'. Precisely the same states of affairs will make true, or false, each of these statements. The statement made by the psychiatrist indicates that he is accepting what John says, but he does not thereby endorse his feelings. When, however, '*x* is virtuous' is used to express an evaluation, (which is its usual function), to accept this is to endorse the evaluation of the speaker. To accept what John says, in that case, is to *agree in feeling* with John – assuming that approvals and disapprovals are feelings.

But utterances that appear to the careless philosopher to be statements about a man's feelings are, in fact, not always to be thus understood. If I addressed a public meeting to argue in support of home rule for Scotland I might present my case by saying: 'I feel most strongly that Scotland ought to be given its own parliament.' To disagree with my statement is to have a different view about the political issue. My statement expresses my feelings about the question of Scotland's independence. My purpose is not to interest the audience in myself: I am trying to interest them in a cause that I consider vital for the Scottish people. The context usually indicates quite clearly whether what the speaker says is meant as an evaluation or as a statement telling people how he evaluates.

The peculiarity of the Subjectivist analysis of evaluative language lies in this, that it claims that evaluative linguistic expressions make statements about the emotions of the speaker. This goes counter to what we normally think, although evaluations are, upon occasion, expressed in language that may seem superficially to make statements about the state of the speaker's emotions. But if the analysis attributed to Hume by Hunter is correct it is extremely difficult to see how '*x* is virtuous' could be construed to express approval,[1] and '*x* is vicious' disapproval. They would rather make statements about the speaker's evaluations.

Let us look again at Hunter's proposed analysis: 'I (Smith) feel a peculiar sort of pain, and I do not feel a peculiar sort of pleasure on contemplating this action' (op. cit., 152). This is logically equivalent, he says, to 'This action is vicious'. He bases this interpretation upon such a passage as the following: ' . . . when you pronounce any action or character to be vicious, you mean nothing, but that from the constitution of your nature you have a feeling or sentiment of blame from the contemplation of it' (THN III, 177/469). Now Hume makes no reference in this statement to the absence of a feeling of pleasure. Hunter is, therefore, improving upon Hume's analysis, in order to avoid the consequence that a man might think the same action virtuous and vicious at the same time.

But there is another aspect of Hunter's analysis which certainly cannot be counted an improvement upon what Hume says: for Hume's 'a feeling or sentiment *of blame*',[2] Hunter substitutes 'I feel a peculiar sort of pain'. Now, there may be many peculiar sorts of pain, and most of them need not be the feeling of blame to which Hume refers. The conditions for the truth of Hunter's analysis might often be fulfilled when it is false to say that the speaker has 'a feeling or sentiment of blame'. Thus, not only is the analysis Hunter attributes to Hume inherently implausible, but the passage in Hume's *Treatise* that comes closest to it is, in important respects, different.

It may also be true that whenever we say '*x* is virtuous' we have a special feeling of pleasure; this is because approval is a special feeling of pleasure. But 'I have a special feeling of pleasure' and 'I do not have a special feeling of pain' does not *mean* the same as '*x* is virtuous'. One must be careful not to confuse statements about approvals and disapprovals and the conditions of approvals and disapprovals with the analysis of the *meaning* of utterances expressing approvals and disapprovals. Hunter's statement is unacceptable as an analysis of the meaning of '*x* is vicious'. It is, all the same, a correct, although not a

---

[1] I here again use the term 'express' in its ordinary sense. It begs no question about the analysis of evaluative expressions. A man would be expressing his approval in saying 'John is a good man' even though we think such evaluative expressions make statements.

[2] My italics.

complete, characterization of the conditions under which it is correct to use this linguistic expression.

In the passage quoted from the *Treatise* the author makes a reference to the speaker's nature. Hume writes 'you mean nothing but that from the constitution of your nature . . .'. To put this in as part of the meaning of 'evaluative' utterances of the kind we are considering, would be justified only if it is meant to stress that *your* nature is such as to approve or disapprove of the thing when you contemplate it; that, of course, others might be entirely different, and that you are making no claim about them. But since one of Hume's main problems in the *Treatise* is to show how in moral evaluation the *natural* bias of each individual's passions is overcome, he surely would not have accepted reference to the speaker's peculiar nature as part of the meaning of such expressions as '*x* is virtuous'.

But might we not be making a mistake in interpreting the passage we are considering from the *Treatise*? Is it not possible that when Hume says 'when you pronounce . . . you mean nothing but . . .' he is making a statement about the expression of evaluation rather than proposing an analysis of the *meaning* of evaluative utterances? Perhaps what he means to convey is simply this: when we have a certain peculiar sort of feeling, which we call a feeling of blame, on contemplating a certain action or individual's character, no more need be present in the situation in order that we may be justified in pronouncing the action or the character vicious. It is a contingent fact that our nature is such that we have this feeling upon contemplating certain actions or characters. This is a description of what entitles us to say '*x* is vicious', but we are not *saying* this. Similarly, one can argue that a peculiar sort of feeling entitles us to say that *x* is vicious, although no part of what we say is 'I have a peculiar feeling'. I am not retracting my earlier contention that 'approval' and 'disapproval' are words that, according to Hume's doctrine in the *Treatise*, stand for peculiar feelings or emotions. But 'I feel a peculiar kind of pleasure' no more *means the same* as 'I feel approval' than 'I see a peculiar kind of colour' means the same as 'I see red'.

I do not think that it is too fanciful to suggest that Hume may have written in such a way as not to distinguish clearly between the analysis of the meaning of an expression, and a description of the conditions that justify its use. The difference is not always clearly brought out by the way we now express ourselves in ordinary language. Sometimes, when we ask a person what he means by a particular utterance, he gives us, in answer, the conditions that led him to make it, and not an analysis of what he said. 'He is an absolute scoundrel.' 'What do you mean?' 'When I asked him to entertain my wife in my absence he took the opportunity to seduce her.' – This is the condition that led to the utterance. We might perhaps, in this case, say it justified the utterance. But it manifestly does not analyse its meaning, in the sense in which Hunter is attributing to Hume an analysis of the meaning of evaluative utterances.

It is not easy to discover precisely what analysis of evaluative utterances Hume wants to put forward, for he says very little explicitly on this topic. He is, in the second two books of the *Treatise*, primarily concerned to provide us with an account of the circumstances within which our feelings and passions arise, and in particular the passions that, for him, constitute approval and disapproval. I think it is clear, however, that he does not believe that we can understand expressions such as '*x* is virtuous', unless we have experienced that peculiar passion which, for him, constitutes an evaluation of character. Once, however, the term 'virtuous' and other value terms have come to be associated with certain conduct, we can make use of them in order to encourage such conduct. Thus, part of the use of evaluative language may be to influence conduct as well as simply to comment upon it. One may, in this connection, recall how Hume claims that politicians indulging in propaganda, and parents in educating their children, may make use of the emotive force of evaluative language, although they cannot, in the first place, give meaning to the evaluative expressions. Only the experiencing of certain emotions can reveal to us their meaning: 'The utmost politicians can perform, is to extend the natural sentiments beyond their original bounds; but still nature must furnish the materials, and give us some notion of moral distinctions' (THN III, 204/500). It is obviously consistent with the Emotionist theory I have attributed to Hume that evaluative language should have more than one use. It need not *only* express an emotion: it may, for example, also serve to arouse one.

I want, in conclusion, to draw attention to certain things that may help us to see why it has proved so difficult to reach agreement about the issues discussed in this chapter.

I have stressed more than once that Hume most decidedly did not think his main concern was with *moral language*. It is Emotionism and not Emotivism that I have all along been attributing to him. He thought he was called upon to explain how *evaluations* were possible, without the postulation of a special order of values or special relations. He wants to show that one can see how evaluations may arise, without having to refer to any principles other than those that are involved in accounting for other aspects of our emotional life. The motives that lead to the adoption of an objective point of view serve to explain both evaluations and perceptual judgments. It has been shown in an earlier chapter how he stresses the similarity between approvals and disapprovals on the one hand, and certain passions such as love or hatred on the other. Approbation and blame are called by Hume 'nothing but a fainter and more imperceptible love or hatred' (THN III, 307/614). Now love and hatred, like all other passions, tend to be biased because of the relation the loved or hated object may have to us. On the other hand approval and disapproval arise only when you have taken up an objective point of view, abstracting from your own special relation to the person loved or hated. If I challenge a person's evaluation, which on this account consists only in having a certain emotion, the only way I can do this is by trying to get him to take up an objective point of view in considering it. If he truly does this, and knows all the relevant facts, Hume seems to think that he will probably come to feel the same way as anyone else who looks at it from the same point of view and who knows the same facts about it. If both have taken an objective view, they can truly say that they approve, that the feeling they have is moral approval. On the other hand, it cannot be this passion if they have been in any sense influenced by a special relation to the object. What if, after all the facts are agreed, two people should still disagree morally? Then the problem cannot be resolved; there is no appeal possible beyond the way the individual feels. It is likely that one or other is biased, and not really feeling approval at all. His utterance, '*x* is virtuous', would then be unjustified because he is not feeling approval, and also, as we might say, because his view of the matter is biased and the facts looked at objectively do not justify the evaluation. Hume appears to think that the peculiar feeling of approval arises only when we have taken an unbiased view of a situation. When this has taken place, we are justified in pronouncing something virtuous, and also have a right to claim that the feeling we have is a genuine feeling of approval, and not some similar feeling such as love. But although whenever we are justified in saying '*x* is virtuous' we are also justified in saying 'I have a feeling of approval in contemplating x', it does not follow that when we say 'x is virtuous' we are *saying* 'I have a feeling, . . .'. I am suggesting that one reason why Hume may have written as if he were putting forward the subjectivist analysis of evaluative utterances about actions and human character is that making the statements 'I feel approval', or 'I feel disapproval', is always and only justified when one is in no way biased, although one may be mistaken or ill-informed about the facts.

Hume seems sometimes to have been over-impressed by an apparent analogy between his own view about the nature of virtue and the doctrine of secondary qualities. This may have led him in places to write as if he were advocating Reflectivism. At one time people thought that secondary qualities such as colours belonged to objects. The doctrine of secondary qualities seemed to show that they really exist only in the consciousness of observers who sometimes mistakenly take them for qualities in the objects themselves.[1] In the same way, people had thought virtue and vice were qualities in the objects we call virtuous and vicious. There are good grounds for thinking that they were mistaken. These qualities are mind-dependent, just like secondary qualities and hence we conclude, from the analogy, that they are qualities in the mind of the person judging. This analogy may go some way towards explaining Hume's curious way of speaking about virtue and vice as if they were discoverable by introspection.

Some of his statements seem, at first sight, to be intelligible only if we consider him to have believed that 'virtue' names a quality of the person contemplating the allegedly good thing, and that 'vice', in the same way, names a contrary quality.

> The vice entirely escapes you, as long as you consider the object. You never can find it till you turn your reflection into your own breast, and find a sentiment of disapprobation, which arises in you, towards this action. (THN III, 177/468-9)

It seems that Hume is saying that 'vice' is the name of 'a sentiment of disapprobation', and that we find the vice in our own breast when we introspect. If the vice must be somewhere, there is nowhere else for it to be, since it is not a quality of external objects. One can easily see how this line of thinking leads to Reflectivism.

---

[1] It should cause no confusion that I call colours, sounds, etc., 'secondary qualities', although Locke uses the term to indicate the power to cause experiences of colour, sounds, etc.

One must not put too much emphasis upon a literal reading of isolated passages, such as the one quoted above. The importance Hume attaches to the analogy with secondary qualities can be easily overestimated, and his reliance upon it misconstrued. Thus Hume's high praise of the doctrine of secondary qualities in this connection is somewhat strange when we remember that, in the first book of the *Treatise*, he is a very stern critic of this doctrine.

It is, perhaps, not inappropriate to quote, side by side, his panegyric in the third book and his condemnation in the first:

> Vice and virtue, therefore, may be compared to sounds, colours, heat, and cold, which, according to modern philosophy, are not qualities in objects, but perceptions in the mind: and this discovery in morals, like that other in physics, is to be regarded as a considerable advancement of the speculative sciences; though like that too, it has little or no influence on practice. (THN III, 177/469)

The doctrine which is here called 'a considerable advancement of the speculative sciences' is described in the following terms in the first book:

> I believe many objections might be made to this system; but at present I shall confine myself to one, which is, in my opinion, very decisive. I assert, that instead of explaining the operations of external objects by its means, we utterly annihilate all these objects, and reduce ourselves to the opinions of the most extravagant scepticism concerning them. If colours, sounds, tastes and smells be merely perceptions, nothing, we can conceive, is possessed of a real, continued, and independent existence; not even motion, extension, and solidity, which are the primary qualities chiefly insisted on. (THN I, 218/227-8)

There can hardly be much doubt as to which of these quotations represents Hume's real view as to the tenability of the doctrine of secondary qualities. It would make nonsense of his most cherished doctrines about our knowledge of the external world, if we took his eulogy of this doctrine in Book III to be an expression of his considered opinion. The fact of the matter appears to be that Hume is here using an *argumentum ad hominem*. If it is admitted that colours and sounds are nothing but perceptions in the mind, there is certainly no objection in principle to considering virtue and vice to be in the same category. He may, here, have Locke's doctrine in mind; but the cases are not really parallel, for Hume is arguing that virtue and vice are 'mind dependent' in a sense in which the secondary qualities are not.

When we approve or disapprove of an agent we take his actions as signs of certain motives or dispositions. Among these signs there are very often secondary qualities; these are qualities we can discover by scrutinizing the object. Virtue and vice, on the other hand, are not natural qualities, like colours, that can be discovered by observation; no scrutiny of external objects will reveal such qualities. Even the mental qualities we infer will not contain the quality, virtue, or the quality, vice. We should not have the concepts of virtue and vice unless we experienced approval and disapproval. But Hume is not suggesting that 'virtue' and 'vice' are names for qualities that appear to belong to external objects (people), but that they really are in the mind of the observer. Too great an emphasis on the analogy with secondary qualities may lead one to believe this. But 'virtue' refers to a quality of mind or character that causes, in an observer, a feeling of approval in special circumstances. One must not take Hume's words too literally when he suggests that one can find virtue and vice only when one turns one's attention to one's own approvals and disapprovals.

There are reasons to believe that Hume never explicitly faced the following problem. Are expressions such as 'John is virtuous', and 'John is vicious', statements about the feelings of the speaker (or other people), or are they to be thought of as *expressing* a feeling and thus as neither true nor false? His most distinguished contemporary critic, Thomas Reid, certainly seems not to have been clearly aware of the difference between these two alternative interpretations, for in one and the same chapter he attributes to Hume both these doctrines.

Reid emphasizes Hume's opinion that moral approbation and disapprobation are not judgments but feelings: ' . . . Moral Approbation and Disapprobation are not Judgments, which must be true or false, but barely agreeable and uneasy Feelings or Sensations' (PWTR, 671). The most important point at issue seems to be whether approvals and disapprovals can be true or false. It is obvious that Reid believes Hume to be denying that evaluations can be described as true or false, to be maintaining that they are not judgments and therefore not expressible in propositions. He is assuming that a judgment unexpressed may be true or false, and, when expressed in words the proposition the words express can be likewise appraised in this way: 'For it [feeling] implies neither affirmation nor negation; and therefore cannot have the qualities of true or false, which distinguish propositions from all other forms of speech, and judgments from all other acts of the mind' (PWTR, 671).

We can express our feelings and emotions in various non-linguistic ways, for example by sighing, smiling, frowning, laughing. We may, however, use language for this purpose, for example 'alas!', 'well done!', 'hurrah!' and various forms of swearing. Reid appears to be maintaining that when language is used in order to express emotions it does not express something true or false – a proposition. His reason for this contention is that we cannot attribute truth or falsity to feelings and emotions themselves. We can, of course, also talk about our feelings and emotions, but we are then using language to express a judgment that can be either true or false. Reid is criticizing Hume for maintaining the, to Reid, erroneous view that approvals and disapprovals are feelings and not judgments, and the correlative view that evaluative verbal expressions are not to be assessed in terms of truth or falsity. He is attributing both Emotionism and Emotivism to Hume.

But Reid, without any warning that he is doing so, credits Hume with a different view in the very same chapter. He contends that Hume confuses two propositions: (1) *'Such a man did well and worthily, his conduct is highly approvable'*; and (2) *'The man's conduct gave me a very agreeable feeling'* (PWTR, 673). Both these statements are regarded by Reid as capable of truth or falsity, and he goes on to point out the difference between them:

> If we suppose, on the other hand, that moral approbation is
> nothing more than an agreeable feeling, occasioned by the con-
> templation of an action, the second speech, above mentioned, has
> a distinct meaning, and expresses all that is meant by moral
> approbation. (PWTR, 673)

Reid, it appears, is attributing to Hume the doctrine of Subjectivism, which holds that moral evaluations are statements about the speaker's feelings. Since, according to Reid, judgments are expressed in propositions, he also, by implication, credits Hume with Reflectivism; and, further, with Emotionism, suggesting that Hume's Emotionism entails Subjectivism. Reid's interpretation of Hume is obviously confused. If I call someone good or virtuous, and am asked why I call him good, I may give an answer by enumerating the valuable qualities that led me to approve of him; but I might also answer by pointing out that I say he is good or virtuous because his conduct gave me a feeling of approval. The first seems to be the proper rejoinder to a challenge of my evaluation. The second would tend to be a statement in justification of my use of the term 'good' in this case. Hume, as I have pointed out, may not have seen clearly enough how necessary it is to emphasize the difference between the two, because he tends to think an approval justified only when it is *genuine* approval, and that biased 'approval' is love and not approval.

It is true that Reid's criticism of Hume does little more than indicate that he seems to have been quite unclear as to what doctrine he thought Hume was proposing. But since he seems unaware of the fact that he credits Hume with two incompatible views, this suggests that the difference between these views was not, to him, a live issue. Perhaps his contemporary, Hume himself, did not see as clearly as twentieth-century thinkers that Reflectivism and Emotionism are clear-cut alternatives. This would help to explain why he appears to express both these views in the *Treatise*. The suggestion that these views are characteristic of different parts of the *Treatise* can be ruled out, for they are, or appear to be, expressed on consecutive pages. Thus Hume's apparent inconsistency on this issue can hardly be attributed to a real change in doctrine. But Reid's interpretation of Hume shows that it was possible for a contemporary to attribute to Hume both Emotionism and an emotive, non-propositional theory of moral language, and that such an interpretation of Hume is thus not necessarily anachronistic.

It must not be forgotten that Hume is attempting to explain the whole of our experiences in terms of the principles of association. Causal inference is an acquired habit, certain experiences have come to be associated in our minds. There is, strictly speaking, no inference from cause to effect. In a similar way, the distinction normally drawn between judgment and feeling is also blurred. Belief, we must remember, is, in some places, characteristically defined as nothing but a lively idea, or perhaps an impression. It would take too long to enter into all the complexities surrounding Hume's view of the nature of belief, but I do not think it can be denied that the view expressed here is to be found in the *Treatise*, and is characteristic. Since the difference between an idea and an impression is only one of force and liveliness, it follows that the idea of a passion and a real passion are not different in kind. If belief is a lively idea or an impression, then, of course, the passion and the belief that you have the passion are not, to Hume, two different things but the same. The judgment that you have the passion is simply having it.[1] It must not be forgotten by those who think that moral

[1] When in this mood Hume tends to write as if only beliefs that are based on experience are real beliefs as opposed to the superstitions inculcated by edu-

judgments were, for Hume, judgments of fact, that he had a very peculiar view about judgments of fact: he is, in a sense, assimilating these to feelings. Thus when Hume says that a certain feeling 'constitutes our praise or admiration', he need not necessarily be denying that to evaluate is to believe that something is the case, that is, that one is having a certain feeling. Looked at from within his theory, the contrast does not seem to arise. On the other hand, it must not be forgotten that, in rejecting that reason discovers morality, he appears to be maintaining that evaluations are neither true nor false in the ordinary sense of these terms.

As to the meaning of the expressions used when we make a 'causal inference' or a 'moral judgment', it seems only natural to think that Hume would explain this, like the rest of experience, in terms of acquired habits: hearing certain sounds tends to lead to having certain ideas; having certain ideas or impressions, coupled with, perhaps, a desire to achieve one thing or another, may lead one to make certain noises. It seems that the only account he could give of language, consistently with his associationist scheme, would be along these lines. The expression 'x is good' is associated with approval (the passion); why should we want to say that it states a fact? Seen within the general context of Hume's theory, it seems rather misleading to say that this and similar expressions are statements of fact. The whole process which leads one to have the feeling that we call approval is conceived of in causal terms. The feelings of others affect us through sympathy, and this helps to produce our approval, which in turn has come to be associated with the evaluative expression. At no point is there any inference, from certain factual characteristics to others, in the ordinary sense.

In attributing Emotionism to Hume, we must bear in mind that he did not consider feeling and thinking to be different in kind; but this does not throw any doubt upon the view that, to him, evaluations are emotions. Hume nowhere suggests that emotions are more like thought than we realize. It is rather the other way round: it is our view about the nature of thoughts that, as Humeans, we should modify. To 'think' is to have ideas, and these ideas are like actual experiences, only fainter

cation. This involves a difficulty about the concept of false beliefs, which it is not our present purpose to discuss. On the account I have given a comparable difficulty arises about biased approvals. It must be noted that I do not restrict the use of the word 'belief' to expectations based on past experience. The truth of any matter of fact can be believed.

or less vivid. Although one can, with some confidence, call Hume an Emotionist, one can not attribute Emotivism to him with equal degree of certainty. Hume's sentimentalist account of thinking fits in well with an expressive, non-propositional analysis of evaluative utterances. It would, in general, fit in well with Hume's associationist scheme when this is applied to the explanation of our use of language. But in attributing Emotivism to Hume, one is not directly interpreting his words, but rather considering what position would be most in conformity with other aspects of his philosophy. For Hume does not give us, in the *Treatise*, a theory of moral language, but an account of the nature and origin of evaluations. If Ethics is defined as the analysis of moral discourse, Hume's *Treatise* does not contain much in the way of Ethics. What it does contain is an account of the way the concepts of virtue and vice have their source in human emotions.

INDEX